Social Work with People with Learning Difficulties

Third edition

PAUL WILLIAMS

MICHELLE EVANS

Series Editors: Jonathan Parker and Greta Bradley

 |

Los Angeles | London | New Delhi
Singapore | Washington DC

Learning Matters
An imprint of SAGE Publications Ltd
1 Oliver's Yard
55 City Road
London EC1Y 1SP

SAGE Publications Inc.
2455 Teller Road
Thousand Oaks, California 91320

SAGE Publications India Pvt Ltd
B 1/I 1 Mohan Cooperative Industrial Area
Mathura Road
New Delhi 110 044

SAGE Publications Asia-Pacific Pte Ltd
3 Chuch Street
#10–04 Samsung Hub
Singapore 049483

Library of Congress Control Number: 2013932596

British Library Cataloguing in Publication Data

A catalogue record for this book is available from the British Library.

ISBN 978-1-44626-757-8 (pbk)
ISBN 978-1-44626-756-1

Editor: Luke Block
Production Controller: Chris Marke
Project Management: Deer Park Productions
Marketing Manager: Tamara Navaratnam
Cover Design: Code 5 Design Associates
Typeset by: Pantek Media, Maidstone, Kent
Printed in Great Britain by: MPG Printgroup, UK

MIX
Paper from
responsible sources
FSC® C018575

Contents

Acknowledgements

Paul Williams would like to thank his friends Roger Peck and the late John Gomm for inspiration, and his former colleagues at Reading University, Linnet McMahon, Alison Cocks, Ann Quinn and Christina Victor for valuable comments and practical support. Francis Phillips, John-Paul Gower, Alison Kerridge, Emily Perl Kingsley and Lynette Hunt very kindly gave their permission for inclusion of their material in the book.

Michelle Evans would like to thank her colleagues at London South Bank University, Kent University and Christchurch University, especially Andrew Whittaker, Joan Curzio, Keith Popple, Annabel Goodyer and Enkanah Soobadoo, colleagues in the Learning Disability, Mental Health and Social Work teams, and past and present students at London South Bank University, especially Zulaika Zurita, Carol Mills, Margaret Kwamina-Crystal, Zephy Polius, Joseph Fitton, Habib Farahmand and Krystle Thomas. Also Ken, Ivy, Joe, Sophie, Jack, Grant, Amelia, Francesca, Felicity and Simon. Thanks are also due to staff of organisations that support people with learning difficulties, including Fionnuala Naicker and Jacqueline Murray; and Tricia Pereira, Annie Knight, Feargal Brady, Winsome Collins, Maureen Harding, Nigel Cox and Graham Smith for being an inspiration during her social work career.

We would like to thank all our family members and friends who have supported us in the enterprise. Paul's thanks go especially to his wife Boni for her inspiration, kind comments, encouragement, support and patience, and Michelle's especially to Alan for his never-ending love and encouragement.

We would like to thank each other for the opportunity to work together on this new edition of the book, a partnership that we hope the reader will find has been very fruitful. We also extend our gratitude to the staff of Sage/Learning Matters, especially Luke Block.

Paul Williams
Michelle Evans

Introduction

Many social workers find work with people with learning difficulties to be extremely interesting and rewarding, and it is a field which has seen dramatic advances in recent years. Horner (2003), in a chapter on 'Social work with people with learning disabilities', charts its successes, particularly in relation to the virtual abolition of large isolated institutions and their replacement with various forms of community care. Up until the early 1970s in Britain, around 60,000 people were accommodated in institutions for people with learning difficulties; now nearly all these places have been closed and the people relocated in much smaller groups in much more ordinary and integrated settings. Horner says:

> In recent years, it has been the view of a number of commentators that social work with people with learning disabilities represents, in many respects, the profession's high water mark...It can be seen that social work, supported by its own value base, and linked to significant and dynamic user movements, has participated in profound and significant developments, many of which would have seemed unthinkable only 30 years ago.

(Horner 2003: 50)

In this book we hope to convey some of the reasons for interest and enthusiasm in this field: the achievements and satisfactions that can be gained, the good relationships that can be formed, and the learning and understanding that can be gained from contact with people with learning difficulties, as well as the need for recognition of vulnerability, the risk of oppression and abuse, and the need for continuing political struggle to establish and protect rights.

The practical aims of this book are:

- to provide a positive picture of people with learning difficulties;

- to describe the very varied roles that a social worker might play in relation to people with learning difficulties;

- to describe developments resulting from the 2001 Government White Paper *Valuing People*, which declared some radical aims for services for people with learning difficulties;

- to present work with people with learning difficulties as potentially long term, offering opportunities for development of relationships and seeing people through life stages that are not so available in other fields;

- to provide information and materials for reflection that relate to the Professional Capabilities Framework;

- to emphasise the importance of values, and to illustrate this with a historical approach;

- to present current policy as the result of a steady build-up of knowledge, skills and understanding through developments in research, philosophy and practice;

- to engender respect for people with learning difficulties and their resilience and achievements;

- to promote equality and partnership in relationships between social workers and people with learning difficulties;

- to provide practical guidance in direct work with people with learning difficulties.

We have tried to present people with learning difficulties as family members and citizens of their community. However, inevitably the space available has meant a focus on the people themselves. Work with families, and work in the context of different cultures, are relatively neglected. We hope that students will learn the importance of these wider perspectives through other sources.

Social workers face many challenges in the current financial, social and political climate. Two of these in particular are highlighted in learning difficulty services. Because these services have been relatively well resourced in recent years compared with services for other groups, they are in the firing line for economic cutbacks, and social workers are often in the forefront of this process. There is a danger that the focus of assessment becomes how to save money rather than objective appraisal of needs. Secondly, in the light of abuse scandals, both within services such as Winterbourne View (where six members of staff were jailed for abuse after a television exposé) and more generally in the allegations against broadcaster Jimmy Savile, the need for protection and safeguarding has been highlighted. There is a danger that preventive measures expected to be pursued by social workers counteract the vital need for relationships for people with learning difficulties to counter the major risk of isolation and loneliness. We hope that this book gives some signposts for social work students in their own approach to resolution of these dilemmas.

This book has been carefully mapped to the new Professional Capabilities Framework for Social Workers in England and will help you to develop the appropriate standards at the right level. These standards are as follows.

- **Professionalism**
  Identify and behave as a professional social worker committed to professional development.

- **Values and ethics**
  Apply social work ethical principles and values to guide professional practice.

- **Diversity**
  Recognise diversity and apply anti-discriminatory and anti-oppressive principles in practice.

- **Justice**
  Advance human rights and promote social justice and economic wellbeing.

- **Knowledge**
  Apply knowledge of social sciences, law and social work practice theory.

- **Judgement**
  Use judgement and authority to intervene with individuals, families and communities to promote independence, provide support and prevent harm, neglect and abuse.

- **Critical reflection and analysis**
  Apply critical reflection and analysis to inform and provide a rationale for professional decision-making.

- **Contexts and organisations**
  Engage with, inform, and adapt to changing contexts that shape practice. Operate effectively within your own organisational frameworks and contribute to the development of services and organisations. Operate effectively within multi-agency and inter-professional settings.

- **Professional leadership**
  Take responsibility for the professional learning and development of others through supervision, mentoring, assessing, research, teaching, leadership and management.

References to these standards will be made throughout the text. You will find a diagram of the Professional Capabilities Framework in Appendix 1, and the relevant extracts from the social work subject benchmark statement in Appendix 2.

Chapter 1

Who are 'people with learning difficulties'?

Introduction

This chapter aims to clarify what is meant in practice by the term 'people with learning difficulties'. It covers debates about terminology, definitions and numbers. An approach is outlined to identifying strengths and achievements of people with learning difficulties, and 'putting oneself in their shoes'. Some of the vulnerabilities of the people and their families are described. The perceptions or 'models' that underlie the practice of different professions and organisations providing services are covered.

Terminology

In the quotation from Horner (2003) in the Introduction, he uses the term 'people with learning disabilities', whereas at the beginning of this chapter, and in the title of the book, we have used the term 'people with learning difficulties'.

There is a movement led by people with learning difficulties themselves which gives them a collective voice (see Chapter 9). This takes the form of 'self-advocacy' groups which are often called 'People First'. One of the issues taken up by many of these groups is that of terminology. There is strong dislike of the term previously in common use: 'mental handicap'.

The alternative that some people said they preferred was 'learning difficulty'. In the early 1990s, the government recognised the dislike of the term 'mental handicap', but instead of adopting 'learning difficulty' they coined the term 'learning disability'; the reason stated was to avoid confusion with use of the term 'learning difficulty' (or usually 'specific learning difficulty') in the education field to refer to people with conditions like dyslexia, affecting the ability to read or write or do maths well, but without affecting intelligence. However, 'learning difficulty' continues to be the term preferred by many within the self-advocacy movement of the people themselves. Sutcliffe and Simons (1993) found that group members had a clear rationale for this: 'disability' means you can't do things, 'difficulty' means you want to learn and be taught how to do things. In this book we will use the term 'people with learning difficulties', except when quoting from other sources where the original terminology will be retained.

The term 'mental handicap' was itself a replacement for the term coined in the 1959 Mental Health Act: 'subnormality'. This term, perilously close to 'subhuman', was in use during the 1960s and early 1970s. Previous terms had been 'mental deficiency' and 'mental defect'. In the first half of the twentieth century, attempts were made to classify degrees of severity of 'mental deficiency' with the terms 'idiot' (very severe), 'imbecile' (severe) and 'feebleminded' (less severe). Other terms in use were 'backward', 'moron', 'moral defective' and (especially in the USA) 'retarded'. Some of these terms lingered on past their sell-by date: a major textbook about people with learning difficulties published in 1974 was still called *Mental Deficiency* (Clarke and Clarke, 1974). The major voluntary organisation concerned with people with learning difficulties in England and Wales is still called 'Mencap', deriving from the term 'mental handicap', and the term 'mentally retarded' is still in common use in America.

ACTIVITY *1.1*

What do you think some of the objections are to the terms mentioned above? Is it possible that the term 'learning difficulties' will eventually need to be replaced?

COMMENT

One of the objections that people have made to the adjective 'mental' is that it creates confusion with mental illness. The term 'handicap' has been felt to have connotations of 'cap in hand', with the image of begging and dependence on charity. The terms 'idiot' and 'imbecile' and 'moron' became widely used terms of abuse in ordinary language. 'Defective', 'deficient', 'retarded', 'backward', 'subnormal' and 'feebleminded' all put a highly negative emphasis on 'something being missing', and again are in use as terms of abuse.

The disability rights movement has developed a 'social model' of disability (in contrast to the 'medical model') (Priestley, 2003; Barnes and Mercer, 2010). This will be explained further later in this chapter. In the social model, the term 'disability' refers to the imposition of restrictions or oppressive experiences on people because of poor attitudes, low skills or unhelpful physical and social structures in society. The term 'learning disability' implies that people are disabled by their learning rather than by society, so it would be rejected in the social model. The term 'learning difficulty' has been chosen by at least some people with learning difficulties themselves, rather than being invented and imposed by others. However, it too may become a term of abuse, or the people themselves may choose another term that they wish to be used.

Other more modern terms you may come across, particularly in a scientific context, are 'intellectual disability' or 'developmental disability'.

Definition

Whatever our terminology, an interesting fact is that 'learning difficulty' can't be defined. Much of the historical terminology implies that the people we are concerned with are primarily people who have low cognitive intelligence. The IQ test, the method that was developed in the early twentieth century to measure cognitive intelligence, was originally devised to identify people of low intelligence for the purposes of providing support, special education or social control.

There is a problem, however. It is not possible to define a level of IQ below which people have learning difficulties and above which they don't. Statistically, about 3 per cent of the population have an IQ below 70 (the average IQ in the population as a whole is 100). This gives a figure of about 1,800,000 people in Britain with this level of IQ. The majority of these people never come to the notice of services designed to support people with learning difficulties. Most people with IQs below 70 are functioning in ordinary society without requiring special services; they are in work, are married with children and live 'ordinary' lives. On the other hand, surveys of people actually receiving services for 'people with learning difficulties' have found that some have IQs above 70. Even in the old institutions it was known that a proportion of patients had IQs above this level (Kushlick and Blunden, 1974).

Without a definition, the numbers of people with learning difficulties cannot be determined. However, numbers are required for the planning of services. For this purpose the concept has been developed of 'administrative prevalence'. This refers to the number of people known to, or actually being served by, specialist services catering for people under the label 'learning difficulty' or equivalent. It would include pre-school children receiving support because of a diagnosis of 'learning difficulty' or 'developmental delay', children receiving special schooling or who have a statement of educational needs under a heading of severe, profound, multiple or moderate learning difficulty (but not 'specific learning difficulty'), and all those adults receiving services labelled 'learning difficulty services' or an equivalent.

Surveys of administrative prevalence have found that around half of one per cent of the population are receiving services for 'people with learning difficulties'; about half of those are defined as having a severe degree of difficulty and about half are said to have milder difficulties (Race, 1995; Emerson et al., 2001). In Britain, with a population of around 60 million people, only around 300,000 people are actually receiving services as a result of being classified as 'people with learning difficulties'.

Numbers

The idea persists, however, that there is a hidden cohort of people who should be described as 'people with learning difficulties' who are not known to specialist services under that name. For example, a survey of people with learning difficulties carried out by the Department of Health (NHS, 2005) states:

> that 2.2% of the adult population of England have a learning disability ... It has been recognised for many years, however, that most adults with learning disabilities are not known to statutory services for people with learning disabilities ... Administrative definitions only include 22% of English adults who we estimate to have learning disabilities (i.e. approximately four out of five adults with learning disabilities are not defined as such by statutory services for people with learning disabilities).

(Supplementary Appendix: 16–17)

It is unclear what advantages there might be to according a higher number of people the label 'person with learning difficulties'. It may be that many more people than at present would benefit from support from services designed for people with learning difficulties, but that has yet to be demonstrated. There seems little point in labelling people as having 'learning difficulties' if there is no evidence it will bring tangible benefits. Being labelled may be accompanied by social stigma and control elements of social policy that can act to the great disadvantage of people (an extreme example was seen in Nazi Germany where people were at risk of extermination – see Chapter 2).

ACTIVITY **1.2**

Can you think of advantages or disadvantages that there may be to defining a larger proportion of people than are served at present as having learning difficulties?

COMMENT

Some of the arguments you might consider include the following.

- *There may in fact be many people who are missing out on needed services, and identification of those people so that their needs can be assessed and provided for is desirable.*

- *Relatively small service input for people with a mild degree of learning difficulty may help more people to achieve independent living or to gain a job.*

- *However, services may have a vested interest in claiming that there is a 'hidden cohort' of potential clients, so that they can argue for a greater role and more finance, and there may be a risk of people unnecessarily being labelled as 'having learning difficulties'.*

- *Serving more people who have milder degrees of learning difficulty may divert attention and resources away from those with more severe difficulties, for whom there may be much greater uncertainty about 'outcomes'.*

Despite such possible reservations, statements that there are over a million people in Britain with learning difficulties have become very common:

About 1.5 million people in the UK have a learning disability.

(Learning Disability Coalition: **www.learningdisabilitycoalition.org.uk**)

We work to ensure the 1.5 million people with a learning disability in the UK have the same rights and control over their lives as everyone else.

(Mencap: **www.mencap.org.uk**)

1.2 million people have mild to moderate learning disability and around 210,000 ... have severe and profound learning disabilities.

(Michael, 2008)

BILD is ... committed to improving the quality of life for the 1.2 million people in the UK with a learning disability.

(British Institute of Learning Disabilities: **www.bild.org.uk**)

If we apply these figures to a population area of 250,000 people, which might be served by a social services community team for people with learning difficulties, they suggest the presence of around 6,000 people with learning difficulties in that area. This figure has little meaning unless we know where the people are and have some idea of their needs. A more realistic picture, representing the actual numbers of people receiving services, is given below. The source of information about children is the Department for Children, Schools and Families (DCSF, 2008) and for adults is Emerson and Hatton (2008).

In a population area of 250,000 people, there would be (approximately):

- 800 children receiving special or supported education for moderate learning difficulties (only some of these will continue to require support as adults);

- 200 children receiving special or supported education for severe, profound or multiple learning difficulties;

- 15 adults in NHS care;

- 200 adults in residential care, in around 30 different registered homes;

- 120 adults supported in their own accommodation, mainly as tenants and often in groups;

- 360 adults in other households, mainly with parents;

- 240 places in day services (likely to be used by a larger number of people, some on a part-time basis), plus some people in work, in work preparation or in further or adult education.

Only some of these people will be in contact with social work services or have a care manager.

Such relatively small numbers are part of the explanation why provision for people with learning difficulties has seen major improvements in the last 30 years (Horner, 2003). Services for other client groups, such as older people, have to cater for much higher numbers.

Determinants

If IQ is not the determinant of who 'people with learning difficulties' are, then what does determine the access of people to services under that label? People are likely to have restricted ability to function in important areas of social activity and personal care as a result of limited understanding rather than physical restriction. In addition, there are factors that may bring people to special notice of authorities or services, such as:

- being diagnosed with a condition that is considered to be strongly associated with having learning difficulties (e.g. Down's syndrome);
- having medical conditions such as epilepsy or cerebral palsy;
- having additional physical impairments or frequent or severe illness;
- exhibiting difficult behaviour;
- having mental health problems or experiencing a high degree of emotional distress;
- having sensory impairments of sight or hearing;
- being unable to communicate well through speech;
- coming from a very poor or neglectful environment;
- having responsibilities that may be difficult to meet without support (e.g. being a parent);
- having difficulty finding or keeping a job;
- needing somewhere to live and being unable to achieve that through family or mainstream resources;
- loss of key resources such as a carer (e.g. when a parent dies);
- being bored and unstimulated with nothing to do during the day;
- being rejected, excluded, bullied or abused;
- breakdown of key relationships in their life.

All these additional factors constitute vulnerabilities over and above a low IQ or lack of cognitive intelligence. It is these additional factors that entail a need for support, and a relative absence of such additional factors may enable a person, even with a very low IQ, to escape a label of 'learning difficulties'. On the other hand, presence of these extra vulnerabilities may mean a person is so labelled in order to receive services, even with a relatively high IQ. This can currently be seen in the case of people with Asperger's syndrome (see Chapters 3 and 4), who may have a high degree of cognitive ability, but whose social vulnerability and needs may be best met (in the absence of specialist services for them) by referral to learning difficulty services. It is these vulnerabilities that are likely to relate to judgements of 'eligibility' for services that social workers may have to make (see Chapter 7 on assessment).

One further aspect of attempts to define 'learning difficulty' is that it is usually taken to refer only to those people who have matched the definition from birth or early child-hood. This is to distinguish 'people with learning difficulties' from people who may have impaired cognitive functioning from accidents or illness in adulthood, and from older people who have developed dementia.

How then can we define a 'person with learning difficulties'?

ACTIVITY 1.3

Have a go at writing your own definition of a person with learning difficulties. If you already know any people with learning difficulties well, base it on your own experience.

COMMENT

To the extent that a definition is needed at all, one attempt in the light of what has been said so far might be along these lines:

A person with learning difficulties is someone who has social and personal vulnerabilities associated with impairment of cognitive understanding or of learning practical skills which has existed since childhood.

This is a rather 'clinical' definition that attributes the 'problem' to the individual. The definition would be rejected by many people with learning difficulties themselves, and more generally by the disability movement.

Definitions more in tune with the 'social model' of disability might be:

A person with learning difficulties is someone who has been labelled as having difficulties in cognitive understanding, but is someone with rights, including the right to maximum control over decisions that affect them, and who may need help and support to claim and exercise those rights.

A person with learning difficulties is someone whom society identifies as having an impairment in cognitive functioning, but whose needs and interests are not well catered for by societal structures or by the interactions of other people; he or she is a survivor of struggles to overcome this disadvantage, and may need help to continue to do so.

Strengths

In the definitions above, we have inserted the word 'cognitive' before 'understanding' and 'functioning'. This is because it can be argued that there are other kinds of understanding or ability that people with learning difficulties may possess in much higher measure. A distinction can be drawn between cognitive intelligence, emotional intelligence and wisdom. Many people believe that each is independent of the others: so, for example, it is possible for someone with very low cognitive intelligence to be very wise, and we can all think of examples of people with high cognitive ability who exhibit very little wisdom. Emotional intelligence includes an ability to be sensitive to the interests and needs of others (Goleman, 1996), and many people who know people with learning difficulties well will attest to their possession often of high ability in this respect. Here are two examples of wisdom and emotional intelligence shown by people with learning difficulties.

CASE STUDY

In an autobiography (dictated to a supporter) by Annette Münch, a Danish woman with learning difficulties, she describes how her parents tried to gain control over her money, eventually resulting in a very upsetting court case. After losing the case, her parents cut off all contact with her. At the end of the book Annette says: 'I don't hear from my parents and this is the best way. Perhaps they will need me later and then I will help them.'

(Münch, 1998: 92)

Having suffered extreme physical, emotional and sexual abuse over many years by the managers of a residential home for people with learning difficulties in which she lived, Dorothy moved to a home of her own after the scandal was discovered. Later she said:

'I've got a very big faith, so strong. I think that's what gives me the energy. I mean, even though...they did cruel things to me, but then if they came to this front door... I would say, "Do you want to come in for a cup of tea?" I would, yes, because isn't that what Christianity is about – forgiveness?'

(Pring, 2003: 186)

One view of the history of the treatment of people with learning difficulties in society, especially in the first half of the twentieth century, is that it represents a conspiracy of highly cognitively intelligent people, but with little wisdom or emotional intelligence, against people perceived as having low cognitive intelligence. The result was great oppression: segregation in large isolated institutions, sterilisation, exclusion from social agencies such as education, severe abuse and even extermination. In Nazi Germany the first group of people to be killed were those with learning difficulties, and the gas chambers were invented for use on them before they were used in the death camps for Jews (see Chapter 2).

In our experience of people with learning difficulties, although they may sometimes exhibit difficult behaviour, most have little interest in power and control over others and certainly not in the use of mass violence in war or genocide. Often their acceptance of our power and control over them, without seeking retribution or reciprocation, is a model to us of wisdom. Criminal or violent behaviour, drunkenness, selfishness, cruelty, dishonesty and ill treatment of others are probably less common among people with learning difficulties than in the rest of the population.

Many people with learning difficulties are skilled in noticing and responding to distress or upset in others, thus demonstrating emotional intelligence. Because of these things, there is much that we can learn from people we encounter with learning difficulties.

Achievements

In addition to any attributes of wisdom or emotional intelligence that people with learning difficulties may possess, many of them have gained more down-to-earth achievements. What constitutes 'achievement' needs to be defined individually for each person with learning difficulties, depending on their particular difficulties, circumstances and opportunities. The standards of judgement of 'achievement' in society generally cannot necessarily be applied. Nevertheless, even in relation to these mainstream standards, there are many examples of achievement by people with learning difficulties, in the creative arts, in sport, in work, in education, in gaining awards, in voluntary work and in relationships. Some people with learning difficulties have learned to read and write, and several have written books or had poetry or autobiographical accounts published (for example, Hunt, 1967; Kingsley and Levitz, 1994; Josephson, 1997; Souza, 1997; Evans, 2005).

Sometimes people show a remarkable and creative ability with words. Here is an example from the autobiography by Nigel Hunt. It was published in 1967 and is thought to be the first published book written by a person with learning difficulties. In this passage, Nigel is describing events he witnessed after leaving his parents' home, without their knowledge, and travelling to London to see the Trooping of the Colour. After his parents reported him missing, he was found and returned home by the police. Here, however, is his marvellous description of what he saw:

> *I sauntered to the Royal Mews and asked where Buckingham Palace is and the man said, 'just keep to the left and you will come to it.' I asked a man to take me across the road; then down the Mall to Horse Guards, and I borrowed a programme off a Coldstream Guardsman. I asked a policeman when the band will be along and he said, 'ten and a half minutes'. So I stood and waited for at least one and a half minutes. I heard a terrific throb and my ears were lifted and with a Biff Biff Bang the band came along, and when they turned the corner up came their oompahs and the miserable trombones and blowed me in the middle of nowhere.*

(Hunt, 1967: 54–5)

At least six people with learning difficulties in recent years have received Honours from the Queen.

- In 1998, Angus Elliot, a man with learning difficulties who had lived and worked for 42 years in a community where people with learning difficulties share their lives with non-disabled people – Camphill Village Community at Botton in Yorkshire – was awarded an MBE for services to that community.

- In 2000, Susan Pipes, a young woman who had won five gold medals at the World Special Olympics for people with learning difficulties, was awarded an MBE for services to sport.

- In 2001, Carol Lee, a member of the self-advocacy group of people with learning difficulties, People First London, was awarded an MBE for her work on the advisory group for the government White Paper *Valuing People*.

- In 2002, Jackie Downer was awarded an MBE for her work in the self-advocacy movement, particularly for stimulating the involvement of Black and Minority Ethnic people with learning difficulties.

- In 2006, Andrew Doyle was awarded an MBE for services to ENABLE in Scotland.

- In 2007, Michelle Chinnery was awarded an OBE (a higher award than MBE) for her work as co-chair of the Valuing People Task Force.

These are just a small sample of the wide range of achievements of people with learning difficulties, more examples of which will be given at various places in this book. A highly recommended book for gaining a flavour of the possibilities for achievement by people with learning difficulties is that edited by Dorothy Atkinson and Fiona Williams (1990).

Vulnerabilities

Later chapters will cover in more detail the experiences of people with learning difficulties that may constitute oppression and social devaluation and give rise to social and practical needs of special relevance to social work. Here, just a sample from one source is described. A survey of adults with learning difficulties in England (Emerson et al., 2005; NHS, 2005; Emerson and Hatton, 2008) gives some statistics about their experiences. The percentages are of a cross-section of people with learning difficulties who were interviewed; this constituted a large and varied sample, but it should be borne in mind that since 'learning difficulty' cannot be defined, the term 'percentage of all people with learning difficulties' has no meaning. The percentages are merely of those people who were interviewed, but they do give an indication of the very different experiences of adults with learning difficulties from those that the rest of us can expect in life. These include:

- 92 per cent had never been married;

- 83 per cent did not have a paid job, and for many of those who did it was only part-time;

- 19 per cent never saw members of their family;

- 31 per cent had no contact with friends;

- 75 per cent did not have any friends who did not have learning difficulties;

- 7 per cent had children, but only half of those had care of their children;

- 43 per cent said they had been bullied at school;

- 32 per cent said they did not feel safe in their home area;

- 32 per cent had experienced rude or offensive remarks towards them in the last year;

- 64 per cent had had no choice over where they lived or who they lived with;

- 39 per cent said they lacked privacy;

- 50 per cent of adults were still living with their parents and a further 12 per cent with other relatives.

Families

The impact of the vulnerabilities of people with learning difficulties may be as much on their families, carers and supporters as on the persons themselves. So social work in this field often involves support to families and other carers. Despite the statistic above, that 19 per cent of people interviewed in the survey had no contact with their family, most families maintain close contact and most people with learning difficulties retain an important role in their family and are greatly loved by their families. Despite any practical difficulties or emotional strains (with which social workers can provide help), it is in families, and to their carers, that many people with learning difficulties make their greatest contribution in the imparting of wisdom and emotional intelligence. Here are extracts from a poem by a mother of a nine-year-old child with learning difficulties (Phillips, 2001). It illustrates the teaching of wisdom by the child, who was initially thought of as 'second best'.

When You Were Born
When you were born another baby died:
She was of course a dream,
With all the hopeful unreality that word implies
(The imagination sometimes lies).
I wept inside.
Well-meaning hands thrust you into a frock
That didn't fit,
And bristling with wires like a Mrs Tiggy Winkle
You and I would sit:
You with your head lolling forward
And your slanting Asian eyes,
I in silent mourning as the dream slowly faded,
Then adapted to fit your fragile size.
That was then.
When did you begin to cast your spell?
Was it when I saw you listening to my voice
As I sang your name over and over again?
Looking back on all those early sleepwalked months,
I cannot tell...
Today our lives revolve around you,
Like satellites around a pocket sun
That glows with warmth and love
(And hasty ill-wrapped gifts)
For everyone
Like an infant deity,
You are enshrined at the centre of our world...
Could I have wished that you had not been born?
Or let you from beneath my heart be torn?
Who then would help make sandwiches for tea?
Who then would sit for stories on my knee?
Who then would keep our hallowed rites alive:
The walk, the duck pond, crisps, the fire at five? ...

Thank you, Cecilia, for inhabiting
Your own special and insistent place;
For teaching me, in so many mischievous
And so endearing ways,
That all is grace.

Mrs Francis Phillips (2001)
Reprinted by kind permission of the author

Models

There are different models for conceptualising people with learning difficulties and their needs that are the primary basis for the practice of different professions. In practice there is great overlap in the use of the models; for example, psychiatry straddles the medical and psychological/educational models.

The medical model

This conceptualisation has had great influence, historically and currently, in defining learning difficulty in terms of 'abnormality' and disease. In this model the body is viewed as a machine, the efficient running of which can be compromised by parts not working properly. In people with learning difficulties the brain is perceived as not working properly, causing a lack of cognitive ability. This can lead to a very negative view of people with learning difficulties: people with lifetime debilitating impairment to a major organ of the body, with devastating consequences that are best avoided if at all possible. Not much place for attributes of wisdom and emotional intelligence here.

However, the medical model is very important for meeting the needs of many people with learning difficulties. It is true that people with learning difficulties are more prone to illness and to conditions like epilepsy and cerebral palsy. Some people with learning difficulties have problems of mobility, hearing, eyesight, respiration, heart functioning, digestion and other issues of a medical nature. It is vitally important for those people to have high-quality diagnosis and medical treatment for these things.

The medical model is also important in the search for the prevention of conditions that affect cognitive functioning. One example of a success story here is the prevention of the effects of phenylketonuria. This condition results from a deficiency of an enzyme in the liver. A substance found in many foods, called phenylalanine, is not properly converted into other chemicals the body needs. Substances called phenylketones are excreted in the urine (hence the name of the condition) and can accumulate in the brain, causing damage and possibly quite a severe degree of learning difficulty. To prevent this happening, all newborn babies are tested for the condition (with a simple blood test) and in the rare event of the condition being found (it occurs in about one in 25,000 births) the baby can be put on a special diet, low in phenylalanine, which prevents damage occurring. There are now very few people with learning difficulties caused by phenylketonuria.

On the other hand there is a big area of controversy in the area of prevention through abortion. Prenatal testing of expectant mothers can identify a number of conditions associated with learning difficulties, the most well-known being Down's syndrome. In this condition the person has an extra chromosome (the carriers of sets of genetic information) in each cell of the body. People with Down's syndrome have distinctive facial and bodily characteristics and are highly likely to have a degree of learning difficulty, though this varies greatly between individuals. If a risk of the foetus having Down's syndrome is discovered during early pregnancy, abortion will be offered to the mother. The ethics of this is a key controversy in the field of learning difficulty.

Professionals whose work is based on the medical model, and with whom social workers are likely to work in partnership in relation to particular needs of people with learning difficulties, include doctors, surgeons, psychiatrists, nurses, physiotherapists, dentists and opticians.

The psychological/educational model

This is concerned with behaviour, emotions and thought processes. Learning difficulty is seen in terms of deficits or excesses of behaviour. Techniques of teaching have been developed to remedy both a deficit in behaviour (lack of skill) or an excess (behaviour problem). For example, attention can be given to adjusting the triggers or antecedents of a particular behaviour, or to the results or consequences of the behaviour, in order to teach a desired skill or change an undesired behaviour. This may seem rather 'cold', but ways have been devised of incorporating such systematic teaching into everyday activities through school education (Wood and Shears, 1986) or 'active support' in daily living (Mansell et al., 2005) and applying it humanely and sensitively, for example through the process known as 'gentle teaching' (McGee et al., 1987; Harbridge, 2001).

> *Gentle Teaching was developed some 20 years ago at Nebraska University by John McGee, Dan Hobbs and colleagues in response to what they saw happening to people whose behaviour was labelled as 'challenging' ... The teacher focuses not on the person's behaviour but on the individual as a person. This means the teacher adopting positive human values in relation to the person and accepting the need to change their own behaviour in order to develop a relationship and achieve a fairer balance of power ... Gentle Teaching requires the teacher to engage closely with the person ... Careful observation of videoed interactions is used to discover the dynamic of the relationship between person and teacher so the latter can adapt their actions: a tiny movement, the tone of voice, the teacher's body position may all be significant. Gentle Teaching has no set formula or hierarchy of rewards. Teachers use all their understanding and skills to appreciate the person and develop and sustain a rewarding relationship.*

(Harbridge, 2001: 33)

A learning pack and manual on Gentle Teaching are available from CL Initiatives, 2 West Park, Minehead, Somerset TA24 8AW.

Particular areas of interest from this educational perspective are the teaching and maintenance of daily living skills, such as dressing and eating, with the general aim of increasing 'independence'; communication, and the development of ways to enhance the communication of people with learning difficulties to others and of others to them; and emotional well-being, including in recent years the development of specialist psychotherapy for people with learning difficulties (Simpson and Miller, 2004).

Professionals whose work is based on this model include psychologists, teachers, further education lecturers, psychotherapists, speech therapists, occupational therapists and nurses with training in teaching people with learning difficulties.

The social model

This is concerned with the place and the experiences of a person in their family and in society. It sees people with learning difficulties as at risk of oppression, social devaluation and many of the 'vulnerabilities' described earlier that have a social origin. The model seeks to reverse the processes of vulnerability by supporting people in valued social roles, for example as family member, citizen, worker, tenant or home-owner (see Chapter 2). This is the primary model on which social work is based, and it is likely to involve partnership with a wide range of other professionals and key people in community life, including support workers, personal assistants, day service workers, employment support workers, advocates and such people as hairdressers, bank and post office staff, shopkeepers or the clergy. Voluntary organisations are likely to subscribe to the social model too, unless they have a remit restricted to a specialised medical or educational issue.

Both in the definition and identification of people with learning difficulties, and in the support and treatment of those people, it is important that the medical or educational viewpoints do not become so dominant that the social perspective is lost or neglected.

Mutuality

The social model of disability rejects the idea that disability is a characteristic of an individual person. A person may have an impairment of bodily or mental function, but that only becomes a disability to the extent that society is not structured to cater well for people with that restriction, and other people's interactions exacerbate rather than overcome any difficulties. People with learning difficulties lack skill in certain areas, but non-disabled people also lack skills of interaction and good relationships with people with learning difficulties. The 'handicap' is thus a mutual one, with a need for support and efforts to overcome difficulties on both sides (Williams, 1978).

ACTIVITY **1.4**

Our Mutual Handicap *(Williams, 1978) is written as if it were a person with learning difficulties speaking, addressing an audience of non-disabled people. For example:*

> One of the things that surprises us most is that you think we are so different from yourselves. We don't think we are. We think we have the same needs, feelings, rights and responsibilities as you. We have a need for somewhere to live, for fulfilling occupation, for affection and appreciation, for a chance to give of our best. We have emotions of sadness, happiness, anger, shame, joy. We believe we have the same rights as you to adequate housing, security, a fair day's pay for a fair day's work, and a right to determine the pattern of our own lives. (Williams, 1978: 1)

Do you think it is valid for a non-disabled person to speculate in this way about what a person with learning difficulties might say? Write down some objections to this enterprise, and some arguments in its favour.

We can never really know what other people think or feel, so any claim to do so must be speculative, and even arrogant. It is also patronising and disempowering if no attempt has been made to discover the views of the people themselves. In fact, Our Mutual Handicap *was based on some early conferences involving people with learning difficulties (Shearer, 1972, 1973; Williams, 1974), representing some of the first attempts to consult people with learning difficulties directly.*

A group of people with learning difficulties was set up to advise the government on its White Paper *Valuing People* (Department of Health, 2001). This group adopted the motto 'Nothing About Us Without Us'. This phrase was used earlier by the disability rights movement, and is the title of a book by Charlton (1998). He quotes Ed Roberts, one of the leading figures of the disability movement in the USA, as saying: *If we have learned one thing from the civil rights movement … it is that when others speak for you, you lose* (Charlton, 1998: 3). So there is something jarring about a person without learning difficulties pretending to speak as if they were a person with learning difficulties. Nevertheless, there are many people with learning difficulties who cannot express their thoughts and feelings in words. Social workers often have to try to 'put themselves in the shoes' of people they are supporting, in an attempt to empathise with them and understand them. The requirements are that it should be done with humility, and that it should not substitute for getting to know the real views, thoughts and feelings of the people themselves. Chapter 9 of this book discusses ways in which we can discover the real views of people with learning difficulties themselves, and includes a number of examples of the voices of the people themselves. In this context, there may be a place for empathetic speculation about the situation of people with learning difficulties as they might express it if they could. Or perhaps not. You decide.

Learning from people with learning difficulties

While there is much mileage in the basic assumption that people with learning difficulties are 'just like us', it is also important to acknowledge their unique experiences and characteristics from which we can learn. As with all groups of people who are different from us, we need to acknowledge and respect the differences, support and cultivate the positive aspects of that difference, and address and remedy the negative aspects of different experiences. People with learning difficulties are likely to have had negative experiences of oppression and social devaluation that we need to acknowledge and address. People with learning difficulties also have their own characteristics and identity – as expressed for example in the self-advocacy movement – which can be explored in order to respect and learn from them.

ACTIVITY *1.5*

List some ways in which you think you might learn from people with learning difficulties. If you already know any people with learning difficulties well, you can base this on your experience with them.

COMMENT

Your list might include things related to wisdom and emotional intelligence, like humility, humour, resilience, patience, responsibility, respect for diversity and enjoyment of simple pleasures. It might relate to gaining an appreciation of vulnerability: how easy it is for people to be rejected or neglected. And it might include practical things, like skills of caring, non-verbal means of communication, counselling, advocacy and negotiation for resources.

CHAPTER SUMMARY

This chapter has discussed the nature and definition of 'learning disability'. Some of the vulnerabilities that bring people to the notice of services are outlined. Strengths and achievements are emphasised, and the mutual nature of difficulties of communication and relationships between people with learning difficulties and non-disabled people is portrayed. The people are presented as people from whom we can learn as well as people who may need our support.

FURTHER READING

Atkinson and Williams (1990) *'Know Me As I Am'* is a superb anthology of writings and art by people with learning difficulties themselves.

Emerson et al. (2001) *Learning Disabilities: The Fundamental Facts* gives comprehensive basic information about people with learning difficulties.

Race (2002) *Learning Disability: A Social Approach* is a good general introduction to services and relevant social policy.

Talbot et al. (2010) *Key Concepts in Learning Disabilities* is a helpful guide to aspects of learning difficulties, arranged in alphabetical order of topics.

WEBSITE

See the list of internet resources at the end of the book.

Chapter 2

The importance of values: a historical account

Introduction

Values are reflected and reinforced throughout this book, but this chapter takes a look at values from a historical perspective. The way in which values have operated to shape services and social policies, resulting in negative or positive behaviour towards people with learning difficulties, will be illustrated. The aim is to demonstrate the crucial importance of positive values within services and in society as a whole in determining the quality of the experiences of people with learning difficulties. The values held by social workers play a vital role in this.

Values and current policy

In 2001 the British government published a White Paper (one that states government policy) on services for people with learning difficulties. It was called *Valuing People*, with the subheading *A New Strategy for Learning Disability for the 21st Century*. In a foreword, the then Prime Minister, Tony Blair, speaks of *our goal of a modern society in which everyone is valued*. So values are officially flagged up as a key issue in current policy and provision. The White Paper will be discussed in more detail in Chapter 3.

Values in history

There is plenty of evidence of negative values in operation in history. The ancient Greeks and Spartans put out their babies onto exposed hillsides so that the weakest would die (Stratford, 1996). Martin Luther believed that people with learning difficulties had no soul, and that *the Devil sits in such changelings where their soul should have been*. He advised about one child: *I should take this child to the Molda River ... and drown him* (Wolfensberger, 1969).

However, Brian Stratford (1996), who has taken a special interest in the place of people with learning difficulties in different societies in history, especially those with Down's syndrome, describes evidence that other societies appear to have revered and worshipped disabled people, including those with learning difficulties. Statues dating from 1500 BC in Mexico indicate that the ancient Olmec civilisation worshipped people with the characteristic features of Down's syndrome. In parts of India, right up to the present day, people with learning difficulties were welcomed at religious shrines, since it was considered they brought special grace to worshippers there. In the Middle Ages in Switzerland, France and parts of England, people with learning difficulties were brought together in communities around monasteries to be cared for by religious orders. Up until the Industrial Revolution in Britain, local communities were by and large accepting of members with learning difficulties and made special arrangements to support them and their families (Wright and Digby, 1996). In parts of Germany, still to this day, people revere statues of a person with learning difficulties, Caspar Hauser, who became well known in early nineteenth-century Bavaria for his spiritual qualities (Wassermann, 1973).

These instances suggest that there have been periods and places in history when people with learning difficulties have been well accepted and treated with respect and even reverence.

ACTIVITY 2.1

By visiting a library or using the internet, find a source of paintings by the seventeenth-century Spanish artist Diego Velasquez. Find the paintings, all housed in the Prado Museum in Madrid, entitled Calabazaz *(1637),* Francisco Lezcano *(1643) and* Barbarroja *(1636). The painting of* Calabazaz *is definitely of a person with learning difficulties, since the gourds (a pumpkin and a squash) were a conventional symbol of learning difficulties used in art at that time. Probably Lezcano and Barbarroja were people with learning difficulties too. What is your impression of how the people are portrayed? What values do you think underlie the paintings? If your source of the paintings has any narrative, how are the paintings described, and what values are implied by the descriptions?*

COMMENT

The paintings, particularly of Calabazaz and Barbarroja, are often titled 'Jester' or 'Buffoon'. This is a later interpretation of who these people were, based on a stereotype of the role of people with learning difficulties in history which is not necessarily true. Velasquez was a painter to the Royal Court of Philip IV of Spain, and it is probable that Calabazaz, Lezcano and Barbarroja were members of the court. There is evidence that the Spanish royal court accommodated large numbers of disabled people, including people with learning difficulties. They were not jesters or clowns, but respected people who it was thought were valuable to have around, as gentle, truthful and reliable people to counteract the political intrigues of the court, and as companions for the royal family, particularly the royal children (Moreno-Villa, 1939; Bouza, 1996).

In the paintings by Velasquez, the people are not dressed as clowns, but are wearing ordinary, even fine, clothes. There is also a convention in paintings of the time that if the picture is painted as if the viewer is looking up at the subject, that is a mark of respect for the person and their status. Particularly in the painting of Lezcano, we see this convention applied. There is therefore evidence that people with learning difficulties, although many outside the court would have led hard lives of poverty, were valued and respected in seventeenth-century Spanish society. It would be difficult to imagine a major artist today painting a person with learning difficulties because they were highly valued in our society.

Charles II of Spain

Spain in the later part of the seventeenth century makes an even more fascinating study, because from 1665 to 1700 there ruled on the throne of Spain a king with learning difficulties. Charles II of Spain (also known as Carlos II) was the only surviving legitimate son of Philip IV when he died, so he automatically became king. He was only four years old, and his mother acted as Regent for him. He was a very sickly child; he could not eat properly due to a deformity of the jaw, and he was late in being weaned and in learning to walk. He never learned to read or write, apart from his signature. He had epilepsy and was infertile and unable to have children. Nevertheless he took the responsibilities of his role seriously. Throughout his life he was guided by his mother and his two wives. He was married to a French princess at age 18, and again to a German princess at age 30 when his first wife died. He himself died aged 39 in 1700 (Nada, 1962).

Typical entries in modern history books or encyclopaedias for Charles II of Spain are along these lines:

Three generations of royal marriages between cousins and nieces produced their dreadful legacy in the pitiful form of Carlos II. Grotesque in appearance, deformed in body and backward in intellect, he seemed barely human.

(Maland, 1966: 227)

He was a foolish and weak monarch at a time when Spain direly needed strong leadership.

(Lopez, 1973: 513)

However, Kamen (1980), in a definitive history of Spain of the time, says of him:

The reiterated attacks of historians on a young man burdened by insuperable infirmities do less than justice to his constant efforts to care for his monarchy.

(1980: 375)

Charles was highly respected by his people. Whenever he was ill, crowds would gather outside his palace in Madrid to pray for his recovery. In 1680, Halley's comet appeared bright in the sky, causing concern among the Spanish people that it was an ill omen for their king and pamphlets were printed to reassure the general population (Kamen, 1980).

ACTIVITY 2.2

Using an internet search engine, find some pictures of Charles II of Spain (use the search terms 'Charles II of Spain' or 'Carlos II'). In works by the famous court painters of the day, you will see him dressed in fine clothing, surrounded by the trappings of royalty. Some paintings show him in grand scenes, mounted on a horse, or taking part in religious ceremonies.

The British Royal Family

In great contrast to this, the British royal family in the twentieth century hid its disabled members away.

CASE STUDY

Katherine and Nerissa Bowes-Lyon were nieces of the Queen Mother and King George VI and first cousins of the Queen. Nerissa was born in 1919 and her sister Katherine was born in 1926. Their father was John Bowes-Lyon, brother of Queen Elizabeth the Queen Mother. The two girls were both described as 'mentally retarded' with 'the mental age of six', and were largely unable to speak. Their father died in 1930 and the girls were cared for privately until, in 1941, when Nerissa was 22 and Katherine was 15, they were admitted to a large hospital for people with learning difficulties, the Royal Earlswood Hospital in Surrey, where they lived from the 1940s to the 1980s. They were not visited by any member of the royal family during that time.

Their sister, Diana Bowes-Lyon, who was not disabled, was a bridesmaid to Queen Elizabeth II (then Princess Elizabeth) on her marriage to the Duke of Edinburgh in 1947, but Katherine and Nerissa did not attend. Later, the family informed Burke's Peerage, which records details of all those who are related to the royal family, that the sisters had died, which was untrue. Nerissa did not die until 1986. She was buried in Redhill Cemetery, near the Royal Earlswood, where her grave was marked with a plastic tag and a serial number, until a headstone was erected 20 years later. Katherine was still alive at least in 2012, living in a nursing home in Surrey.

CASE STUDY *continued*

(Information from the internet encyclopaedia Wikipedia – **www.reference.com/browse/ wiki/Nerissa_Bowes_Lyon** *and* **www.reference.com/browse/wiki/Katherine_Bowes_ Lyon** *– and from an article by Mackay, 2002).*

Burke's Peerage *now mentions the names of Nerissa and Katherine but has no other information about them. When Mackay (2002) was writing his article, he enquired about the two women to the Queen Mother's office and Buckingham Palace but was told they had never heard of them.*

We include this story here as an illustration of the way in which different values can affect people. We do not intend to heap blame on Nerissa and Katherine's family. At the time they were born it was the height of the eugenics movement that regarded people with learning difficulties as a threat to society (Mazumdar, 1992). In the 1940s when the girls were admitted to an institution, and even much more recently than that, it was common for parents to be told by professionals (including social workers): 'Put them away and forget about them.' Visitors were often discouraged from going to see people in institutions (Morris, 1969; Jones and Fowles, 1984). And in Nazi Germany, thousands of people with learning difficulties were being led to their deaths in gas chambers. It is not surprising that the weight of the negative values towards people with learning difficulties that were held in society generally were reflected in the royal family's behaviour towards its own members. Nevertheless, we can speculate on the great boost that might have been given to the status of people with learning difficulties in Britain if two young women with learning difficulties had been bridesmaids at the wedding of Princess Elizabeth, or if they had stood on the balcony of Buckingham Palace waving to the crowds at the Coronation, or even if they had been regularly visited by King George VI, the Queen Mother and the Queen at their home in the Royal Earlswood.

ACTIVITY **2.3**

As a social worker in the field of learning difficulty you will find yourself working with a very wide variety of people. Imagine yourself as a social worker to the wider Bowes-Lyon family, including King George and the Queen Mother, in the 1940s. How might you advise the family, taking into account their needs and interests and those of the women in the family with learning difficulties? What might be your aims? What values would underlie your work?

Nazi Germany

The historical low-point in societal values relating to people with learning difficulties was reached in Nazi Germany. A key source of information is the Center for Holocaust and Genocide Studies at the University of Minnesota in Minneapolis, USA (**www.chgs.umn. edu**), from which the following account is derived.

It is a little known fact that gas chambers were first invented to kill large numbers of people with learning difficulties, before the technology was developed for the mass killing of Jews. The first gas chambers were developed by doctors, nurses and technicians within institutions for people with learning difficulties in Germany and Austria. Because of their experience, some of the nurses and administrators from these hospitals were later sent to design and supervise the setting up of the gas chambers in the death camps in Poland for exterminating the Jews. For example, Michael Hermann, formerly Chief Male Nurse at Hartheim Castle, an institution for people with learning difficulties in Austria, was sent to establish and run the gas chambers at Sobibor, one of the death camps for killing Jews in German-occupied Poland.

Many doctors, particularly psychiatrists, were members of the Nazi party, and even members of Hitler's special protection army, the SS. As part of their belief in the purification of the Reich they were already practising 'euthanasia' of disabled people on a large scale. This was an extension of a programme introduced by the Nazis in 1933, only six months after they came to power in Germany, to sterilise the 'hereditarily sick'. This programme is thought to have resulted in the forced sterilisation of 200,000 people with learning difficulties, 100,000 people with mental health problems, 60,000 people with epilepsy, 21,000 people with physical impairments and 20,000 people with sensory impairments.

On 1 July 1940, it was ordered that all patients in institutions had to be reported to the Reich Task Force of Sanatoriums and Nursing Homes if they suffered from schizophrenia, epilepsy, congenital syphilis, mental retardation, encephalitis, Huntington's chorea and other incurable neurological diseases. More than 60 staff were charged by the Reich Task Force with inspection of the registration forms filled out by the institutions. A red '+' mark (ironically, the international symbol of lifesaving – the Red Cross) resulted in a decision for 'euthanasia'. The decision for life or death of a patient was made by someone who had never met them. All registration forms showing the red '+' mark were handed over to the Gemeinnützige Krankentransportgesellschaft (charitable ambulance service, known for short as 'Gekrat') which provided for the transfer of the patients. The Gekrat buses had their windows covered by cloth or painted so that the local population could not see the people inside. The buses drove into specially constructed garages at the killing institutions, from which passages led directly into the main buildings.

A statistical record found after the end of the war showed that over 70,000 people with learning difficulties or neurological conditions were killed; of these, 10,000 were killed in Hadamar, the main hospital for people with learning difficulties in the German province of Hesse-Nassau. It was chosen as a killing institution because of its geographical location and the enthusiasm of the authorities that ran the institution for the euthanasia policy. After its own patients had been killed, it began to accept people from other institutions. These arrived on the Gektrat transport and were killed within a few hours. First, they had to get undressed. Then they were photographed and doctors recorded a 'cause' that allegedly led to their death. After this procedure, they were taken to the gas chamber. The gas chamber was disguised as a shower room. A perforated gas pipe, fixed at a height of about a metre, went through the room. The pipe was connected with gas containers in the room next door. Carbon monoxide entered the room through the holes in the pipe. Up to 60 people were crowded into the 14 metre square room which was locked by steel doors. Through a control window in the wall, the doctors and administrators watched the people die. It took several minutes before they were all dead. Afterwards, a fan extracted the gas from the chamber. Death certificates were issued for the families, but the data on them about cause, time and place of death were false.

It is known that some social workers in Germany actively colluded in these events, and at the very least there was little protest from social workers about what was happening (Kunstreich, 2003; Johnson and Moorhead, 2011).

The eugenics movement

Although mass killing of people with learning difficulties on this scale only happened in Nazi Germany, sterilisation of large numbers of people also happened elsewhere. During the twentieth century, there were large programmes of sterilisation practised in North America, Scandinavia and other parts of the world (Gottshall, 1995). Sweden had a strong sterilisation programme, sterilising around 62,000 individuals over a period of 40 years until as recently as 1976. Other countries that had active sterilisation programmes include Canada, Australia, Norway, Finland, Estonia, Slovakia, Switzerland, Iceland, and some countries in South America, including Panama (**en.wikipedia.org/wiki/Compulsory_ sterilization**). In the United Kingdom, Winston Churchill was among those advocating sterilisation, but an attempt to legalise it in the 1913 Mental Deficiency Act was defeated through the efforts of dissenters, including the writer G.K. Chesterton. Widespread debate about the desirability of sterilisation as part of the 'eugenics movement' in the early years of the twentieth century (Mazumdar, 1992) led to successful opposition to sterilisation in Britain. Instead, a policy of segregation of people in institutions was pursued to prevent people from breeding (Mencap, 2008).

Leaders of the eugenics movement held some extremely negative views about people with learning difficulties. For example, these statements were made by two prominent psychiatrists in the USA, Schlapp and Fernald, both in 1915:

> *It is among those unfortunate members of society who fall so far short of the line of normal mentality as to be an inherent social menace, that there flourishes the real peril to the mental and moral stamina of our nation. The problem is the most serious facing the country today.*

(Schlapp, quoted by Wolfensberger, 1969: 103)

> *We now have state commissions for controlling the gypsy moth and boll weevil, the foot-and-mouth disease, and for protecting the shell-fish and wild game, but we have no commission which even attempts to modify or control the vast social, moral and economic forces represented by the feeble-minded persons at large in the community.*

(Fernald, quoted by Wolfensberger, 1969: 106)

ACTIVITY 2.4

Write down what you consider to be your values in relation to the following. When you reach the end of this chapter you can review what you have written to see how far it agrees with some of the values that appear to underlie current policy and practice in services.

The place of people with learning difficulties in society
The nature of community
Equality and anti-discrimination
Spirituality
Relationships
Protection of vulnerable people

Positive values

This has been a depressing account of the application of negative societal values towards people with learning difficulties, and it is time to turn to examples of more positive attitudes. Positive values can be seen in the ideas and actions of a number of pioneers of services for people with learning difficulties.

Jean Itard

A well-known story in the early history of education for people with learning difficulties is that of 'the wild boy of Aveyron'. Between 1797 and 1800 in the Aveyron region of France, a young boy was occasionally seen running naked in the woods. He was captured several times but always escaped. Finally in 1800 he was caught and sent to be examined by doctors in Paris. He was about 12 years old and had apparently fended for himself, perhaps in the company of wolves, for several years, probably after being abandoned in the woods by his family. He had no speech and spent much of his time in a crouching position, rocking to and fro. He was declared by those who examined him to be an 'idiot', but one young doctor, Jean Itard, took him into his home and tried to devise ways of teaching the child, whom he named Victor. Itard had considerable success, and he wrote an account of his work which was very influential in fostering optimism about the possibilities of education for children with learning difficulties. Itard wrote:

> [It has been] as much my desire as it was my duty to prove, by the success of my first experiments, that the child on whom I have made them is not, as is generally believed, a hopeless idiot, but a being highly interesting, who deserves … the attention of observers, and the assiduities which are devoted to him by an enlightened and philanthropic administration.

(Itard, 1801; English translation, 1972: 93)

Samuel Howe

In 1866, Samuel Howe gave a speech on the opening of an institution for disabled people in America. It was for blind people, but it could just as well have been for people with learning difficulties, for whom similar institutions were being established at the time. Howe's words were 100 years ahead of their time:

> *All great establishments ... where the sexes must be separated, where there must be boarding in common, and sleeping in congregate dormitories, where there must be routine and formality and restraint and repression of individuality, where the charms and refining influences of the true family relation cannot be had – all such institutions are unnatural, undesirable and very liable to abuse. We should have as few of them as possible, and those few should be kept as small as possible ... Beware how you needlessly sever any of those ties of family, of friendship, of neighbourhood ... lest you make a homeless man, a wanderer and a stranger. Especially beware how you cause him to neglect forming ... relations of affection with those whose sympathy and friendship will be most important to him during life ... If the field were all clear, and no buildings provided, there should be built only ... school rooms, recitation rooms, music rooms and workshops, and these should be in or near the centre of a dense population. For other purposes ordinary houses would suffice.*

> (Howe, 1866; quoted in Wolfensberger, 1969: 138–41)

Langdon Down

Dr John Langdon Down gave the first systematic description of Down's syndrome, which is named after him. From 1858, he was superintendent of the first large residential establishment in Britain for people with learning difficulties – Earlswood Asylum in Surrey, which later became the Royal Earlswood Hospital (where the Queen's cousins lived). In 1868 he left to set up his own service which would better reflect his ideas on care. He bought a large house – Normansfield – in south-west London which he lived in with his family while developing residential accommodation in small rooms in the house and in extensions that were added over time. Support staff were attached to each small group, and were expected to live with them each day, sharing in meals and all activities, and sleeping in as required.

Langdon Down and his family frequently ate meals and joined in activities with the people with learning difficulties. The idea was to replicate family care for those who could not live at home with other family members (Ward, 1998). Photographs of the 'patients' taken by Langdon Down show them to be immaculately dressed with smart hairstyles. Conor Ward in his biography (1998) says that *residents of Normansfield were intended to live the lives of young ladies and gentlemen*. Normansfield closed in 1997; among other uses it now houses the headquarters of the Down's Syndrome Association (see Merriman, 2007).

Rudolf Steiner and Karl Koenig

During the twentieth century a number of people developed philosophies that stood in great contrast to the negative values expressed in the eugenics movement. Among them was Rudolf Steiner. Born in Austria in 1861, Steiner developed a philosophy and set of principles for daily living that he called 'anthroposophy', meaning 'human wisdom'. This concept can be applied to recognise the wisdom that can be possessed by people with low cognitive ability (as discussed in Chapter 1), and the virtue of inclusion of all people equally in 'community'. Steiner said that social structures should promote brotherhood and social relationships based on human rights, *inspired by a concern for equality – not equality of spiritual capacity or material circumstances, but that sense of equality that awakens through recognition of the essential spiritual nature of every human being* (Davy, 2005).

In 1939 Karl Koenig founded the Camphill movement to apply this concept in services for people with learning difficulties. Koenig was an Austrian paediatrician and educator. He fled the Nazi invasion of his own country and settled in Aberdeen, Scotland, in 1939 with a group of young doctors, artists and caregivers. There they founded the first Camphill community, where people with learning difficulties and non-disabled people live together. Members of the communities teach and learn from each other in a process of mutual interaction. The needs of each person are met through living in a cooperative community – each individual contributing his or her own special gifts and talents. The international Camphill movement now consists of more than 100 communities in 22 countries (**www. camphill.org/?p=34**).

ACTIVITY 2.5

Camphill has been criticised for advocating 'special' communities which segregate and isolate people from the 'ordinary' community. As we have seen, Samuel Howe, back in 1866, argued powerfully against this. Write down your ideas of possible advantages and disadvantages of 'special' communities for people with learning difficulties.

COMMENT

You might consider that people will be well treated and respected in such communities, avoiding the risks of bullying and rejection that they might experience in the 'ordinary' community. Some people living in special Camphill villages have made major long-term contributions to community life there, and are greatly appreciated for that (see the mention in Chapter 1 of an MBE awarded to Angus Elliot for his contribution to a Camphill community). On the other hand, people are isolated from their home communities and families, and those communities lose the opportunity to know and to serve the people with learning difficulties who are taken away. Whatever our views on segregated 'special' communities, the concept of 'life-sharing' between people with learning difficulties and non-disabled people which underlies Camphill, derived from Rudolph Steiner's enlightened philosophy of community and equality, is a model of good relationships that reflects high values towards people with learning difficulties.

Jean Vanier and L'Arche

The concept of 'life-sharing' is also promoted by Jean Vanier. Like Rudolf Steiner, he emphasises the potential spirituality of relationships between people with learning difficulties and non-disabled people. Vanier was born in Canada in 1928, the son of a former Governor General of Canada, Georges Vanier. He served in the British and Canadian navies before studying philosophy in France. In 1964 he moved into a house in the village of Trosly in France with two men with learning difficulties – Raphael Simi and Philippe Seux – whom he had befriended. The house was named L'Arche ('The Ark') and it was the beginning of the worldwide movement for life-sharing with people with learning difficulties known by that name. He has written:

> *Those who are rejected heal and transform us, if we enter into relationship with them. [It is] the vocation of our people and [our] mission ... to create communities, networks of friends, with and around the weakest. There we learn to love and carry one another, to share our life together and thus become a sign in a world of competition and individualism, that love is stronger than hate. This is our way of struggling for justice and peace.*

(Vanier, 2004)

It may seem a heavy burden to thrust on disabled people to be the pioneers of a new world of love, acceptance, justice and non-violence. Such a romantic notion is likely to be rejected by many disabled people, who see themselves, and wish to be seen by others, as equal citizens with equal rights, not as special, holier-than-thou alien creatures. However, Vanier's philosophy stands in great contrast to the dominant negative attitudes towards disabled people, and people with learning difficulties in particular, in recent history.

ACTIVITY **2.6**

L'Arche is based on fostering relationships of equality and sharing. This approach might be contrasted with current policy in Britain, which is to pursue 'standards', prescribed by government and enforced by an inspectorate (Care Standards Act 2000), and to require 'professionalisation' of the care workforce (through training and eventually registration). Which do you think offers the best protection of vulnerable people from harm? What values underlie each approach? Do you think the two approaches can be made compatible? If you are not familiar with the Care Standards, try to find out more about them. (They are currently applied and monitored by the Care Quality Commission – see **www.cqc.org.uk**.*)*

COMMENT

Those responsible for current policy in Britain would probably share the basic values of Jean Vanier towards people with learning difficulties. We can remember Tony Blair's statement from the Valuing People *White Paper:* our goal of a modern society in which everyone is valued. *However, it seems to us that there is a great difference in emphasis between the methods suggested to achieve this.*

Perhaps the more bureaucratic approach of official policy statements like *Valuing People* and the Care Standards can work alongside the more inspiring relationship-based words of L'Arche:

> *We develop relationships of mutuality in which people give and receive love. We create homes where faithful relationships based on forgiveness and celebration are nurtured. We seek to reveal the unique value and vocation of each person. We are active in changing society by choosing to live relationships in community as a sign of hope and love.*

(From a statement by L'Arche in America, **www.larcheusa.org**, quoted by Williams, 2002: 57)

Jack Tizard

Opposition to the eugenics movement grew in Britain in the 1930s and 1940s, and more optimistic and positive attitudes towards people with learning difficulties began to emerge. The 1940s also saw the beginnings of parents' groups, including the organisation that eventually became Mencap, the major charity in Britain representing people with learning difficulties and their families.

A key development was the setting up of a research team in 1948 by the Medical Research Council under the direction of Sir Aubrey Lewis. He recruited, among other researchers, a young psychologist from New Zealand – Jack Tizard (Williams, 2005b, 2005c). Tizard began researching the potential of people with learning difficulties to do a job of work, reported in a book (O'Connor and Tizard, 1956) whose title – *The Social Problem of Mental Deficiency* – still reflected the old negative thinking of the eugenic era, but whose content was much more positive. It led to an emphasis in day services for people with learning difficulties on constructive work-based activities.

Tizard was disturbed by the poor quality of provision that he saw in institutions, and he was instrumental in supporting a report by the National Council for Civil Liberties (now called just Liberty) in the early 1950s called *50,000 Outside the Law* (1952). This documented the poor treatment and lack of rights for people with learning difficulties living in institutions. It led in part to the setting up of a Royal Commission to review the law, which resulted in a new Mental Health Act which accorded many more rights to people with learning difficulties or mental health problems. In 1959, Tizard initiated a famous research project – the Brooklands experiment. A group of children living in a large institutional hospital were transferred to live in a much more homely environment in a large house called Brooklands. Staff were taught to have a developmental, rather than custodial, approach to the children. The children's progress was monitored in comparison with a comparable group of children who remained in the hospital. Impressive gains in ability were recorded in the Brooklands children (Lyle, 1960).

The development of community care

Tizard was later appointed Professor of Child Development at London University Institute of Education. He initiated many research projects to demonstrate the potential of people with learning difficulties and the possibilities for provision of much better services for them. In 1964 he published a key work – *Community Services for the Mentally Handicapped* – which set out a blueprint, based on research knowledge, for a comprehensive pattern of community-based services for people with learning difficulties.

In 1971, the government produced a White Paper called *Better Services for the Mentally Handicapped*, which set out a plan for a partial reduction in the numbers of people in institutions and their relocation into community-based provision. Just before its publication, a group of young people with radical ideas about people with learning difficulties and their need for social inclusion, equality and rights, set up a pressure group for the improvement of services. They called the group Campaign for the Mentally Handicapped (later renamed Values Into Action). One of their first publications was called *Even Better*

Services for the Mentally Handicapped (1971), arguing for the complete closure of institutions. The late 1960s and early 1970s also saw the establishment in Scandinavia, Britain and America of projects to explore the feasibility of caring for people with severe degrees of learning difficulty in community settings, opening up the possibility of the complete closure of institutions. One of the researchers sponsored by Jack Tizard was Maureen Oswin, who continued to document the very bad conditions in hospitals for people with learning difficulties, especially children, in her books *The Empty Hours* (1971) and *Children Living in Long-Stay Hospitals* (1978). Her work illustrated the slowness of progress towards better services, but it also provided a boost to efforts to close the institutions.

These forces together – the work of pressure groups, the establishment of demonstration projects and studies of people's experiences in institutional care – began a general move towards the complete closure of the institutions and the relocation of their residents into community settings. The role of social workers in this process of closure and relocation has been documented by Horner (2003).

Normalisation

A framework was needed for the establishment of new community-based services, based on the more positive values that were becoming established towards people with learning difficulties. This was provided by a set of ideas or principles known as 'normalisation'. The concept had been spoken about and used in planning services in Scandinavia in the 1960s, but the first written exposition of it was in a paper by Bengt Nirje (1969). He defined the principle of normalisation as *making available to the mentally retarded patterns and conditions of everyday life which are as close as possible to the norms and patterns of the mainstream of society*. In other words, the same values that are held by most people in society about their experiences of everyday life should be applied to the opportunities for experience that are offered to people with learning difficulties. This principle again focused attention on institutional care, where the homeliness of buildings and the activities and routines of the day departed in very obvious ways from mainstream norms and patterns. The principle of normalisation was embraced in the planning of many services designed to offer a more community-based alternative to institutions. One of the people who developed the concept was the German-born American psychologist Wolf Wolfensberger. He edited a book (Wolfensberger, 1972) which expanded the concept of normalisation and detailed its application in many different areas of service provision.

Social role valorisation

In a previous paper on the origins of institutions, Wolfensberger (1969) had outlined some negative or unhelpful social perceptions of people with learning difficulties that he argued underlay the eugenics movement and the growth of institutional care in the first half of the twentieth century:

- as a sick person;
- as a subhuman organism;
- as a menace;

- as an object of pity;

- as a burden of charity;

- as a holy innocent.

Wolfensberger realised that unless these perceptions were challenged and were changed, people would be as much at risk of social exclusion and poor everyday life experiences in newly created services as they were in the institutions. In other words, the bad experiences of people were not attributable to institutions per se, but to negative or unhelpful attitudes towards groups of people in society. Furthermore, this did not just apply to people with learning difficulties, but to many other groups who were 'societally devalued'. Wolfensberger thus developed the idea of normalisation into a framework or set of principles to address this societal devaluation. Because the term 'normalisation' no longer fully expressed this aim, he proposed a new term: 'social role valorisation' (Wolfensberger, 1983). The framework has since been developed into a sophisticated set of ideas and principles, derived from empirical evidence of what influences social perceptions of people (Wolfensberger, 1998; Race, 1999; Flynn and Lemay, 1999).

The institutionalisation of people with learning difficulties is only one, albeit extreme, expression of their societal devaluation; there are many other ways in which people are rejected, isolated, denied opportunities and poorly treated. Jean Vanier called these negative experiences of people their 'wounds', and this term has also been used by Wolfensberger in a detailed analysis of the negative experiences that constitute devaluation. This analysis will be described in Chapter 7 in the context of assessment of people's needs. Normalisation and social role valorisation are, however, sets of positive principles for avoiding societal devaluation. They involve giving attention to the size, design, appearance and location of buildings; to the nature of activities and the possessions people have; to the groupings of people within services, the identity of support staff and the nature of relationships with people; to support for people in their presentation of themselves to others; to terminology used about people and services; and to rights and autonomy. The two main strands of social role valorisation are achieving conditions that maximise opportunities for the development of competence in people to participate equally in society, and structures, settings and practices that promote positive and helpful images and messages about people and their human and social worth and status (Wolfensberger and Glenn, 1975; Wolfensberger and Thomas, 1983, 2007).

Accomplishing an ordinary life

John O'Brien produced a version of these ideas in the form of what he calls 'service accomplishments' (O'Brien, 1987). He delineated five areas of accomplishment which encapsulate the main ideas of normalisation and social role valorisation: presence in the community; skills and competence; rights and choice; respect and dignity; and participation in community life and activities.

Utilising the concept of normalisation, the influential policy research and advice organisation in Britain, the King's Fund, produced a document called *An Ordinary Life* (King's Fund Centre, 1980). It stated:

Our goal is to see mentally handicapped people in the mainstream of life, living in ordinary houses, in ordinary streets, with the same range of choices as any citizen, and mixing as equals with the other, and mostly not handicapped, members of their own community.

This document was adopted as a guide by many health and social service agencies in planning new services, and considerable progress was recorded in a follow-up book *An Ordinary Life in Practice* (Towell, 1988).

Part of the movement towards greater acceptance and inclusion of people in mainstream community life has been a reappraisal of the meaning of 'community'. One of the foremost thinkers and activists in this has been the American writer John McKnight. Here is an extract from his book *The Careless Society* (McKnight, 1995: 172):

There is a mistaken notion that our society has a problem in terms of effective human services. Our essential problem is weak communities ... We all know that community must be the centre of our lives because it is only in community that we can be citizens. It is only in community that we can find care. It is only in community that we can hear people singing. And if you listen carefully, you can hear the words: 'I care for you, because you are mine, and I am yours.'

The pursuit of normalisation, social role valorisation and 'an ordinary life' is thus very much community work, as well as work with individuals, their families and services. It is compatible with, and complementary to, the social model of disability proposed by the disability movement, in which disability is not seen as a characteristic of the individual but as a consequence of society's attitudes and behaviour towards people with impairments (Race et al., 2005).

Anti-oppressive practice

This can be linked to frameworks for anti-oppressive or anti-discriminatory practice. One framework for doing this is known as the WISE principles (Williams 2004; Nzira and Williams 2009). They incorporate the two main strands of social role valorisation – promotion of competence through appropriate and effective support, and promotion of positive imagery:

- W is for Welcome: the welcoming of diversity and the welcoming of groups and individuals with particular identities, through knowledge and appreciation of their history, culture and contribution to society.

- I is for Image: the promotion of positive messages about groups or individuals, through knowledge of their strengths and achievements.

- S is for Support: the provision of whatever support people need to function equally in social situations.

- E is for Empowerment: the according of a voice to groups or individuals, and listening to and acting appropriately on what people say.

ACTIVITY 2.7

Think of a situation or setting in your own daily life: a leisure activity, your home and family life, your work or your education. Think through the four elements of the WISE principles and how you might apply them in relation to people with learning difficulties being included in that setting or activity:

How might you welcome people?

How might you promote a positive image of them to others? Is there any knowledge that would help in this, of the history, strengths, achievements and contribution of the person? Are there generalisations that can be made about the positive characteristics, strengths, achievements and contribution of people with learning difficulties in general that would help?

What supports might we give people to enable them to function equally in that situation?

How can we help to give people a voice in that setting, and ensure that it is listened to? How can we accord people rights and protection to ensure they are treated equally and with respect?

COMMENT

Your answers will depend on the situation or setting you choose, but there are many examples of inclusion of people with learning difficulties where these issues have been thought through. For example, the Open University has run distance-learning courses for people with learning difficulties, and Anglia Polytechnic University has run courses for people to improve self-confidence through use of media such as photography. These open up university facilities to people who might be excluded. They involve welcoming people to a university environment, having a positive image of their potential and contribution as students, giving appropriate support to enable them to benefit from university facilities, and empowering them to play a full role as university students. (See also Wilson et al. 2012.)

CHAPTER SUMMARY

This chapter has reviewed the values underlying social policy through a historical account of attitudes and practices towards people with learning difficulties in different societies and at different times. Ostensibly, there are high values of equality and inclusion underlying current policies, and social workers have helped to bring about the prominence of these values in official statements and intentions. However, we will need to continue striving for the actual implementation of these values in real services on the ground, and in the real experiences of people with learning difficulties and their families. We need to do this in the knowledge of how easy it has been in the past for negative values to predominate in society's responses to its vulnerable members: hence the vital importance of a strong values base to social work practice.

Department of Health (2001) *Valuing People* is the government's statement of policy and principles to underlie services for people with learning difficulties. It is essential reading for everyone with an interest in this field of work.

Department of Health (2009d) *Valuing People Now* updates this policy.

House of Lords and House of Commons Joint Committee on Human Rights (2008) *A Life Like Any Other?* is an interesting commentary by politicians on how they see the needs of people with learning difficulties.

Race (2003) *Leadership and Change in Human Services* is an edited collection of the writings of Wolf Wolfensberger who has had a great influence on the development of services through a values-led approach.

The website of the Center for Holocaust and Genocide Studies at the University of Minnesota in Minneapolis, USA, **www.chgs.umn.edu**, describes in detail the fate of people with learning difficulties in Nazi Germany.

Chapter 3
Policy and legislation

Introduction

Not only is it essential for social workers to understand the law and its role in practice but the law also sets boundaries for social work practice itself. Human rights and justice are fundamental to law; thus having an understanding of law and its application to practice are essential (Johns, 2011). Whilst this is the case within all aspects of social work practice, people with learning difficulties have historically experienced discrimination and trauma from failures of services (Talbot et al., 2010). Therefore an understanding of policy and legislation is essential for students and practitioners to enable them to support people with learning difficulties in a person-centred individualised way.

ACTIVITY **3.1**

Task 1: Define what is meant by legislation

Task 2: Define what is meant by policy

Task 3: Define what is meant by law

COMMENT

Thompson (1996) defines legislation as the process of making laws, *policy as* course or principle of action adopted or proposed by government *and law as* rule enacted or customary in a community and recognised as enjoining or prohibiting certain actions and enforced by the imposition of penalties.

The social worker's professional role includes intervention to protect or support the service user themselves, their family, carers or others. When working with people with learning difficulties a substantial part of the role incorporates supporting people to achieve independence, choice and well-being, to understand and access their rights, to be socially inclusive and to achieve equal opportunity with respect for diversity and difference (Talbot et al., 2010). However, how can this be achieved without a framework to adhere to? That is where the law and an understanding of it significantly impact the social worker's role. By understanding what laws are applicable in each individual case and how to use them in practice the law then becomes an invaluable and useful tool.

Putting knowledge into practice

> **CASE STUDY**
>
> *Ben is a 21-year-old man who wants to move into supported housing. Ben has Down's syndrome and learning difficulties, but he is active, going to college, having many friends including a steady girlfriend, and engaging in several hobbies at home. He has some health issues which include congenital heart defect, long-sightedness, some hearing loss and recurring ear infections. He has been used to regularly attending hospital and clinic appointments initially with his Mum and now with his personal assistant (PA) accessed through direct payments (Department of Health, 2009b).*
>
> *Ben's Mum, Lisa, is supportive of Ben moving to supported housing as not only has she always encouraged Ben to be as active and independent as possible, she is also concerned that one day she will be too old to care for him herself.*

> **ACTIVITY 3.2**
>
> *What policies or legislation do you think you could use to support Ben's choice? Outline the process of preparing a report or representing Ben at a funding panel.*

> **COMMENT**
>
> *First of all, it is essential you communicate with Ben. Find out his thoughts and feelings. In order to demonstrate Ben's views one option may be a tool such as multi-media advocacy to create a portfolio, which allows for person-centred pre-planning. Ben could provide a PowerPoint presentation or use a digital camera to explain his choices (Mickel, 2011).*

Amongst the policy and legislation you may have considered are:

- National Assistance Act 1948;
- Chronically Sick and Disabled Act 1970;
- Disabled Persons Act 1986;

- Human Rights Act 1998;

- National Health Service and Community Care Act 1990;

- Community Care (Direct Payments) Act 1996;

- Disability Discrimination Act 1995 (2005 amendment).

It is important to note that whilst an act may stipulate that certain services need to be provided, it does not necessarily stipulate how these services are delivered, which is where difficulties can arise with people receiving different services in different areas (Johns, 2011; Brayne and Broadbent, 2002; Brayne and Carr, 2012; Jones, 2009).

In the next section we will primarily focus on:

- *Valuing People* 2001 and *Valuing People Now* 2007 and 2009;

- The Health and Social Care Act 2012;

- The Equality Act 2010;

- The Autism Act 2009.

We will also briefly consider the role of the Equality and Human Rights Commission and the implications of personal independence payments. Finally, we touch on concerns about how people with learning difficulties fare if they come into contact with the criminal justice system.

Valuing People

Firstly we will consider *Valuing People* (Department of Health, 2001) as it could be argued this was a turning point in improving lives for people with learning difficulties. One of the key features of this government White Paper was that people with learning difficulties themselves, and representatives of their families, were closely involved in the groundwork behind it. A Service Users Advisory Group was set up, comprising of members of several self-advocacy groups, with a small number of supporters and advisers experienced in facilitating people with learning difficulties to express their views. This group produced a report called *Nothing About Us Without Us*. As we described in Chapter 1, this is a motto taken from the wider disability movement that expresses a primary need of people to be involved in all decisions that affect them.

Valuing People had many facets that indicated values officially accepted to underlie service provision in principle. It stated four 'key principles': rights, independence, choice and inclusion. Mechanisms are suggested for giving people more control over their lives and the services and support they receive, for example through advocacy, individualised person-centred planning and direct payments. Attention is given to improving health services for people with learning difficulties, and to the needs of people from minority ethnic groups. Intentions are expressed to develop more leisure services, more opportunities for employment, more choice in housing options and more support for carers. Priorities in the use of new funding are the modernisation of day services, the closure of the few remaining institutions, developing better services for people living with older carers, promoting advocacy, supporting the introduction of person-centred planning, developing local specialist provision for people with behaviour difficulties and integrating health and social services for young people with complex needs.

Despite mechanisms in place to ensure the *Valuing People* agenda was pursued, for example the appointment of a full-time National Director to oversee implementation and the creation of a Taskforce which included representation of people with learning difficulties themselves (see Chapter 7), there has been disappointment in the progress achieved. For example, 'modernisation' of day services has meant in some areas the closure of day centres without adequate alternative provision and with a narrowing of eligibility criteria, leaving some people without day provision at all.

Valuing People Now

In 2007 the government published a consultation document outlining proposals to rejuvenate the implementation of *Valuing People*; this was called *Valuing People Now* (Department of Health, 2007b). It covered the areas of personalisation; what people do during the day; better health; improving people's housing situation; advocacy and rights; partnership with families; inclusion; citizenship; and transition into adulthood.

Whilst there is no doubt that this government strategy document has contributed to major policy shift, there has been criticism of it for not setting targets or committing resources. However, it has kept the ideas, values and principles in *Valuing People* alive. For a comprehensive analysis and critique of *Valuing People Now* see Congdon (2008). A revised version of *Valuing People Now* was published in 2009 (Department of Health, 2009d).

Whilst the policy aims to act on what people with learning difficulties and their families have said, has this really been the case in practice? Three of the areas in which people with learning difficulties wanted their lives improved were employment, community learning and housing. Let's consider these.

Employment
The *Valuing People* team has published new practical tools to assist local partners to support people with learning difficulties with regard to employment; these include:

- the business case for local authorities to support more people with learning disabilities into work and invest in supported employment, which evidence suggests can save money for social care;

- a 'How To' Guide with learning and practical information from the *Valuing People Now* employment demonstration sites (including Getting A Life, Jobs First and Project Search);

- a guide for local authority commissioners;

- the government's new best-practice guidelines for supported employment and job coaching.

For more information see Valuing People Now Update: **www.y-gen.co.uk/pages/ resources-archi-valuing-people-now-update-496.html**.

The Valuing People Now Update guidance raised awareness of the role of the British Association of Supported Employment (BASE). BASE is the national trade association which represents agencies involved in securing employment for people with difficulties and disabilities. Its aim is to raise awareness of supported employment, represent the sector on a collective basis, inform members, and encourage best practice. (For more information see **www.base-uk.org**.)

Community learning

The Department for Business Innovation and Skills (2011) has provided information on how to access educational and employment support in a document *Review of Informal Adult and Community Learning* (for more information see **www.bis.gov.uk**).

The review highlights that people with learning difficulties may experience complexity participating in informal learning which can result in isolation or social exclusion. This could be due to *inaccessibility of buildings and lack of reasonable adjustments to learning materials* and *they may also have attitudinal barriers such as low expectations and the fear or prejudice of others* (2011:10).

Whilst the conclusion of this review stated that the overarching aim was to *support flexible, innovative informal adult learning that develops social and economic capital at an individual, family and community level and supports the development of the Big Society* (2011:12), it could be argued that this depends on what support is available in the area where the person with the learning difficulty lives. Also it could depend on how pro-active the people who support the person with the learning difficulty are, whether they are aware of what is available and the extent to which support is accessible.

Housing

The Valuing People Now Update also highlights the importance of housing and information about housing and knowing how to get the money and support to make it happen. Housing Options is a charity providing a housing advisory service for people with learning disabilities, their families and their supporters. For more information see the Housing Options Website: **www.housingoptions.org.uk**.

The equivalent of *Valuing People* in Scotland is called *The Same As You?* (Scottish Executive, 2000). It has been followed up with a number of implementation reports (see **www.scotland.gov.uk/publications**).

ACTIVITY 3.3

Take a few minutes to critically reflect upon what you have learned so far and how you would use the legislative and policy framework to support Ben. Remember being reflective enables you to see what will work and what won't, what you can do better in the future by learning from the past and allows 'awareness, analysis and evaluation' (Brown and Rutter, 2008: 21).

Health and Social Care Act 2012

The introduction of the Health and Social Care Act 2012 (H&SCA) has brought about significant changes in the provision of Health and Social Care as it is the most extensive reorganisation of the structure of health and social care to date.

A major change for the social work profession was the abolition of the General Social Care Council in August 2012 and the introduction of the Health and Care Professions Council (HCPC), thus changing the regulatory body responsibility for the regulation of social care workers (H&SCA, Section 209). For more information see **www.hcpc-uk.org**.

However, the introduction of this Act raises questions; what are the implications of this Act for people with learning difficulties? Does it work in harmony with the overarching aims of *Valuing People* and *Valuing People Now?* Under the Act (Section 179), by 2013 Primary Care Trusts will be disbanded (Samuel, 2012). This will impact social work in general as much work has been done to engage in multi-agency partnership working between health and social care, with networks being built up and often budgets being pooled to provide the best cost effective service. With the new system GP consortia will be introduced in which there will be statutory bodies with responsibility for commissioning most health services, made up of GP practices (Samuel, 2012). GP practices will have autonomy to decide the boundaries of their consortia. Whilst councils will take on the role of public health duties, Health and Wellbeing Boards have the responsibility to ensure that multi-agency partnership working continues between health and social care (Sections 195/196).

The Act highlights that this reform will give people greater choice, putting them in control of their care and will build on progress already made with regard to personal budgets. For people with learning difficulties specialist support and services are needed to enable them to do this. Promotion of the changes and continued joint working is essential to contribute to this as often people with learning difficulties and their families only get support at times of crisis (McGill, et al. 2010).

Whilst organisations such as Mencap welcome changes that may improve lives for people with learning difficulties, they recognise that for them and their families support is increasingly difficult to access, as demand for social services grows while care budgets are cut (see **www.mencap.org.uk/news/article/mencap-responds-health-select-committee-social-care-report**). Mencap's *Death by Indifference: 74 deaths and counting – a progress report 5 years on* (2012) (following *Death by Indifference*, 2007) relates how a lack of basic care, poor communication, and failure to recognise pain are but a few areas in which the needs of people with learning difficulties are not met, with disastrous results. Thus whilst positivity is felt with regard to the introduction of the Health and Social Care Act the need for reform for people with learning difficulties is not only welcome, but essential.

Mencap has also highlighted that people with learning difficulties regularly face discrimination, with as many as 9 out of 10 people with a learning difficulty having been victims of hate crime or bullying. Whilst much campaigning is being done by Mencap and other organisations to address this, greater reform is still needed. (See **www.mencap.org.uk/standbyme.**)

Equality Act 2010

The Equality Act 2010 simplified the way people were protected with regard to discrimination. Under this law a person with any kind of impairment, including learning difficulties, who can show the issues they have in carrying out every day activities, is defined as a 'disabled person' and is protected under the terms of the Act. An important aspect of the Act is that it protects people from 'indirect discrimination', which is where policy or practice is applied in the same way to all persons, but may put someone with difficulty at a disadvantage. For example, information may be provided in written format, but there may be no easy-to-read version for people with literacy difficulties.

The Act means that if someone with a learning difficulty is treated unequally, unfairly or unfavourably, the person can make a claim for 'unlawful discrimination'. For example, if a person with a learning disability applies for employment and reasonable adjustment could be made to enable that person to be employed, e.g. specialised computer software, communication or technological support, there may be a case for unlawful discrimination if this doesn't occur. However, it is important to note that all cases are taken on an individual basis and the Act as a whole needs to be considered to gain the fullest of understanding. (For more information see Equality Act 2010: What do I need to know as a customer? **www.equalities.gov.uk**.)

The Equality and Human Rights Commission

This Commission, established in 2007, brought together the Disability Rights Commission, the Commission for Racial Equality and the Equal Opportunities Commission. Its overarching aims are to:

- bring together equality and human rights experts and act as a single source of information and advice;

- be a single point of contact for individuals, businesses and the voluntary and public sectors;

- help businesses by promoting awareness of equality issues, which may prevent court and tribunal cases;

- tackle discrimination on every level – some people may face more than one type of discrimination;

- constitute a national body which includes the tackling of age discrimination (**www. equalityhumanrights.com**).

For people with learning difficulties, their families, carers, supporters and professionals working with them, the Commission can be accessed to prevent inequality and unfair treatment, thus contributing to improving experiences and ensuring greater autonomy, independence and well-being.

Autism Act 2009

Autism is known as a 'spectrum' condition, meaning that it can vary from mild to profound. It is said to involve a triad of difficulties: in social interaction, communication and imagination. Some 75 per cent of people with autism also have learning difficulties (Talbot et al., 2010; Baron-Cohen, 2008). There is a closely related condition that affects people with higher intellectual ability, called Asperger's syndrome (Attwood, 2008).

The fact that this condition is complex requires specialist skill and services to meet needs. In the past these specialist services have not been widely available, and consequently many people with autism or Asperger's syndrome have been the responsibility of learning difficulty services, whether they have learning difficulties or not. The Autism Act committed the government to publishing an autism strategy to transform services for adults with autism. Following the publication of this strategy changes have been made to enhance the experiences of people with autism. However, there is still room for improvement as is testified by further additions to the strategy (see a report from the National Audit Office: **www.nao.org.uk/publications/1213/adult_autism_strategy_progress.aspx**).

People with autism and those with Asperger's syndrome have different needs. Following the strategy some specialist teams have been set up for people with Asperger's syndrome, acknowledging that they need different support and services from people with autism. However, services are still often located uncomfortably within learning difficulty or mental health teams (see the National Autistic Society website: **www.autism.org.uk/working-with/autism-strategy/the-autism-strategy-an-overview/adult-autism-strategy.aspx**).

The National Audit Office's progress report on the autism strategy (2012) highlights that whilst the Department of Health is the policy lead for autism, the nature of the strategy means that the responsibility is shared across departments, creating the flexibility of delivering services in a localised way. There is an Adult Autism Strategy Programme Board, whose members include government departments, people with autism, and representatives of carers and autism charities set up to oversee progress against the Strategy and facilitate local delivery.

Personal Independence Payment

From April 2013 the government is introducing a new payment called the Personal Independence Payment (PIP) which replaces Disability Living Allowance (DLA) for people of working age, 16–64 years. At present there are no plans to change the way DLA is provided for children less than 16 years. There will be an assessment of individual need carried out by a trained independent assessor, with contributions also being made by health, social care and other professions involved in the person's care. The focus of the assessment will be based on the person's ability to carry out a range of activities and skills used in everyday life.

This again is a major change to the way disability benefits are provided, and until the system is in place it is difficult to say what the implications for people with learning difficulties will be. However, this is where policy and legislation are a useful tool, because whilst changes are inevitable, legislation and policy can ensure people with learning difficulties are treated fairly and equally and their experiences are improved (**www.dwp.gov.uk/policy/disability/personal-independence-payment**).

Policy and legislation in practice

Refer again to the case study of Ben at the beginning of this chapter. Having gained a greater understanding of the policies or legislation that could assist Ben in his choice, how would you support him?

COMMENT

The first thing to remember is that all people with learning difficulties are 'people first'. All have different needs, hopes and aspirations. Whilst working within the law to ensure you contribute to the best possible outcome, you also need to balance this with risk (see Chapter 6). Valuing People *and* Valuing People Now *show the importance of service user involvement. It is essential that just because you think something would work well, you don't just continue without really listening to and considering the person with whom you are working.*

An important piece of legislation in this respect, which will be referred to in later chapters, is the Mental Capacity Act 2005.

In Ben's case you could consider contacting specialist organisations such as:

- The Down's Syndrome Association (**www.downs-syndrome.org.uk/information/for-professionals/social-care.html**);

- Action on Hearing Loss (**www.actiononhearingloss.org.uk**);

- Sense, the charitable organisation campaigning for deaf blind people (**www.sense.org.uk**).

You can also use research that has already been carried out. This will help you as a practitioner to think outside the box and maybe come up with fresh and innovative ways to support the person you are working with.

RESEARCH SUMMARY

How adults with learning disabilities view independent living (Bond and Hurst, 2009)

> *Nine people with learning disabilities talked about their own lives:*
> *they talked about the good and the bad things;*
> *they said it was sometimes hard but better than living in residential care;*
> *they want people who provide services to know that it can be hard living alone.*

Bond and Hurst highlight that whilst the key principles outlined in Valuing People *and* Valuing People Now *aim at enabling people with learning difficulties to have greater choice and control over their lives, in reality this is not always the case. They quote the* Down's Syndrome Association, *who acknowledge the aspirations of people with learning disabilities, but express concern at the level of support available and whether this will meet the needs of people with learning disabilities (Bond and Hurst, 2009: 286).*

Understanding legislation and policy not only sets out clear guidelines and a framework for social workers to practise within, but it also, through the court system, ratifies decisions made by social work agencies (Johns, 2011). However, it does need to be made clear that the law does not advise social workers what to do in every case, or in each individual circumstance. For example, when working with Ben, if the social worker chose not to explore and apply a particular piece of policy or legislation Ben and his family are unlikely to know that it could have been. Social workers also have to remember that the person with the learning difficulties has choice (balanced with risk) and if Ben made an informed choice to disregard how the law could be used in his case, that should be respected.

The criminal justice system

One specific area of legislation and related policy concerns what happens when someone with a learning difficulty enters the criminal justice system.

RESEARCH SUMMARY

Learning disabilities and criminal justice: custody sergeants' perceptions of alleged offenders with learning disabilities (Hellenbach, 2012)

Hellenback carried out a qualitative research study in which 15 custody sergeants from Cheshire, Merseyside and Greater Manchester were interviewed to find out their opinions and attitudes towards people with learning difficulties who are alleged to have committed a criminal offence. In his findings it emerged that:

- *there was a lot of confusion about what characterises a person with learning difficulties;*

- *the provision of support to offenders with learning difficulties, particularly the availability of an appropriate adult, depended on the custody sergeants' professional knowledge;*

- *pressure resulting from performance targets further compromised a detainee's needs for support being sufficiently considered by custody sergeants when processing arrestees.*

As background to this research, Hellenbach comments that *during the last decade, the mental health of individuals, and to a lesser extent their intellectual functioning, has received increased attention by the government resulting in improved access to services and support within mainstream society as well as within the criminal justice system.* The Police and Criminal Evidence Act 1984 (PACE) defined for the first time that a person not able to *understand the significance of what is said, of questions or of their replies ... should be treated as mentally vulnerable and an appropriate adult called* (§1G PACE). The Mental Capacity Act (2005) and the Mental Health Act (2007) further clarified what characterises learning disabilities and what safeguards should be put in place to recognise the vulnerability of those affected. In 2009, Lord Bradley's Review made a substantial number of recommendations regarding the treatment of arrestees when in police custody, court or prison (Nash and Williams, 2010; Bradley, 2009). The report suggests better awareness training of all criminal justice professionals, improved cooperation and exchange of information among mental health and learning disability services and criminal justice agencies to allow early identification of offenders with special needs and more consistency in the treatment of alleged offenders with a learning disability throughout different jurisdictions in England (Hellenbach, 2012: 16).

Hellenbach's findings suggest that amendments in law do not automatically result in changes of professionals' attitude. They highlight that if greater awareness had been achieved, some of the people with learning difficulties that are currently in the criminal justice system might have avoided this route altogether.

The Prison Reform Trust (PRT, 2012) has produced a document entitled *Fair Access to Justice? Support for vulnerable defendants in the criminal courts*. As well as giving recommendations for the better treatment of people with learning difficulties throughout the criminal justice system, it also raises concern about their welfare in prison. The report states that 7 per cent of adult prisoners have an IQ less than 70 and a further 25 per cent have an IQ between 70 and 79 (though see Chapter 1 for caution about the interpretation of such statistics).

CHAPTER SUMMARY

This chapter has discussed legislation and policy that are important to understand and integrate into practice when working with people with learning difficulties, not only to support people to achieve the best possible goals and aspirations in their lives but also in specific circumstances such as entry to the criminal justice system. Whilst there is much more progress to be made in improving the experiences of people with learning difficulties, policy and legislation contribute to these improvements being made. Campaigning work of organisations working with people with learning disabilities has impacted the past and will undoubtedly contribute to the future. A key factor is the contribution people with learning difficulties themselves make. One of the key features of the 2001 government White Paper *Valuing People* was that people with learning difficulties themselves, and representatives of their families, were closely involved in the groundwork behind it. They are the experts on their experiences and it is essential that their contributions are considered for future policy and legislation to really make a difference.

FURTHER READING

Johns (2011) *Using the Law in Social Work.*

This book is part of the Transforming Social Work Practice series written specifically to support students on social work degree courses. It aids students to understand how the law interacts with social work and impacts on their practice. The table of legislation will prove useful for quick reference and direction through the complexities of the legal system required within social work.

Barber et al. (2012) *Mental Health Law in England and Wales.*

This is a complete guide to the Mental Health Act 1983, as amended by the 2007 Act and is a comprehensive and up-to-date reference work for mental health professionals. This revised edition includes Mental Health Tribunal Practice Directions and information regarding the Care Quality Commission and the Health Inspectorate (Wales).

Pickford and Dugmore (2012) *Youth Justice in Social Work*.

This book analyses and puts in context several pieces of new legislation such as the Criminal Justice and Immigration Act 2008, The Youth Rehabilitation Order 2009 and the new Youth Condition Caution. This book enables the reader to follow complex and often difficult legislation and law.

Chapter 4

The role of the
social worker

A C H I E V I N G   A   S O C I A L   W O R K   D E G R E E

This chapter will help you to develop the following capabilities, to the appropriate level, from the **Professional Capabilities Framework**:

- **Values and Ethics**, Apply social work ethical principles to guide professional practice
- **Diversity**, Recognise diversity and apply anti-discriminatory and anti-oppressive practice
- **Justice**, Advance human rights and promote social justice and economic well-being
- **Intervention and Skills**, Use judgement and authority to intervene with individuals, families and communities to promote independence, provide support and prevent harm, neglect and abuse
- **Critical Analysis and Reflection**, Apply critical reflection and analysis to inform and provide a rationale for professional decision making.

It will also introduce you to the following standards as set out in the 2008 social work subject benchmark statement.
5.1.1 Social work services and service users
5.1.5 The nature of social work practice
5.5.1 Problem solving skills
5.6 Communication skills
5.7 Skills in working with others

Introduction

This chapter introduces a wide range of areas of work with people with learning difficulties in which a social worker might be involved. These are organised under the headings:

- support for people with particular characteristics;

- support for people with particular needs;

- support for families, family care and relationships;

- support for education, leisure and community inclusion;

- support for one's own home, work and daytime activities;

- support for empowerment and service development.

The chapter ends with an account of the roles and relationships of social workers in a particular project, as a further illustration of the variety and possibilities involved in this field of work.

What is a social worker?

In England, the title 'social worker' is now restricted by law to those who are registered with the Health and Care Professions Council, having obtained a recognised qualification in social work. The HCPC sets standards of proficiency for practice (**www.hpc-uk.org**). A social worker must be able to:

- practise safely and effectively within their scope of practice;
- practise within the legal and ethical boundaries of their profession;
- maintain fitness to practise;
- practise as an autonomous professional exercising their own professional judgement;
- be aware of the impact of culture, equality and diversity on practice;
- practise in a non-discriminatory manner;
- maintain confidentiality;
- communicate effectively;
- work appropriately with others;
- maintain records appropriately;
- reflect and review practice;
- assure the quality of their practice;
- understand the key concepts of the knowledge base relevant to the social work profession;
- draw on appropriate knowledge and skills to inform practice;
- establish and maintain a safe practice environment.

Critical reflection on one's own views, values and feelings, and on the outcomes one achieves, are also vitally important (Brown and Rutter, 2008).

It is difficult to be precise about the organisational framework for social work these days. In many local authorities, the former social services departments have been broken up, with children's services being allied to education, and adult services remaining separate or being allied with health. In unitary authorities, adult social services are allied with housing. In addition there are numerous private agencies or voluntary organisations that a social worker might work for. It is also possible to be self-employed and to sell one's skills to whoever needs them.

In this book, we do not take a fixed view of what role a social worker might be in. To us, a social worker is someone with certain knowledge, skills and values as a result of certified training. The knowledge, skills and values required for work with people with learning difficulties are in the areas:

- assessment of need;

- listening;

- problem-solving in partnership;

- supporting valued social roles;

- empathetic understanding of the existential identity of people;

- commitment to anti-oppressive practice;

- capacity for unconditional positive regard for clients.

For some roles, further training will be needed, and may be available in the form of post-qualifying courses. Other training courses in additional specific skills, for example counselling or careers guidance or service management, are also available.

Social work roles

Social work knowledge and skills are relevant to most people with learning difficulties in a wide range of situations. The main role for social workers at present is that of care manager in a local authority multi-disciplinary team (usually called a community team for people with learning disabilities, or CTPLD). This role involves assessment of need for community support services and commissioning services according to criteria of eligibility, availability and cost, together with more direct support and advice to individual clients and families. However, social workers also work in a wide variety of other services, whether primarily involving assessment, advice, advocacy or direct service provision. One of the features of social work with people with learning difficulties that many social workers appreciate highly is the opportunity to work with people over the long term – occasionally throughout their lives. This presents possibilities of relationships that are rarely available in other more short-term forms of social work. This theme will be explored later in this chapter. Chapters 5 and 6 present an account of possible needs of people with learning difficulties and their families across the lifespan, and give an impression of what lifelong work with a person might involve.

Areas of work

We will consider the wide range of areas of work that a social worker might get involved in or specialise in. Each is accompanied by a brief comment, with occasional case studies, research summaries or exercises. Some of the areas will be considered further in Chapters 5 and 6. Many of the areas are likely to involve close collaboration and team work with others: nurses, doctors, therapists, care staff, day service staff, counsellors, teachers, inspectors, employers, advocates, researchers, volunteers, members of the public, families, and of course people with learning difficulties themselves. Work with people with learning difficulties involves multi-disciplinary, partnership-based approaches.

As you read through the areas of work covered below, consider for each one the relevance of the social work skills and values listed above (assessment of need, listening, problem-solving in partnership, supporting valued social roles, empathetic understanding of the existential identity of people, commitment to anti-oppressive practice and capacity for unconditional positive regard for clients) and how they might be applied.

Support for people with particular characteristics

People with physical impairments or health issues

People with learning difficulties of any degree of severity may have additional physical impairments or have illnesses such as epilepsy or diabetes. Specialist knowledge of the needs of these people and appropriate treatment, care and support for them is necessary. For example, Doran and Williams (2005) give an outline of the kind of information that is needed by people working with people with learning difficulties who have epilepsy:

> *How can epilepsy be explained to people with learning difficulties? Are there any accessible materials for this? How can people be reassured before and after a seizure? How can the importance of regular medication be conveyed? What are some of the issues of consent for this group? ... Practical advice is needed on such things as pressure pads on beds or listening devices in bedrooms to warn of fits at night. Should helmets be worn? How can people be helped to be safe when cooking, bathing, swimming or riding in a car? And what are the issues in balancing safety considerations against restriction of opportunities or negative imagery (as in the case of helmets)? What are the issues of rights, respect and privacy for this group?*

People with sensory impairment

Problems of eyesight and hearing are much more common among people with learning difficulties than in the general population. We discuss this topic in detail in Chapter 8.

People with profound and multiple impairments

Some people have a very severe degree of learning difficulty or additional physical or sensory impairments that make them very vulnerable to isolation, lack of activity and stimulation, and lack of communication to and from others. Work with such people is challenging but can be very rewarding.

Caldwell (2005b) describes the use of a technique called 'intensive interaction' which involves close observation of the person's use of their body to create their 'inner world' of communication with themselves. This may involve making sounds, moving their eyes, touching or moving their hands or feet: it will be highly individual to each person. The carer or supporter then enters this world of communication by using the same sounds, touches or movements to begin a conversation with the person. An impressive video is also available showing this process in action (Caldwell, 2005a).

People with autism or Asperger's syndrome

As mentioned in Chapter 3, autism involves difficulties in understanding in areas of relationship and emotion, resulting in behaviour that is sometimes unusual or obsessional. There is a spectrum of severity of the condition itself, and it can be accompanied by any degree of cognitive intelligence. Autism accompanied by average or high cognitive ability is known as Asperger's syndrome. Some people with learning difficulties also have autism. Because of a lack of specialist services, people with autism, including those with Asperger's syndrome, may be referred to learning difficulty services for support. However, understanding the needs of people with autism and providing appropriate care and support requires particular knowledge and skills.

The novel *The Curious Incident of the Dog in the Night-time* by Mark Haddon (2003) gives an impression of what autism is like. Other reading we would recommend includes Hermelin (2001), Johnston and Hatton (2003), Rankin (2000) and Attwood (2008). The publishing firm Jessica Kingsley specialises in books on autism and Asperger's syndrome (**www.jkp.com**).

People with additional mental health problems

A much-needed special area of support for people with learning difficulties is in relation to additional mental health issues. People with learning difficulties experience mental health problems more frequently than other groups (Holt et al., 2006a, 2006b), and accurate diagnosis, and effective treatment and support, require specialist knowledge.

RESEARCH SUMMARY

James Hogg and Maureen Philip from the University of Dundee carried out a research project under the auspices of the Foundation for People with Learning Disabilities, called the Well-Being Project. The question they researched is: What leads carers to identify changes in emotional and mental well-being in young people with profound and multiple learning disabilities and how do they respond?

Indicators used by parents and carers include changed communication and social behaviour, disruption of sleep and mealtime activities and challenging behaviour. Situations reported as affecting mental health included bereavement, losing relationships, boredom and important transitions in life such as leaving school. The person's physical condition often affected emotional well-being while poor mental well-being could lead to poor physical health.

However, parents and carers reported that they had little confidence in professional advice when their son or daughter experienced difficulties in their mental health, and many sought their own solutions.

The project resulted in a manual to help carers identify mental health problems (Philip et al., 2005).

Offenders with learning difficulties

People with learning difficulties who have committed offences have special needs for advocacy and advice, support in their contacts with the police and the justice system, work on prevention and rehabilitation, and – for some people – care in conditions of greater security. A few people with learning difficulties are in high security hospitals under sections of the Mental Health Act.

Older people with learning difficulties

The recognition of the needs of older people with learning difficulties, and provision of appropriate care and support, requires special knowledge and awareness (Crawford and Walker, 2008). This is discussed further in Chapter 6.

Members of Black and Minority Ethnic communities

People who are disabled and also Black may find that their needs and interests are not fully catered for in services or activities either for disabled people or for Black people. There is thus a need in provision for people with learning difficulties for special consideration to be given to support for members of Black and Minority Ethnic communities. This may involve the provision of information about services to those communities, anti-oppressive policy development, protection of rights, knowledge of and sensitivity to culture, knowledge of different languages and support for inclusion in relevant community groups or activities. A helpful resource is the National Learning Disability and Ethnicity Network (**www.lden.org.uk**).

Lesbian, gay, bisexual or transgendered people

There is a need for special support for people with learning difficulties who have a sexual orientation or identity which is associated with a risk of discrimination or oppression from others (Partners in Advocacy, 2004).

Support for people with particular needs
People with terminal illness

An area of specialism is in support for people with learning difficulties who have life threatening or terminal illnesses. A number of resources for this work have been produced (for example, the workbook by Brown et al., 2005), and there is a group of palliative care professionals with a special interest in this area (see Blackman and Todd, 2005).

Bereavement counselling

In the past it was often thought that many people with learning difficulties could not understand the concept of death, did not experience grief and were best protected from the trappings of death. One of the seminal works of the pioneer researcher on the needs of people with learning difficulties, Maureen Oswin, was called *Am I Allowed to Cry?*

(1991). Nowadays the vital importance of supporting people through bereavement and a grieving process is more recognised. The Royal College of Psychiatrists, together with St George's Hospital Medical School, have produced materials to help people with learning difficulties, and those who support them, in bereavement: *When Mum Died* and *When Dad Died* by Sheila Hollins and Lester Sireling (2004a, 2004b), and *When Somebody Dies* by Sheila Hollins et al. (2003).

People in hospital

Health service personnel do not necessarily know much about the special needs of people with learning difficulties, and so they need support and advice when they encounter them (Michael, 2008). This is especially so when a person with learning difficulties is admitted to hospital. Their means of communication, degree of skill, preferences, care needs and value as a person all need to be communicated to hospital staff. In extreme cases, people need protection from neglect when in hospital (Wolfensberger, 2005).

People who have been abused

Unfortunately, people with learning difficulties are vulnerable to abuse. The survey of people with learning difficulties mentioned in Chapter 1 (NHS, 2005) found that 43 per cent of adults had been bullied at school and 32 per cent did not feel safe in their home area. Some people suffer serious physical, sexual or emotional abuse (Turk and Brown, 1993; Pring, 2003). Recognition, prevention of and response to abuse is an important part of social work with people with learning difficulties.

Formed in 1991, Respond is a voluntary organisation specialising in advice and therapy for people with learning difficulties who have been abused. It provides a range of services to child, adult and older victims and perpetrators of abuse who have learning difficulties, and training and support to those working with them (**www.respond.org.uk**). Other organisations concerned with people with learning difficulties who have experienced abuse include the Ann Craft Trust and Voice UK (see the list of internet sites at the end of this book).

Psychotherapy

Psychologically based therapeutic work with people with learning difficulties has long been recognised as a need. A major textbook on learning difficulty over 50 years ago included a chapter on this (Gunzburg, 1958). Many people with learning difficulties have gone through traumatic experiences; the negative consequences of their impairments or other people's reactions to them may have had a severe impact on their self-esteem or psychological functioning. A psychoanalytic approach to these issues was given a boost by the publication of a book by Valerie Sinason in 1992:

> *Handicapped adults and children are still too rarely seen to have words and thoughts of value inside them and only too rarely provided with a means of interpreting them or having them interpreted. It is not surprising that they can give up the exhausting and unequal struggle for communication and keep their thoughts locked up in their heads.*

> (Sinason, 1992: 3)

Work with people with difficult behaviour

Some people with learning difficulties have behaviours which present problems to themselves or others. Examples would be aggression towards others or destructiveness of property or self-injury. There has been much research into the treatment and management of such behaviours (Emerson et al., 1993; Harris et al., 2001). Work with people with difficult behaviour is a challenging area of practice, requiring particular vocational skills and values. (See the account of 'gentle teaching' in Chapter 1.)

Support for families, family care and relationships

Pre-natal or peri-natal counselling

Nowadays pregnant women are offered a range of tests to discover if their baby is likely to have an impairment. Women may need counselling or advice about the tests themselves and their implications, or about abortion, or about the consequences of impairment, the possible characteristics and potential of a child with the impairment, the management of uncertainty, or relationships with partner and family. A woman and her family may need support and advocacy in pursuing their decision to terminate the pregnancy, to continue or to seek adoption. Advice and support may be needed during pregnancy and at the time of birth. A social worker with good knowledge of the potential of people with learning difficulties and positive regard for them may be particularly helpful in preventing decisions based on negative information.

Fostering and adoption

Children with learning difficulties may require fostering or adoption, occasionally from birth, if their families are unable or do not wish to care for them. Many children for whom adoption is sought nowadays have impairments, and there are some specialist fostering and adoption agencies dedicated to this (**www.baaf.org.uk/info/disability**).

Support to families

At all stages of childhood and adulthood, the families of people with learning difficulties are likely to need support, including:

- practical support (for example to access benefits or gain aids or adaptations in the home);

- advisory support (for example on managing difficult behaviour or teaching skills or giving equitable attention to all family members);

- emotional support (through feelings of loss, uncertainty, loneliness); and

- advocacy support (in battles to achieve effective support and good experiences for the person).

Short-term ('respite') care

Regular short breaks for a person with learning difficulties away from parental care can be very helpful for families. It needs to be of high quality and of benefit to the son or daughter too if parents are to use the opportunity for relief of stress and worry (Oswin, 1984).

RESEARCH SUMMARY

Among the findings of Maureen Oswin's research into short-term care for children with learning difficulties is the following:

Parents had little or no opportunity to discuss their worries related to their children's special needs as handicapped children, and although they sometimes filled in forms about their children's care, they were not certain how and if this information was used. Professionals tend to underestimate the love that parents and their handicapped children feel for each other and the painfulness of their being separated.

(Oswin, 1984: 58)

Oswin found that regular placements of children with short-term foster families rather than in residential care settings provided the best way of ensuring good care for the child and reassurance to the parents.

Maureen Oswin's findings have been confirmed by more recent studies. For example:

Respite care was generally perceived as an inadequate service.

(Treneman et al., 1997: 548)

Respite care often fails to facilitate the maintenance of socially supportive relationships.

(McNally et al., 1999: 1)

Use of respite care ... appeared to engender a degree of emotional stress.

(Hartrey and Wells, 2003: 335)

Support for siblings of people with learning difficulties

The brothers and sisters of people with learning difficulties may have particular issues that require support or advice. They may feel neglected because of the care and attention their brother or sister requires within the family. They may have worries about heredity, about bringing friends into the home, about relationship or marriage prospects, about responsibility for future care of their brother or sister, and so on (Hames and McCaffrey, 2005).

Befriending

People with learning difficulties have a great need for friends (Firth and Rapley, 1990; Bayley, 1997), and there are schemes to recruit people to befriend individuals.

RESEARCH SUMMARY

A research study, sponsored by the Joseph Rowntree Foundation, of 234 befriending schemes in the UK reported:

Befriending services use a variety of criteria to match volunteer and user, including shared leisure interests, a similar personality, and age … Staff, volunteers and users all stress the importance of talking, and of the befriender taking a personal interest in the user … Mostly this occurs alongside a leisure activity which is based in the user's home neighbourhood. Befriending was found to be highly valued by the people who are befriended. The personal relationship formed with the volunteer is important to the user, as is the opportunity for social activities and new experiences. Most expect their current befriending relationship to continue and would ask for another befriender if something happened to end the relationship. To admit to loneliness is difficult, but a number of the users interviewed revealed they have few other visitors.

(Dean and Goodlad, 1998; excerpt from a summary at
www.jrf.org.uk/knowledge/findings, ref. SCR038, p.3)

Sex education, counselling and protection

People with learning difficulties require special help, advice and teaching in understanding emotional and sexual relationships. They may need support and advocacy in gaining opportunities and privacy for the development of relationships, but they may also need protection from exploitation or abuse. Counselling around appropriate behaviour or disappointment at not achieving desired relationships may be needed.

Marriage and relationship support

Some people with learning difficulties will be in a stable long-term emotional relationship with a partner, or may wish to get married, or may be married. Janet Mattinson (1970) wrote a book about social work support for people in such relationships, which remains a key study of marriages of people with learning difficulties. There is much support and advice that can be given to maximise the chances of relationships lasting and being satisfying to the people involved.

RESEARCH SUMMARY

Mattinson (1970) interviewed 35 married couples where at least one partner had received services under a label of having learning difficulties. She concludes her book with the summary:

The success of many of these marriages seemed to be related to the initial expectation not having been too high. That they had done so much better than most people had expected them to do gave them enormous satisfaction. Some failure was not as distressing to them as it might have been to other people whose aims were higher and who might have had a better model in their childhood ... 'To me you are mine, even if you cannot read and write,' was something very important to preserve, particularly when they found themselves to be more effective than when they were single. Singly, they once [had been seen as] defective in social living; paired, with renewed motivation to succeed, and ... reinforcing each other's strengths, many of them established marriages which were by no means defective.

(1970: 201)

Support for parents who have learning difficulties

Some people with learning difficulties have children. In the survey mentioned in Chapter 1 (NHS, 2005), 7 per cent had children, though only half of those had care of their children. Pioneer researchers in the area of support to such parents have been Tim and Wendy Booth (1994, 1998, 2005). Much attention is being given at present to support for parents with learning difficulties to avoid child protection concerns and the possibility of the children being removed from the care of their parents.

Some of the conclusions of the work of Tim and Wendy Booth are:

- *Parents with learning disabilities are at risk of having their parental responsibilities terminated on the basis of evidence that would not be used against non-disabled parents.*

- *People with learning disabilities are likely to have their parenting skills judged against much harsher standards and criteria than non-disabled parents.*

- *There is a presumption that parents with learning disabilities are incapable of parenting because of their disability; services tend to place an emphasis on people's deficits rather than on what people can do.*

- *Family and childcare problems are often ascribed to the limitations of the parents, when they owe more to environmental pressures or deficiencies in the support system.*

- *The organisational division between children and family teams and disability teams often results in parents not receiving the expertise and support they need to fulfil their parenting role.*

(Summarised from Booth, T. and Booth, W., 1994, 1998
and Booth, W. and Booth, T., 1998)

Support for the children of people with learning difficulties

A specialist area of social work with children and families is the welfare of the children of parents who have learning difficulties. This will involve practical support and advice to the parents on child rearing, and also may involve direct work with the children on issues of development, relationships with peers, care of their parents, or other worries or concerns.

Support for education, leisure and community inclusion

Pre-school provision

Good care and stimulation are very important for young children with learning difficulties, and advice on or introduction to methods of helping their children are likely to be very helpful for families. This is covered further in Chapter 5.

Educational welfare

Whether in mainstream or special schools, children may have social needs related to behaviour, motivation, performance, bullying, home–school contact, health or personal development.

Further education

Adults receiving further education may need social support in areas such as getting along with fellow students, managing the curriculum, taking part in college-based social events, avoiding bullying or discrimination, behaving appropriately, liaison between college and home, generalising skills to community life, or using transport independently.

Alternative communication methods and IT

Speech and language therapists are the experts in alternative means of communication, but social workers can also be involved in the development, teaching and use of these. There are many systems in use, and different people will need different systems. The most common system is a simplified version of British sign language, called Makaton, which enhances communication through the use of hand signs (**www.makaton.org**). Other systems use pictures, photographs or symbols. They are described in more detail in Chapter 8. The development of computer software and other technological aids for learning, communication or enjoyment by people with learning difficulties is a related area of work.

Creative activities: dance, music, art, writing, theatre

Some people with learning difficulties show special aptitude in the creative arts. Some write poetry (e.g. Josephson, 1997; Evans, 2005). Several people have written autobiographies (e.g. Kingsley and Levitz, 1994). An anthology of writings and art work was published some years ago by the Open University (Atkinson and Williams, F. 1990). There are several theatre and dance groups of people with learning difficulties which tour the country giving high-quality performances (Goodley and Moore, 2002). Some people with learning difficulties play musical instruments and have formed bands. Some are good artists who have exhibited and sold their work. Sally Johnson, who sadly died when she was 25, was a person with Down's syndrome who was a talented artist. She exhibited and sold many of her paintings, including one which was bought by John Major when he was Prime Minister to hang in No. 10 Downing Street (Anderson, 2003). Support of people in these creative endeavours is a growing and interesting field of work.

Sport

Opportunities for sport are helpful for health, enjoyment, self-esteem and social contacts. There are sports clubs for people with learning difficulties in many areas of the country, feeding talent into national and international competitions especially for people with learning difficulties. These take place under the auspices of the UK Sports Association for People with Learning Disability (UKSA – **www.uksportsassociation.org**), and Special Olympics Great Britain (**www.specialolympicsgb.org.uk**). In 2002, England won the World Football Championship of the International Sports Federation for People with Intellectual Disability, held in Japan. Simon Beresford, a young man with Down's Syndrome, has run in a number of international Marathons, raising over £20,000 for the Down's Syndrome Association (DSA, 2008).

Community inclusion

One of the most devastating experiences for people with learning difficulties is exclusion from 'ordinary' community facilities and activities, with subsequent loneliness and isolation. Community work to increase the skills of communities in including disabled people, and negotiation and support for the inclusion of individual people in specific community settings or activities, are needed.

Support for one's own home, work and daytime activities

Supported living and housing

Increasingly, people with learning difficulties are being helped to achieve ownership or secured tenancies of properties, so that their housing is relatively secure and is more in their control. Unlike residential care, in which housing and care are provided in a single package, in supported living whatever care people require is provided separately from their housing. People may need support in understanding and managing their housing arrangements, and many people will have the same needs for long-term care and social work as those in residential homes. Current issues in this area are discussed by Young (2008).

Adult placement

Most local authorities, and some voluntary organisations, have schemes to place adults with learning difficulties with families who will care for them when they are no longer able, or no longer wish, to live with their own family members. Arranging and supporting these placements is sometimes a specialist social work role within local authorities or other agencies (Baldwin, 2005).

Residential care

About 50,000 people with learning difficulties in England live in places registered as residential care homes (see Chapter 1). These vary in size, but many nowadays consist of ordinary houses accommodating small numbers of people, sometimes just two or three or four. This enables principles of 'normalisation' to be followed (see Chapter 2), where good relationships with neighbours and a range of ordinary community activities can be supported. Social work knowledge, values and skills are very much needed in such settings. Care homes provide opportunities for long-term work with a small number of individual people, based on close relationships and a detailed understanding of their history, identity and needs. This kind of in-depth residential social work is poorly paid but can be extremely rewarding.

Post-school transition and careers guidance

School leavers require support in moving on to work or further education or other daytime activities. *All Change – Transition into Adult Life* by Robina Mallett et al. (2003) is a resource for young people with learning difficulties, family carers and professionals. Transition can be a particularly complicated and stressful experience for a young person with disabilities and his or her family. *All Change* looks at the process of transition in England and the main issues and choices that may arise, both in the lives of young people with learning difficulties and for their families. It covers what happens when the young person leaves school, the choices they might need to make about further education, work, housing and leisure, the transition to adult services and the different options and types of support that are available.

Work preparation

Most day services will include schemes to prepare people for work, where this is considered appropriate. This preparation includes social aspects of appropriate behaviour, getting along with colleagues, presenting oneself well, communication skills, relating to the public, handling money, etc.

> **CASE STUDY**
>
> *The mother of a 26-year-old man with learning disabilities contacted her local supported employment agency as her son, Michael, wanted a job. The agency spent a significant amount of time establishing a rapport and identifying coping mechanisms to enable him to manage a transition into work. They agreed that in the first instance a work experience placement with a local employer would help. The agency approached an employer to explain how the agency would support Michael if they could 'carve' a job incorporating a variety of tasks in which Michael wished to gain some experience. The company was very open to ideas. Work adjustments were made by the agency and the employer with Michael during the placement and it became clear that Michael was not only enjoying the work but was demonstrating potential that the employer considered worthy of pursuing further. Near the end of the placement the employer tabled an offer of part-time employment to Michael.*
>
> *Michael's ever-growing confidence soon meant that 15 hours per week work was not enough for him. The supported employment agency helped him negotiate longer hours and a transition from benefits to wages. He is £77.46 per week better off than when he was on benefits. The agency continues to support Michael and the company is training and developing him further. He has worked for the company for nine months and now has the confidence to be considering leaving the family home. (Adapted from a report on employment by the Scottish Executive, 2003)*

Support in work

There are schemes to support people in work, through on-the-job training, mentoring, allocation of a supporter or fellow worker to assist or supervise, etc.

> **CASE STUDY**
>
> *During a presentation in Wiltshire in November 2005, John O'Brien from Responsive Systems Associates in Georgia, USA, told the story of Kenny. Kenny is deaf and blind and used to spend his time lying in a box banging his head, for which he wore an unsightly helmet. Through the support of a circle of friends, he learned to communicate by touch and gained a job collecting and sorting eggs on a farm. John ended the story with a slide of Kenny swigging a bottle of beer with his mates, wearing a wide grin and no helmet.*
>
> (Williams, 2006)

Day services

Adults with learning difficulties who are not in work or further education need activities during the day. There used to be large 'day centres' for people with learning difficulties in most local authority areas, but efforts have been made in recent years to provide a wider range of activities in more dispersed and integrated settings. Social work knowledge and skills are very relevant for staff in these settings. *Changing Our Days* by Andrea Whittaker (1999) is a book designed to explain alternatives to day centres to people with learning difficulties themselves.

CASE STUDY

Kevin is a young man in his 30s. He lives at home with his mother. He had not received any services for 15 years, had no regular activities and no social life. He couldn't talk or hear very well. Then he began to get help from staff who work with people by going to their homes. He had a lot of help with speech and language and learned to use symbols. This meant he could make real choices about what he wanted to do. Kevin particularly enjoys art and has joined mainstream art and pottery classes at his local college. He goes out for cups of coffee with his classmates. He is good at computers and has learned to hold conversations with people using typed messages. He goes swimming regularly and visits a neighbour. Kevin had an exhibition of his artwork and pottery at the café he often goes to. Family and friends came to see the exhibition and his picture was in the local newspaper. (Whittaker, 1999: 19)

Support for empowerment and service development

Support for self-advocacy

Individual people with learning difficulties can be taught skills and can be supported in order to represent their own interests and choices. In addition, the last two decades of the twentieth century saw the growth of self-advocacy groups of people with learning difficulties, often called 'People First' groups, which give a voice to people in pursuing their rights and needs (Williams and Shoultz, 1982; Dybwad and Bersani, 1996; Goodley, 2000). These groups benefit from the sensitive support of non-disabled advisers and helpers. Self-advocacy is covered further in Chapter 9.

Professional or citizen advocacy

Social work often involves advocacy on behalf of people (Brandon and Brandon, 2001). A person may in some circumstances need professional advocacy from others, for example a solicitor or benefits adviser. There are, however, limits to professional advocacy in the form of time constraints and possible conflicts of interest. A powerful alternative is citizen advocacy which involves recruitment of volunteers from the general public to represent the interests of a vulnerable person (Wertheimer, 1998; Williams, 1998; Gray and Jackson, 2002). Advocacy is discussed further in Chapter 9.

Financial and budgeting advice and assistance

As in many fields of social work, people may need advice on managing their finances. For people with learning difficulties this may involve teaching the value of money, recognition of different notes and coins, and simple maths to calculate totals and change, as well as planning skills to manage their budget. For those for whom direct handling of finances is not possible, support can be given in the form of trusteeship or financial management on behalf of the person. An important aspect is ensuring the person and their family have access to benefits to which they are entitled.

Management of direct payments

A few people with learning difficulties receive direct payments to enable them to purchase support services that are chosen by them and are in their control (Bewley and Holman, 2002; Gramlich et al., 2002; Duffy, 2003). People can be supported in the financial and management aspects of this by others, including social workers. This is likely to be an expanding area of work in the future. It is particularly promoted in the White Paper *Valuing People*.

Brokerage

This is a concept that originated in Canada (Brandon and Towe, 1989; Brandon, 1995). A broker is someone who negotiates the provision of a particular service or package of services for an individual. The broker is an independent person who combines advocacy on behalf of someone and a specialist knowledge of available or effective services. Some of the work of social workers in care management roles is similar to brokerage, but the concept adds an element of independence from agencies; brokers are likely to be self-employed or employed by advocacy organisations. Brokerage can be particularly helpful when someone is receiving direct payments.

Staff training

One possible role for a social worker with specialist knowledge of people with learning difficulties is in teaching others. These may include other professionals, student social workers or staff in social care roles. Many people working in residential care, day services or domiciliary support do not have a professional qualification, and training in skills, knowledge and values at a variety of different levels is important for them.

Service evaluation and inspection

Some social workers may develop a special interest in evaluating the quality of services. This can be done in partnership with service providers as a support for their improvement of the service offered. There are many tools for service evaluation. There is an instrument called PASSING (Wolfensberger and Thomas, 1983, 2007) which determines the extent to which a service is supporting valued social roles for the people served (see Chapter 2). There are measures of the extent of engagement of people in daily activities (Mansell et al., 2005). There are sets of official care standards, enforced by inspectors (some of whom are social workers), for residential care and domiciliary support services (Ridout, 2003).

Roles and tasks

As an extension of Activity 4.1, choose one of the areas of work listed above which particularly interests you. Imagine what sort of activities it would involve for you as a social worker. Write down a more detailed account of what the role might involve.

COMMENT

Depending on which area you chose, the work might involve:

- *assessment of need and the commissioning of services to meet the need;*
- *more detailed assessment in order to plan specific programmes of support;*
- *working closely with other professionals in a multi-disciplinary team;*
- *counselling or psychotherapy skills;*
- *practical advice;*
- *specialist care skills;*
- *skills of teaching;*
- *advocacy;*
- *support for self-advocacy;*
- *skills of negotiation or management;*
- *developing specialist knowledge about people with particular characteristics or needs;*
- *direct work with people with learning difficulties themselves;*
- *work with families;*
- *community work;*
- *work with agencies to achieve inclusion.*

So we can see the very wide scope for social work in relation to people with learning difficulties. You should not think too narrowly about what your role might be – there is plenty of opportunity to develop areas of work in which you are especially interested or have particular knowledge and skills.

The following research summary gives some findings on the formal role of social workers in one particular project. The study is limited, in that it does not cover work with families or support for people with severe degrees of impairment. It does, however, give an indication of some key tasks in direct social work with people with learning difficulties.

Atkinson (1989) carried out a study of the tasks performed by social workers as members of teams supporting people with a relatively mild degree of learning difficulty following their discharge from long-stay hospitals to live in community settings. She found that the formal role of the social workers had six main components: practical help, financial assistance, provision of, or referral to, services, mediation skills, crisis intervention and personal advice and support.

Practical help

Social workers had got involved in helping people order items for their home, accompanying them shopping, doing repairs in the home, helping people to contact landlords or contractors to carry out repairs, and giving help with correspondence and keeping in touch with family and friends. The social workers had to make judgements about when help was necessary and when it might encourage over-dependence or be seen as interference.

Financial help

As well as help to claim benefits, people needed advice on their entitlements, help to access their money and help with budgeting. If people got into financial difficulties, their social worker would give advice and support, refer the person to more specialised services and act as advocates and intermediaries. As with practical help, a fine judgement often had to be made between helping and protecting a person, and allowing them to experience independence and learn from possible problems.

Provision of, or referral to, services

For example, daytime activities, leisure activities, teaching of skills, befriending, medical or psychiatric help, and housing and care arrangements.

Mediation skills

Social workers were involved in resolving difficulties, disputes or complaints concerning neighbours, shopkeepers or others in the community where people lived. Most of these incidents were of a minor nature and were fairly easily resolved.

Crisis intervention

Sometimes urgent action was required. During the course of Atkinson's study there were four fires, several falls or injuries sustained by people, occasional serious illness and the deaths of two people at home. The role of the social worker was partly to prepare people in advance for possible crises: ensure people knew what to do and who to contact, and that people nearby would be available and willing to help.

Personal advice and support

People often turned to their social worker as a personal counsellor or confidant(e). Atkinson describes this as a key element in the social work task. Social workers played an important role in reassurance and seeing people through periods of disappointment, loneliness, self-doubt, communication difficulties, frustration, problems with sexual relationships, unemployment or lack of meaningful daytime activity. Some people needed help with personal appearance, hygiene or behaviour, or with keeping their home clean.

Friendship

One finding of Atkinson's research is that the social workers she studied developed close personal relationships with the people they were supporting. Sometimes in social work there is an emphasis on keeping clear boundaries, not letting work encroach on our personal lives and maintaining 'professional' or 'objective' relationships with people. Much work with people with learning difficulties illustrates that this may not always be necessary or desirable. We remember what a useful lesson it was to one of our students on placement in a community learning disability team, when he arrived for supervision by his practice teacher to find her in tears. She explained that she had just learned of the death of a person with whom she had worked as her social worker for many years. She had become a family friend. They had attended each other's weddings, had visited each other's homes informally outside the context of work and had spoken frequently on the phone to exchange news as equals. Our student saw social work in a new light. (There is further discussion of this issue in Chapter 6.)

Atkinson says:

> The social worker's task was characterised by informality. [It] took place within longterm relationships which involved frequent and regular contact. Many people had their social worker's home address and/or telephone number … All social workers called the people with whom they worked by their first names, and many service users reciprocated … Many social workers … described themselves as 'friends' of the people with whom they worked. Some service users shared this view, and came to see their social workers as their 'friends' too.

> (Atkinson, 1989: Chapter 6)

However, Atkinson also counsels that we should consider what friendship really means.

ACTIVITY 4.3

Consider what would constitute a relationship of 'friendship'. How might it express itself? You might use as a model some friendships you have in your own life. List the possible benefits and risks of considering the relationship between a social worker and a person they support as 'friendship'.

COMMENT

Atkinson says that a relationship of friendship should have components of warmth, sharing of interests and intimate aspects of our lives, mutual liking and reciprocity. It should persist even through major changes in circumstances; otherwise it may contribute to experiences of loss. True friendship is thus a major and long-term commitment. Where contact is likely to be short-term (as it will usually be for a student on placement) or strictly limited to a 'business' relationship, Atkinson says that we should make that clear and explicit to people from the outset. It is important for students to maintain a sense of professional boundaries until the experience is gained to judge the appropriateness of a friendship relationship.

However, long-term, frequent and close contact can lead to genuine friendship. This can be very beneficial to people, with an important proviso: the relationship should not be a substitute for the fostering and maintenance of other more 'ordinary' friendships for a person. Indeed, friendship between the social worker and the person supported should *be used to encourage other friendships, through personal introductions, role modelling, and practising and transfer of friendship skills* (Atkinson, 1989: 70–1).

A relationship of friendship with people with learning difficulties we support runs the risk of upset and loss if it cannot continue in the future. However, many people with learning difficulties have few friends (Firth and Rapley, 1990; Bayley, 1997) and they need the experience of friendship. Some people have gone further and suggested that provision of friendship is a major role for professionals and other staff in this field. David Pitonyak is a consultant and trainer from Vermont, USA, particularly on support for people who present difficult behaviour. He attributes much of people's difficulties to loneliness, resulting from the absence in their lives of close relationships. His publications have names such as *The Importance of Belonging* and *Loneliness Is the Only Real Disability* (Pitonyak, 2004, 2005). In his presentations, he describes many of the people with learning difficulties he knows as 'my friends' and he tells stories of how this friendship is expressed in experiences that are reciprocal and mutually rewarding (Williams, 2006).

CHAPTER SUMMARY

This chapter has reviewed the wide range of roles, tasks and activities that might be undertaken by a social worker in supporting people with learning difficulties and their families. We hope it has conveyed the scope for developing particular interests within this field of work, and some of the rewards that can come from the relationships involved.

FURTHER READING

Atherton and Crickmore (2011) *Learning Disabilities: Towards Inclusion.* A collection of chapters by a range of professionals illustrating the variety of services available.

Grant et al. (2010) *Learning Disability; A Life Cycle Approach.* An edited collection reviewing research and practice relevant to people with learning difficulties from childhood to older age.

Perry et al. (2010) *Caring for the Physical and Mental Health of People with Learning Disabilities.* A practical guide to working with people who have additional physical or mental health problems.

Thomas and Woods (2003) *Working with People with Learning Disabilities* gives a comprehensive account of this field of work, written by two social workers.

Turnbull (2004) *Learning Disability Nursing.* Despite its emphasis on health issues, this book gives a useful overview of work with people with learning difficulties.

David Pitonyak's papers (e.g. 2004, 2005) give a refreshing and interesting view of work in this field. They can be accessed at **www.dimagine.com**.

For light reading we would recommend **Mark Haddon's** novel (2003) *The Curious Incident of the Dog in the Night-time.*

Chapter 5
Working with children and families

Introduction

Social work practice with children and families is one of the most challenging, skilled and rewarding areas of social work practice (O'Loughlin and O'Loughlin, 2012: xi). One thing all children will have in common is that they are vulnerable and need support. In this chapter we will explore a life-stage perspective on need experienced by children and families. We will adopt what is sometimes called a systems approach, seeing the person not as an isolated individual but as part of a family, a local community, a particular background and culture, and wider society as a whole. Additionally the essentiality of safeguarding/protecting children and the multi-agency nature of work in this field will also be clear.

The following vignettes illustrate the need for a holistic or systems approach to work with families. Issues for one member are likely to have major impact on the other members too.

Keith attends a residential school and so is away from home during the week during term time. His parents travel a round journey of over 100 miles to bring him home on Friday evenings and take him back on Sunday evenings. They also have him home in the holidays. He requires constant attention because of epilepsy and overactive behaviour. His parents thus have very little time together. They also worry about the care he is receiving when he is away from home.

Susan has a younger brother with learning difficulties whom she loves very much. However, she has always been reluctant to bring friends home because she fears their reaction to meeting him. She is now 16 and is increasingly worried about telling boyfriends she has a disabled brother.

Tom and Sarah have a one-year-old daughter with Down's syndrome. The day-to-day task of caring for her is not too onerous, and they are delighted to have such a happy and loving child. However, they have not spoken to or seen Tom's parents since their daughter was born, after they expressed the view that Sarah should have terminated the pregnancy or had the child adopted or sent away to a home. Sarah's parents are no longer alive and Tom and Sarah would like their daughter to benefit from having grandparents.

Before birth

There are a number of areas where a social worker might be involved during a pregnancy, for example antenatal care, and during pre-birth screening.

Antenatal care

A first consideration in relation to all pregnancies is to ensure that the mother receives good antenatal care. There may be circumstances in which a particular mother or family requires support or advocacy in order to ensure this. These might include situations where the mother herself is disabled; experiences social deprivation; English is a second language; is very young; is drug/alcohol dependent; a lone prospective parent or may be reluctant to access antenatal care for other reasons. A social worker may also be the person to whom anyone might go for advice and support if they feel the antenatal care they are getting is poor.

Pre-birth screening

One of the most controversial areas in relation to pregnancy and learning difficulties is that of antenatal screening. The majority of women attending antenatal services will be tested, with ultrasound and/or blood tests, to identify the possibility of the baby having a condition associated with learning difficulties after birth. Not all such conditions can be detected, but some, such as Down's syndrome, can. If a likelihood of impairment is identified, it is current antenatal medical practice to offer the mother additional tests to enable consideration of termination. A social worker working in a multi-agency environment with medical, nursing and other colleagues may be involved in support or advocacy in a number of circumstances. This may concern the tests themselves, e.g. explaining the nature of the tests and discussing test-related anxiety; test reliability, e.g. the possibility of inaccurate results; risks of side effects associated with the tests; or supporting and advocating for women who do not want the tests. It may also involve giving information about particular conditions (like Down's syndrome, for instance), termination related counselling, supporting women after termination, and supporting women who continue their pregnancy knowing their child is likely to have learning difficulties. The need for support is likely to extend to the wider family. Sometimes facilitation may be required to resolve differences of views among family members.

A further area that social workers may be involved in before birth is in giving information and counselling about termination alternatives when the parents do not wish to keep the child. Opportunities for fostering and adoption of disabled babies do exist, and information and support can be given if this is what the parents would like to explore (for more information see **baaf.org.uk**).

ACTIVITY 5.1

Some women who have chosen to continue their pregnancy, knowing their child will have a condition associated with learning difficulties, have described the 'incredulity' of doctors and nurses at their decision (Williams, P. 1995). Why do you think that some professionals might take this view? What should be a social worker's position on this issue?

COMMENT

Many professionals involved in antenatal care will have been brought up in the traditions and values of the medical model (see Chapter 1). Learning difficulty is likely to be seen as an abnormality, akin to a disease, and its prevention a matter of good public health (for the benefit of society) and good medical practice (for the benefit of the mother and family and to avoid suffering by the child). Few professionals are likely to be familiar with positive expressions of the benefit and contribution to family and community life by people with learning difficulties (covered in Chapter 1). While claiming that they are merely offering a free choice to prospective parents about whether to have a child with likely learning difficulties, medical and nursing personnel may in fact exert strong pressure for termination (Williams, P., 1995). In order to be more objective and helpful in all circumstances that occur, a social worker should develop a balanced view of the positives and negatives of being a person with learning difficulties, of having a person with learning difficulties in the family and of the presence of people with learning difficulties in the community and in society.

At birth

There is a well-known piece that creates an analogy of giving birth to a person with learning difficulties. It was originally written by Emily Kingsley, a mother of a young man with Down's syndrome.

Welcome to Holland

By Emily Perl Kingsley
©1987 by Emily Perl Kingsley. All rights reserved.
Reprinted by permission of the author.

I am often asked to describe the experience of raising a child with a disability – to try to help people who have not shared that unique experience to understand it, try to imagine how it would feel. It's like this …

When you're going to have a baby, it's like planning a fabulous vacation trip – to Italy. You buy a bunch of guide books and make your wonderful plans, the Coliseum; the Michelangelo David; the gondolas in Venice. You may learn some handy phrases in Italian. It's all very exciting.

After months of eager anticipation, the day finally arrives. You pack your bags and off you go. Several hours later, the plane lands, the stewardess comes in and says, 'Welcome to Holland.'

'Holland?!?' you say. 'What do you mean Holland?? I signed up for Italy! I'm supposed to be in Italy. All my life I've dreamed of going to Italy.' But there's been a change in the flight plan. They've landed in Holland and there you must stay.

The important thing is that they haven't taken you to a horrible, disgusting, filthy place, full of pestilence, famine and disease. It's just a different place. So you must go out and buy new guide books. And you must learn a whole new language. And you will meet a whole new group of people you would never have met.

It's just a different place. It's slower-paced than Italy, less flashy than Italy. But after you've been there for a while and you catch your breath, you look around … and you begin to notice that Holland has windmills … and Holland has tulips. Holland even has Rembrandts.

But everyone you know is busy coming and going from Italy … and they're all bragging about what a wonderful time they had there. And for the rest of your life, you will say 'Yes, that's where I was supposed to go. That's what I had planned.'

And the pain of that will never, ever, ever, ever go away … because the loss of that dream is a very, very significant loss.

But … if you spend your life mourning the fact that you didn't get to Italy, you may never be free to enjoy the very special, the very lovely things … about Holland.

The welcome

Because many people have a very negative perception of learning difficulties, the birth of a child with learning difficulties will nearly always be seen as a tragedy, a disappointment, something to be regretted and mourned. A social worker can help in these situations by taking a realistic but positive view. It is important for the future well-being and happiness of the child and the family that the baby is welcomed and seen as a valuable person in his or her own right. Parents may need support in bonding with their child, in telling family members and friends about the birth in a positive way, and in responding to the baby with love and a positive perception. Many parents may find this extremely difficult and need great support, since they may be experiencing strong feelings and reactions of grief and disappointment at the loss of the imagined child they were expecting. This type of loss is described as 'non-finite loss', i.e. grief that is ongoing and changing as life consistently falls short of expectations (Collins, 2008; Bruce and Shultz, 2001; Evans and Whittaker, 2010). Empathy with this while helping to achieve a positive welcome for the child into the world is a skill that social workers involved at this time need to develop.

Some newborn children with conditions associated with learning difficulties may not have a high expectation of life. They may die at birth, after a few hours, days or months, or in the early years of life, and the loss is 'finite' (Evans and Whittaker, 2010: 54). Again, the prognosis for the child should not obviate the benefits of bonding and love by the parents, a welcoming of the child into the world, and a positive view of their value and contribution to family and community life. If and when the child dies, social workers may be able to help with the process of grief and loss (Thompson, 2002; Parker, 2005; Weinstein, 2008), and with practical arrangements for the funeral and memorial. There may also be a need for facilitation of discussion about having further children.

Infancy

Most children born with learning difficulties will survive into childhood and adulthood. One of their great needs in infancy, however, will be good and equitable health care. There has been evidence in the past of discrimination against children with learning difficulties, for example in whether to perform heart surgery when needed, because of a negative view by the medical profession of prognosis or 'quality of life' (Williams, P., 1995). Nowadays it is increasingly recognised that children with learning difficulties should have an equal right to medical care with all other children. If parents feel they are not getting this for their child, then a role for a social worker may be advocacy for the child's rights. Every child should have regular, expert, high-quality assessment, followed by remedial treatment if necessary, of nutrition, hearing, eyesight, mobility, teeth and general health, and a social worker can help to achieve these if they are not in place. Many parents value knowing something about the cause of their child's condition; this helps them to know they and their child are not alone, to learn about the condition, to join organisations concerned with people with the condition and to meet with other children and families with similar experiences and needs. Social workers can help families to find and access information and resources that relate to a specific diagnosis of their child. (For more information see **www.cafamily.org.uk**).

Stimulation

An example of a home-based scheme to help parents enhance their child's development is Portage, a home-visiting educational service for pre-school children with additional support needs and their families, first developed in Portage, Wisconsin, USA in the early 1970s. There are now 140 schemes in the UK (**www.portage.org.uk**).

Portage Home Visitors undergo training in the method. They visit families, initially at least weekly, to work with the parents in meeting developmental needs. Usually the aim of each home visit is to decide on an activity which the family can practise and enjoy together. The activities are based on play grounded in everyday situations to provide fun and success for the child. Each activity may represent a small step towards one of the family's planned goals and families using Portage usually choose to practise activities between weekly visits. Parents may use charts or diaries as a reminder of the activity and a record of what happens between visits. In this way a family can build a shared record of their child's involvement with Portage.

Some families find the Portage approach too formal and demanding for their needs, and prefer less structured home-visiting support.

Social support

The social development of the child is also of great importance. Every child needs experiences from an early age of meeting other people and being with other children of the same age, learning to play cooperatively with them. A social worker needs to be aware of unnecessary isolation of the child, problems of relationships with other children, or difficulties for the child in developing skills of play or interest in play. Considering the wider 'system' of the family and local community, there may be issues of relationships within the family, such as weak bonding by a parent, or difficulties experienced by or from siblings, or unhelpful behaviour towards the child or family by neighbours. Some families are at risk of becoming isolated from community networks, if care of the child restricts their social life, or if social contacts outside the home are not supportive.

There is a government programme called 'Early Support', designed to improve services to disabled children under five and their families (**www.gov.uk/help-for-disabled-child/early-support-programme**).

Childhood

School

For most children, starting school is usually a time of celebration and eager anticipation. The child may have fears and sadness at leaving the cosiness and security of home, but everyone expects there to be great benefits to the child's cognitive, social and physical development. Starting school is also a public community rite of passage. However, for a child with learning difficulties starting school may be seen as presenting great problems. Will he or she be able to go to the same school as his or her siblings or the neighbours' children? Will he or she get the right kind of education at the local school? Will he or she be bullied by other children, or not be able to cope with the teaching or other activities in school? Will he or she be disruptive to other children, and hence resented by those children, their parents and the teachers? What are the alternatives? Is there a special school available? Would it involve a long, tiring journey? Might not the same possible issues of suitability, bullying, disruptiveness or resentment arise as much in the special school as in the ordinary school? Won't the child get isolated from other children in the local neighbourhood, with damage to his or her social development and friendships?

The segregation of disabled children in 'special' schools has sometimes been severely criticised (Whittaker and Kenworthy, 2002; Smith, 2011). Many parents firmly believe in the benefits of inclusive education and will strongly press for their child to go to the local mainstream school with their siblings and neighbours' children. A social worker may be involved in supporting this choice and advocating for the family, perhaps in the face of much opposition by the school or education authority. Some families do believe strongly that a special school will be best for their child. The most helpful role for a social worker in that situation is to ensure the parents have full information, that the child's needs – both social and educational – are properly assessed and that the consequences of the choice are fully discussed. The choice may be due to poor support for inclusion in the local school, in which case there may be a need for advocacy on the family's behalf for adequate support to be provided. Or the choice may be based on genuine preference and good evidence that there will be benefits for the child, in which case there may be a need for advocacy to help the parents achieve their wishes. There are strong arguments for the benefits of inclusion. John McKnight and others have written about the concept of 'the competent community', arguing that it is in the interests of all of us to develop the capacity for our local community to include all its citizens in its basic functions of home, work, leisure, use of local amenities, education, safety and basic health (McKnight, 1995).

In Chapter 2 we outlined the WISE principles for anti-oppressive practice: welcome, image, support and empowerment. All schools should be welcoming to disabled children. Schools and teachers should have a positive image of the achievements that can be made by disabled children and the social and educational benefits to the child and to other children in the school. Adequate support should be provided to enable disabled children to function as equally as possible with other children in the school. And disabled children should be empowered to access resources and experiences that are necessary or helpful to their social and educational welfare, through rights, advocacy and involvement. Disability rights legislation applies to schools and all other educational establishments.

The support required for the education of a disabled child is detailed in a Statement of Special Educational Needs, following assessment, usually by an educational psychologist. In 2011 a government Green Paper *Support and Aspiration: A New Approach to Special Educational Needs and Disability*, proposed a change from the statement of educational needs to a single assessment from early childhood to adulthood, linking educational, health and care needs (see **www.education.gov.uk/childrenandyoungpeople/send/b0075291/ green-paper**). It also proposes giving more control to parents, e.g. through direct payments.

Once in a school, whether mainstream or special, the child may have a more detailed need for support in managing the learning and in relationships with teachers and peers.

Community, family and social life

Children with learning difficulties should be able to partake fully in the life of the local community. This may mean inclusion in places of worship; shops; leisure facilities; primary health care resources; children's clubs and organisations, e.g. scouts, brownies and guides. Any difficulties a family is encountering in achieving this access for their child may be helped by a social worker in the role of negotiator, advocate or commissioner of any special resources required.

A social worker can also keep an eye on inclusion of the child in home and family life. As with any child, unless there are very exceptional reasons, a child with learning difficulties will benefit from full inclusion in family mealtimes, bedtime processes, watching television together with family or friends, having friends in to play or stay overnight, having birthday parties, visiting relatives, going on outings, and so on. Individual children may have specific difficulties for which a social worker could give advice or direct the family to other professionals or sources of support. These might include sleep problems, eating problems, mobility problems, health issues, difficulty in communicating or issues of relationships with siblings, for example. If a social worker feels a child is unnecessarily isolated or denied opportunities for inclusion in family or community life, there may be a case for following procedures for managing concerns about children (see later in this chapter). On the other hand, many families and communities may provide models of good practice which we can learn from and share with others.

CASE STUDY

Following an enquiry from a mother about possible residential care for her 11-year-old daughter Jane with learning difficulties, a social worker from the Children and Families team who specialised in disabled children visited the family. Rather than carrying out an assessment of Jane, she interviewed the parents to get a picture of the whole family. She discovered that the father was out of work and the mother had only a part-time cleaning job, and they were in debt, causing some friction between them.

She was able to put them in touch with a debt advice agency. She also learned that a second daughter, Shirley, aged 14, had recently been brought home by police at 1 a.m. having been found drinking cider with some older children in the local town centre.

Shirley had increasingly been staying out late at night, saying that she was embarrassed to bring friends home as they would be put off the friendship by seeing Jane. The parents had also not cooperated with the drawing up of a Statement of Educational Needs for Jane's progression to secondary education, because Shirley had said she did not want her sister to come to the same school.

The social worker arranged to see Shirley on her own. She spoke to her about her fears and tried to convey that having learning difficulties need not be viewed entirely negatively. People could be helped to be proud of their identity, and others could admire

---

their resilience and efforts to overcome their difficulties. She said that Shirley could greatly benefit Jane's development by helping her to meet and take part in activities with non-disabled children. She told her that children are prejudiced against disabled people more often out of ignorance than out of embarrassment at seeing them, and that meeting Jane would benefit Shirley's friends too. She suggested that Shirley could play an important role in helping her school to plan and arrange the resources and supports Jane would need in order to attend. Finally, she invited Shirley to come with her to an exhibition of art by people with learning difficulties being held at a local college, to show her the kinds of achievements that might be possible for Jane.

Adolescence

For most young people, adolescence is a time of growing understanding of their body and how to manage it, increasing independence and freedom, experimentation with relation-ships, and often some rebellion and challenging of authority. With common sense, and love and good advice from family and friends, most young people survive this period having learned a great deal about themselves and the skills and knowledge and responsibility required for adulthood. In particular, access to a very much greater quantity and variety of relationships will have been opened up. A problem for many young people with learning difficulties is that they may not have this adolescent experience and development. They may be sheltered and protected in what is believed to be their best interest, and hence may not have the experience to gain the confidence and skill to manage freedom, form adult rela-tionships, resist authoritarian behaviour towards them or care responsibly for themselves or others. If a young person is successfully guided to develop these things they are very lucky, and it may save them from a restricted, sheltered and possibly lonely life.

As childhood progresses, a person with learning difficulties will have an increased risk of isolation from community relationships. It will be harder for their family to secure inclu-sion in mainstream education at secondary level than it was at primary school. Clubs and other facilities for young people may become more reluctant to accept and include the person. 'Special' provision may be provided for needs in these areas, such as clubs for people with learning difficulties, but they will inevitably involve segregation and isolation from 'ordinary' community life. There are two consequences: the person with learning dif-ficulties does not experience how to function well in community settings and activities, and 'ordinary' community members do not experience interactions and relationships with people with learning difficulties. This is the beginning of a rift between different sections of a community ('our mutual handicap') that may take tremendous efforts to overcome.

RESEARCH SUMMARY

Janet Carr (1995) reports on a longitudinal study of all the children with Down's syndrome born in the county of Surrey in 1964, matched with a sample of 'ordinary' children. She followed up both groups, each numbering 54 children, till the age of 21. Here are some findings illustrating how the experience of adolescence can differ between people with and without learning difficulties.

At 21 years, only about a quarter of the young people with Down's syndrome had received sex education, knew about contraception and knew that a baby could result from sexual intercourse. Half of the sample, but none of the control group, had never had a girlfriend or boyfriend. Of those who had, all involved relationships with other disabled people, mainly attending the same day centre.

At age 21, only 24 per cent of the young people with Down's syndrome had non-disabled friends, compared with 100 per cent of the control group. Among those with Down's syndrome, the proportion with non-disabled friends had dropped from 54 per cent at age 11.

At age 21, only 5 per cent of those with Down's syndrome had a job, and only 12 per cent were in further education. Five per cent were still attending a school, 5 per cent remained at home all day, and 73 per cent attended segregated day centres. (Summarised from Carr, 1995)

Transition

Greater efforts than in the past are made now to support young people with learning difficulties in the key life stage of transition from school to post-school opportunities. However, the risk of spending large amounts of time in segregated settings is still very real.

RESEARCH SUMMARY

In 2002 the Joseph Rowntree Foundation published a review by Jenny Morris of relevant research studies on the experiences of young disabled people, including those with learning difficulties. Here are her conclusions relating to transition:

'Although it is a legal requirement that all young people over the age of 14 with a Statement of Special Educational Needs have a transition plan, a third of young people in one study of 283 families did not (Heslop et al., 2001). Education and social services departments are often not working well together in transition planning. There is also often poor co-ordination between children's social services and adult social services. Young disabled people are often not involved in planning for their future. This is particularly so for those with communication and/or cognitive impairments. Assessments often cover what a young person cannot do because of their impairment, rather than identifying disabling barriers which could be tackled. Topics covered in transition planning are frequently not those of most importance to young people and their families. Friends and sexual relationships are important issues for young people but transition planning, assessments and services rarely address these concerns.

(From Morris, 2002: **www.jrf.org.uk/knowledge/findings/foundations/512.asp***)*

The Department for Education and Department of Health are now working on the Special Educational Needs and Disability single assessment process (called Pathfinder) proposed in the Green Paper mentioned above. The Statement of Special Educational Need ceases when compulsory schooling ceases, whereas the Pathfinder assessment process will carry on with the young person into college up until they are 25. Social workers need to note that early transition planning is essential for young people with learning disabilities in order for them to achieve their full potential. Identification of transition needs should begin no later than the child's fourteenth birthday to enable sufficient planning, referral to adult services and access to resources.

Career support and advice

The countrywide Connexions service was a structure set up to help young people especially those with extra needs such as learning difficulties, providing general support services to young people aged 13–19 through an advisor. However, services are now more variable. In some parts of the country the service is still called Connexions, in other parts it is called Youth Advice or has its own branded name. In some areas careers advice is only provided to the most vulnerable young people, e.g. young people who do not attend any school or college, with young people who do attend school or college assumed to receive careers advice in-house. In other areas youth careers advice is provided within a multi-agency team, incorporating housing, substance misuse and linking into charities such as Family Action. For children in care, local authorities are required to have a service for care leavers under the Children Act 2004, supporting children up to the age of 22. Social workers may be involved in providing signposting for young people and families to access resources and to pursue suggestions for future options.

RESEARCH SUMMARY

Wilson, H, Bialk, P, Freeze, T, Freeze, R and Lutfiyya, Z (2012) Heidi's and Philip's stories: transitions to post-secondary education. British Journal of Learning Disabilities *Vol. 40(2) pp87–93*

This research outlines the experiences of two young people, Heidi and Philip, with learning difficulties who made the transition from post-secondary education to higher education. It includes their recommendations to other young people with learning disabilities who aspire to higher education. Heidi and Philip studied at an advanced level, decided on real careers and, in the process, helped a university to redefine its role in the community.

COMMENT

*The experiences of Heidi and Philip highlight that a person with learning difficulties is a person first with hopes, aspirations and ideals. In order for their goals to be realised, support needs to be provided to enable access and options for transition. Social workers need to practise from a person-centred perspective, providing a tailor-made service based on the social model of disability. This helps societal views to change so that people with learning difficulties experience inclusion (Swain et al., 2007). Awareness is necessary of what is available in the local area, and of relevant organisations that can be accessed for support, e.g. People First (**www.peoplefirstltd.com**).*

In summary, some important needs of people with learning difficulties during adolescence with which a social worker may be able to help are:

- to participate as much as possible in inclusive activities of education, family life, leisure and community membership;

- to have a range of developmental experiences that will equip them for adult life;

- to have relationships and friendships;

- to have planned support and resources for a good transition from school and childhood into adulthood and adult activities.

The Children Act 2004

This Act expanded on the Children Act 1989 to improve the way services are delivered at local level, ensuring that local authorities lead on integrated delivery through multi-agency working, implement a Common Assessment Framework, and particularly focus on looked after children, with greater devotion of social work time, more support for carers and improved education opportunities.

The revised Act followed the government Green Paper *Every Child Matters* (Department for Education and Skills, 2004), which in turn followed the inquiry into the tragic death of Victoria Climbié (Laming, 2003). *Every Child Matters* states that all children should have the right:

- to be healthy;

- to stay safe;

- to enjoy and achieve;

- to make a positive contribution;

- to achieve economic well-being.

There is a campaign called Every Disabled Child Matters run by four leading organisations working with disabled children and their families – Contact a Family, the Council for Disabled Children, Mencap and the Special Education Consortium, to ensure these principles are also applied to all disabled children (**see www.edcm.org.uk**).

Children and Families Bill

In 2012 the government put forward proposals for a new Children and Families Bill, some of the aims of which will be to:

- replace Special Educational Needs (SEN) statements and learning disability assessments (for 16–25 year olds) with a single, simpler 0–25 assessment process leading to an Education, Health and Care Plan;

- provide statutory protections comparable to those currently associated with a statement of SEN up to 25 in further education – instead of being cut off at 16;

- require that local authorities and health services jointly plan and commission services that children, young people and their families need;

- give parents or young people the right to a personal budget for their support;

- strengthen the role of the Children's Commissioner;

- reform family law to speed up care proceedings.

(See **www.education.gov.uk/inthenews/inthenews/a00208753/childrens-bill-family-support**)

Child protection/safeguarding

Disabled children with additional needs are known to be more vulnerable to abuse (Bernard, 1999). However, Morris (1995) argues that disabled children are not as likely to be represented in child protection investigations. This may be because a child's account may not be believed; children with learning difficulties may not be considered as credible witnesses; and the child's ability to recount what has happened may be limited. However, whether a child is disabled or not they have a right to protection under legislation and guidance.

In a bid to overhaul child protection procedures, Professor Eileen Munro was commissioned to carry out a review (2011). In her report *Moving towards a child centred system* (2012) she identified that *we have to have realistic expectations of how well professionals can protect children and young people. The work involves uncertainty; we cannot know for sure what is going on in the privacy of family life, nor can we predict with certainty what will happen* (2012: 3). However Professor Munro made 15 recommendations to contribute to child protection reform. Among these were:

- extensive overhaul of safeguarding procedures and joint working;

- a new investigation framework should examine the child's journey and examine how the feelings of the children and young people inform and shape the provision of services;

- employers and higher education institutes should work together so that social work students are more prepared for child protection work and practice placements are of a high quality.

An essential part of child protection social work practice is to be able to identify what constitutes child abuse. Under the 1989 Children Act there are four categories of child abuse: neglect, physical, sexual and emotional. The Children Act 1989 brought about fundamental changes in child law (White et al., 2008). The process of unified jurisdiction gave much-needed guidance and structure to the way children were safeguarded. Section 17 of the Act focuses on the needs of the child. Section 47 places duties on local authorities to investigate where *risk* of significant harm is suspected. *Where a local authority has reasonable cause to suspect that a child who lives or is found in their area is suffering or is likely to suffer significant harm, the authority shall make or cause to be made, such inquiries as they consider necessary to enable them to decide whether they should take any action to safeguard or promote the child's welfare* (Children Act, Section 47; see O'Loughlin and O'Loughlin, 2012).

ACTIVITY 5.2

Consider which legislation and guidance you would use to safeguard this child:

Xianthippe is six years old and has a severe learning disability. She is an attractive and outwardly cheerful child, but is unable to walk or talk. She communicates by eye pointing. She lives with her parents and two older brothers. She attends the local primary school and has a teaching assistant to help her in class. It is suspected that Xianthippe may be being sexually abused as you have had a referral from a GP outlining concerns. What legislation would you draw upon to help you in your approach/intervention?

COMMENT

Under section 47 of the Children Act 1989 risk of significant harm is grounds to begin an investigation and take action if necessary to safeguard or promote a child's welfare (White et al., 2008). In Xianthippe's case it would take time and patience to ensure an accurate account of what has happened. Assessment would involve liaising with all the agencies, professional and non professional, relevant to Xianthippe, talking to her parents, making sure all meetings are communication friendly, and considering Xianthippe's capacity.

A structured procedure can ensure that social workers practise ethically and legally, adhering to all relevant agency procedures and protocols. A number of tools have been provided by the Department of Health to guide social workers and other professionals in their practice. These include *Working together to safeguard children* (Department for Children, Schools and Families, 2010) and *What to do if you are worried a child is being abused* (Department of Health, 2003b). The first of these includes specific guidance on cases involving a disabled child. The second includes a helpful diagram of the process that should be involved (see Figure 5.1).

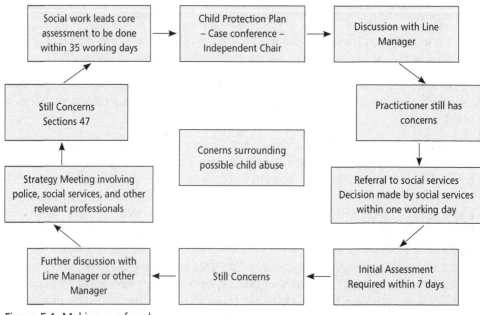

Figure 5.1 Making a referral

In all child protection work we would stress the importance of discussion with your line manager, regular recorded supervision, and multi-agency working and networking.

Parents with learning difficulties

A challenging issue in social work is the parenting capacity of parents who have learning difficulties. Mayes and Llewellyn (2009) highlight that parents with learning difficulties are considered as being at greater risk than any other parents of losing parental custody of their child. A common view is that parents with learning difficulties are not able to parent well enough or appropriately to meet their child's needs.

As long as the prevalent attitude of current and future parental incompetence continues to exist, having a child taken away – permanently – remains a real possibility for many parents with intellectual disability (Mayes and Llewellyn, 2009: 92). However, the authors argue that the consequences and effects for the children and their parents when children are removed are significant, with children experiencing lasting effects of being removed from their parents, often never to see them again, and the parents experiencing severe depression, self-harming or contemplating suicide.

This area requires further research in order to explore the effects of these experiences. However, with Department of Health guidance in place such as *Valuing People* (2001) and *Valuing People Now* (2009d) and legislation such as the Children Act 1989/2004 and the Children and Families Bill, it should be possible for support to be put in place that ensures parents with learning difficulties can parent well enough and appropriately. It is our responsibility, within a multi-disciplinary and multi-agency approach, to ensure that this support is available, and that stigma is not still attached to a parent who has learning difficulties. (See also the research by Tim and Wendy Booth described in Chapter 4.)

Conclusion

Whilst work within children and families can be challenging, it can also be highly rewarding. The Social Work Task Force recommended that *unless practitioners have enough time to bring their professional skills to bear, to carry out the analysis and reflection that lead to good judgement, the impact of increasing other resources will be limited* (Department of Health 2009a: 28). This is all the more so when working with children that are not only vulnerable but also have a learning disability. An essential aspect of working with children with learning difficulties is to support them through key life stages, really considering their views, ensuring appropriate and individual communication methods are used, and ensuring the welfare of the child is paramount (Children Act 1989 Section 1).

CHAPTER SUMMARY

This chapter has considered the needs of children at key stages of their development, policy and legislation specifically relevant to children and families and to disabled children in particular, and the need for awareness of procedures and good practice in child protection, and their specific application with children with learning difficulties and their families.

FURTHER READING

Grant et al. (2010) *Learning Disability: A Life Cycle Approach* is a comprehensive book of contributions relevant to the themes of this and the next chapter.

Hothersall and Maas-Lowit (2011) *Need, Risk and Protection in Social Work Practice*.

It is important that social work students and practitioners understand the issues surrounding need, risk and protection. This book provides guidance to understanding these issues with numerous practical examples from legal issues and policy and practice contexts, to debate surrounding ethical dilemmas faced by social work practitioners.

O'Loughlin and O'Loughlin (2012) *Social Work with Children and Families*

This book is part of the Transforming Social Work Practice series written specifically to support students on social work degree courses. Working with children and families whilst rewarding can also present challenges with social workers being confronted with difficult decisions to make. This book gives guidance, knowledge and practical tips for undertaking work in this area.

Taylor (2011) *Working with Aggression and Resistance in Social Work*.

Social workers have roles that require them to engage with clients and families who may be 'reluctant clients', ambivalent or reluctant towards those seeking to help and protect. This includes safeguarding roles in relation to children and vulnerable adults, and work to engage with marginalised groups such as young offenders and those with mental health and substance misuse problems. This book provides a blend of practice and theory to direct practitioners in this complex role.

Chapter 6
Working with adults

Introduction

This chapter will cover some major areas of work with adults with learning difficulties. The importance of valued social roles will be emphasised. Employment, relationships and the impact of negative experiences will be discussed. Health needs and needs in older age will be covered. Risks to adults and the need for safeguarding will be presented in the context of the need to avoid isolation and preserve benefits of social integration and community membership. Avoidance of discrimination and the management of problem behaviours are other topics that will be touched on.

CASE STUDY

Peter is 30 years old and has severe learning difficulties. He lives in a house where he has a joint tenancy with two other men and he is cared for by a 24-hour supported living service. Peter has a twin brother, James, who is a solicitor. They have always been close, and James and Peter visit each other's homes often. Carl is Peter's Care Manager in the local Community Team for People with Learning Difficulties who helped arrange

> ### CASE STUDY *continued*
>
> *his tenancy and commissioned his support service. Mary is a member of the team that supports Peter and she acts as his keyworker. All four are Black British people whose parents were immigrants from the Caribbean.*
>
> *James is getting married and wishes Peter to be his Best Man; however, in the past, Peter has chosen not to go to church by refusing to wear appropriate clothes if this is suggested. Carl and Mary had initial doubts whether Peter would be able to participate in the Best Man role, because of his lack of understanding of the marriage ceremony and concerns about his behaviour.*
>
> *A meeting was held between Carl, Mary, James and Peter to discuss the possibility. Peter seemed happy with the plan that was devised. He had enough in his account to afford a new fitted suit. Carl took him to a well-respected men's outfitters where he was measured for a fine suit with waistcoat, a process Peter seemed to like. Carl and Mary borrowed several wedding videos from friends and Mary played them to Peter, pointing out the Best Man and saying 'That will be you, Peter'.*
>
> *At the wedding rehearsal, and again on the day, Peter agreed to put on his suit, was accompanied by Carl and Mary to the church and was assisted by them to perform all the tasks required of Best Man. He was heartily welcomed by the members of the local close-knit Black community who made up most of the family members and guests present at the wedding.*

Valued roles

As we saw in Chapter 2, the concept of 'valued roles' is a very powerful one. People with learning difficulties, particularly in adulthood, are at risk of being seen in one or more negative social roles: as a nuisance, an object of pity and charity, a dependent non-contributor, a drain on community resources, an eternal child, an object of dread or embarrassment, a sick person, a trivial person without the usual human sensitivities, and so on (Wolfensberger, 1992; Race, 1999). If we can help people to achieve positive social roles they are likely to have better experiences and relationships in life generally (Wolfensberger, 1998).

> ### ACTIVITY *6.1*
>
> *There are thousands of valued roles that we have in everyday life – such as partner, lover, parent, uncle, aunt, neighbour, follower of a religion, worker, volunteer, houseowner, philatelist, artist, photographer, gardener, friend, teacher. Make a list of some of the valued social roles that you have. Try to come up with at least 20.*
>
> *Make some notes alongside each one with ideas on how a person with learning difficulties might be supported to achieve and maintain each role. Can you identify any problematic issues in working towards these roles?*

Some roles are likely to be more difficult for people with learning difficulties to achieve than others. Becoming a partner or lover might be more difficult than being a good neighbour. Within the framework of 'social role valorisation' (Wolfensberger, 1998), the important principle is that as many valued roles as possible should be sought and supported to compensate for any that are too difficult to be achieved.

The issue of choice can be raised. Should we ever try to impose roles on people against their apparent wishes? This difficult question – of choice versus what we might judge to be in a person's best interests – is covered further in Chapter 9. At the very least, people should be involved as much as possible in decisions that affect them: the 'Nothing About Us Without Us' principle. In the case study of Peter, we can gain a sense that the good relationships between Peter and those supporting him are likely to have involved constantly testing out whether Peter was happy with what was happening. However, they did not just accept at face value his apparent refusal to attend church; they worked with him on a plan to achieve what they believed would be of benefit.

Needs

In this chapter we will consider five particular areas of possible need to illustrate the richness and variety of social work with adults with learning difficulties. Each is related to being socially valued, but each also has a more personal or psychological element concerning self-esteem and self-worth. They are: needs around work or valued daytime activity, needs around close personal relationships, needs arising from past negative experiences, needs arising from ill-health, and needs in older age.

The chapter will end with a consideration of concepts of risk and safeguarding in relation to adults with learning difficulties.

Work

Apart from its economic function, work is a highly valued social activity. It signals to others that we are contributors, that we have skills, that we can learn, that we are responsible, and it signals to ourselves that we are wanted, have a place in society, are like our family members and friends and are contributing to community life. Even if the economic function cannot be achieved and the experience of work has to be obtained through subsidised or sheltered means, the other benefits are still there, especially if we take care to capitalise on them.

We can easily damage the possible benefits from work, especially in the signals given to others about the value of the people working. The work can be demeaning or have a negative connotation, for example of dirt or of boring repetitiveness. People can be transported to work in special vehicles that publicly portray them as different. People can work in a building that is not sited in a work area of town, or that looks like a school rather than a place of work. The work may start later and finish earlier than similar neighbouring work for other people. Social activities associated with work, like lunch or after-work sports or events, may take place in a segregated, isolated way. In all these ways we can fail to capitalise on the social benefits of work.

Furthermore, there has been a widespread view that work is impossible or inappropriate for many people with learning difficulties. Daytime activity for most people with learning difficulties has tended to be provided in multi-purpose centres, carrying out education, providing leisure facilities, acting as a social club, facilitating drama, music, dance, art and pottery, organising outings, establishing self-advocacy groups and so on. While many of these activities can constitute valued alternatives to work, it is much more difficult to give out the 'signals' of value to the local community, and there is a risk that people are seen as going to day services merely to be occupied because they have nothing else to do.

ACTIVITY 6.2

Make a list with work at the top, but including other activities that you think would constitute valued alternatives to work. For example, adult education, homekeeping activities, hobbies, sport, being a social club member …

Brainstorm some ways in which such activities, including work, might be organised for people with learning difficulties in order to send out a strong signal of the value of the people involved.

Think about avoiding segregation and isolation. Think about separating different activities that don't usually belong together in the same building or at the same time. Think about buildings or venues, their location, design and names. Think about how people might get there and the timing and duration of activities. Think about end products and publicity.

Think about the most appropriate identity and skills of staff in a supporting role.

There is a revival of interest in work for people with learning difficulties (as indeed there is for other groups at risk of unemployment and dependency). There are a number of schemes promoting training for work, and providing support for people in work (O'Bryan et al., 2000; Ridley and Hunter, 2005; Beyer and Kaehne, 2008). An objective stated in the White Paper *Valuing People* is:

> *To enable more people with learning disabilities to participate in all forms of employment, wherever possible in paid work, and to make a valued contribution to the world of work.*
>
> (Department of Health, 2001: 84)

Personal relationships

We have already seen that people with learning difficulties may end their childhood with few friends, with little knowledge about sex and with little or no experience of having a boyfriend or girlfriend. Given the importance of these things to nearly all of us without learning difficulties, we need to view this issue as one of great priority (Katrak and Fanstone, 2003).

Each person is of course a unique individual and we cannot really know their needs, wishes and best interests without getting to know them well. Some people with learning difficulties may have little interest in deep emotional or sexual relationships, though they may be very loving, and loved, people. Other people may have a degree of learning difficulty that makes it very unlikely that they would understand the concepts and consequences of marriage, sexual intercourse, pregnancy, childbearing or child rearing. That said, there are many people whose opportunities to consider these things have been greatly restricted by the attitudes of family, carers or society.

There is a range of areas of need that people may have. The first is protection. People who are likely to be sexually active with another person need education and practical support with the ordinary requirements for protection against unwanted pregnancy and sexually transmitted disease. Unfortunately, people with learning difficulties are also vulnerable to others taking advantage of them against their wishes. People therefore need extra education, advice and support in their actual relationships with others, including assertiveness and in some cases supervision. There also need to be clear mechanisms for people to report abuse, and to have their experiences listened to and appropriate action taken. Achieving these things while not denying people the privacy, choice, experimentation and risk conducive to their development and fulfilment is an extremely difficult skill for families, carers and other professionals. A social worker who develops knowledge and skill in this area is likely to be highly needed and valued. (See Fanstone and Katrack, 2009.)

The second area of need is education. Materials are available for teaching people with learning difficulties about sex and relationships (for example, the CD-ROM *All About Us* from FPA, **www.fpa.org.uk**). Social workers may be able to advise on needs, advocate for the right of people to receive this education and negotiate for it actually to happen. The fears and anxieties of family members may need to be discussed and resolved.

A big problem for many people with learning difficulties is that even when they have had good education on sex and relationships and are well protected against unwanted events, they may still be extremely restricted in opportunities. There are a few schemes acting as 'dating agencies' for people with learning difficulties, for example Stars in the Sky in Haringey, London (**www.starsinthesky.co.uk**), and the Relationship Support Service, a joint venture between Mencap and Hertfordshire NHS Trust (see Jenner and Gale, 2006). Most such projects are for people with only a moderate degree of learning difficulty and are based on a restrictive assumption that people with learning difficulties can only form close personal and emotional relationships with other people who also have learning difficulties.

The question of how to expand the opportunities available to people to meet others, and support them in developing their relationships to a deeper level, perhaps involving sex, is one where social workers may be able to play an important role, both in advocacy and in practical support. For most people, deep relationships and loving sex are sources of great fulfilment, enjoyment and happiness. Hopefully this can be the same for many people with learning difficulties if we can remove the fears and anxieties that others may have.

Inevitably, there will be some people with learning difficulties who, despite their ideal wishes and desires, are unable to find a partner for a deep or sexual relationship. These people have a 'wound' to their identity and self-esteem (see below), which may require special love and understanding of the person by family, carers and other professionals. Portrayal to them that celibacy and virginity are acceptable and valued lifestyles may be helpful.

Occasionally, people with learning difficulties will engage in unacceptable sexual behaviour. A summary of the issues here and possible approaches to take to help such people is given by Brown (1998). At the other end of the spectrum, it is being increasingly recognised that people with learning difficulties can experience marriage or partnership, have children and be good parents (Roy, 2000). The research work of Tim and Wendy Booth in this area was described in Chapter 4.

Negative experiences

In Chapter 2, we mentioned Jean Vanier, the founder of the L'Arche movement of services involving life-sharing on an equal basis between people with and without learning difficulties. He has called the negative experiences that people with learning difficulties may have suffered their 'wounds'. As we noted above, having to accept that one may never achieve a deep or sexual relationship with a partner may be one such wound.

Many people with learning difficulties will have experienced wounds, in their families, in the community, in services or as a result of insight into their limitations and other people's perceptions of them. Examples could include rejection, isolation, bullying, name-calling, being ignored, being spoken of always as 'a problem', having little choice, receiving segregated services, having to live with people you haven't chosen to live with, being forced to spend long periods of inactivity, being treated as a child, or being physically attacked or sexually exploited. Some of these experiences are well recognised as constituting abuse, and we discuss these risks and the need for safeguarding later in this chapter.

In the Department of Health survey of people with learning difficulties described in Chapter 1 (NHS, 2005), 19 per cent of those included had no contact with their family and 31 per cent had no contact with friends. This illustrates a particular wound for people with learning difficulties, that of abandonment. Avoidance of this risk involves making every effort to retain family relationships and friendships, and fostering new friendships, networks, social relationships, advocacy, communality and community participation. Where people have no family or contact cannot be renewed, the importance of services like Adult Family Placement come into play (Baldwin, 2005; Fiedler and Lockwood, 2004). Similarly, if people have no or few friends, there needs to be action to foster friendships, perhaps through a befriending scheme if there is one available (Firth and Rapley, 1990; Bayley, 1997; Florides, 2012).

On top of any direct wounds, many people with learning difficulties know that they are perceived as having something 'wrong' with them, that they are seen as 'a problem' and are of low social status. This may be combined with frustration and regret at things that their impairments may not allow them to do.

> *The awareness of being handicapped, the insight into being mentally retarded, is expressed in possibly distorted self-concepts or defeated utterances or through defence mechanisms, closing in on inner sorrows.*

> (Nirje, 1980: 32)

In developing a perspective on the needs of people with learning difficulties we should be aware of their experience of 'wounds'. Those currently being experienced need remedying, and those in the past need compensatory action. A framework for exploring this will be outlined in the next chapter, based on the strategy of social role valorisation described in Chapter 2.

Social workers need to be especially understanding and appreciative of the resilience and survival skills of many people with learning difficulties, but also their strong need for love, teaching, care, choice, opportunity, relationships and inclusion that will serve to compensate for disadvantage. A particular interest for social workers in this respect might be the development of psychotherapeutic counselling with people with learning difficulties. This is rarely available, or even considered to be needed, at present. One of the pioneers of such an approach has been Valerie Sinason at the Tavistock Clinic in London (Sinason, 1992). See also Simpson and Miller (2004).

Ill-health

Some people with learning difficulties are more likely to develop physical impairments or illness than is usual in the general population. This may be due to genetic or physiological factors which are related to the cause of the learning difficulty itself. People with Down's syndrome are more likely than other people to develop dementia in middle age (though it should not be assumed that all will). In other syndromes there is an increased risk of certain kinds of cancer. Epilepsy is more common in people with learning difficulties. Some people with learning difficulties are prone to respiratory diseases or heart conditions. Overall, there is a greater risk of ill-health than among other people.

On top of this 'natural' risk, there are risks that ill-health will not be recognised, diagnosed correctly and treated effectively. There are several stages in the recognition and treatment of illness, at each of which there needs to be good practice and effectiveness for the person's health to be protected. Without this many people with learning difficulties are likely to be at risk of serious ill-health and even unnecessary death. Surveys have shown that screening for cancer is offered much less often to people with learning difficulties than to others. Conditions such as breast or cervical cancer in women, and testicular or prostate cancer in men, are likely to be picked up less frequently in people with learning difficulties than among other people. As a result, people with learning difficulties are four times more likely to die from treatable illnesses than others (Mason and Scior, 2004; Laurance, 2005; Disability Rights Commission, 2006).

The first stage is the enablement of people to recognise signs of ill-health in themselves. There are several sources of information on illnesses and on how to check one's own health available for people with learning difficulties to use with whatever help they may need. The Elfrida Society has a number of leaflets designed for people with learning difficulties explaining illnesses and medical procedures (**www.elfrida.com**), and the Royal College of Psychiatrists publishes a series called Books Beyond Words on health issues, devised in conjunction with St George's Hospital Medical School in London (**www. booksbeyondwords.co.uk**). The British Institute of Learning Disabilities and FAIR Multimedia based in Edinburgh are other sources.

Next is the need for people in direct contact with a person with learning difficulties – their family, their carers, their friends, advocates and any professionals in regular contact – to be aware of signs of ill-health. People who know the person well can be sensitive to changes in the person's behaviour that may indicate pain or discomfort. Referral then needs to be made to expert medical diagnostic and treatment services.

Third is the need for people with learning difficulties to be supported in taking up screening services which are available.

Professionals and other personnel in health services need to be welcoming and sensitive to people with learning difficulties who come to them. Medical staff need to have skills of recognition of health needs among people with learning difficulties. Investigations to determine diagnoses may need to be more complex and lengthy than with other patients, families and carers may need to be more involved in identifying and interpreting symptoms, and specialist opinion may need to be sought from professionals with special experience or knowledge of people with learning difficulties.

Treatment then needs to be effective and non-discriminatory. The communication methods of people with learning difficulties need to be known to hospital staff, and families and carers need to be involved in order to provide such information. Some hospitals have begun to appoint liaison nurses specifically for patients with learning difficulties to ensure their special needs are recognised and met. Medical and nursing treatment needs to be of high quality and applied without erroneous assumptions about the 'quality of life' of people with learning difficulties being inevitably poor (Brown et al., 2005). To guard against the possibility of stereotyped prejudice or failures of communication or recognition of need, the presence of advocates for the person may be needed. These could be family members, carers or independent friends and supporters. Wolfensberger (2005) has written a guide to possible needs and actions in such circumstances.

Older age

Older people with learning difficulties are likely to have special needs; this topic is covered in more detail in the book in this series *Social Work with Older People* (Crawford and Walker, 2008).

Dementia may occur earlier in some people with learning difficulties, particularly those with Down's syndrome, than is usual among the general population. This is something that those supporting older people with learning difficulties should be aware of and prepared for when it happens. On the other hand, we need to guard against assuming that any problems being experienced by those people are due to the onset of dementia. Each person needs a high-quality individualised assessment of their physical or mental health, without assumptions about the consequences of either older age or learning difficulties (Holland and Benton, 2005; Kerr and Wilkinson, 2005).

The concept of valued social roles will continue to be important and people will need to be supported in family roles (great aunt, for example) and community roles (senior community member with long experience, contribution and memories). Some people in older age will develop new roles and will have new needs for consequent support. For example, people in their families may move from a dependent to a caring role (Lifetime of Caring, 2005).

Important throughout life, but especially in older age, is the maintaining of good records of the person's life: family tree, photographs, life history, community networks, past friends and contacts, well-known places, memories, valued possessions and so on. People should be supported through times of bereavement when friends or family members die (Oswin, 1991; Thompson, 2002; Hollins et al., 2003; Parker, 2005). Many people are likely to wish to attend, and benefit from attending, the funerals of people close to them.

High standards of palliative care and care of dying people should apply to people with learning difficulties at the end of their lives (Blackman and Todd, 2005; Brown et al., 2005; Tuffrey-Wijne, 2009). Their funerals should be occasions of celebration of their lives and their contribution to society. Unless it goes against the person's wishes if they have expressed them, or the wishes of their family, efforts should be made to inform the wide range of people in their social network that they have died. It is a mark of the value in which many people with learning difficulties are held by those who know them that their funerals will often be very well attended. Among those mourning their passing but celebrating their lives may well be their social worker.

CASE STUDY

At the funeral of a man with severe learning difficulties who had died aged 54, a eulogy was given by a friend who had known him all his adult life. It included the following, emphasising his positive contribution and the valued social roles he held:

> Nowadays, John would probably not be born. His birth would be regarded as a tragedy, tests would be done and abortion strongly recommended. But we are here to celebrate John's birth and life. It would have been a tragedy if he had not been born, because his life was one of achievement, love and benefit to others. I believe that all of us here, and many other people too, are better people for having known John. We are gentler and more affectionate and more resilient to the upsets we experience, because we have learned from John's example, his patience, his gentleness and his sense of humour ... Let us remember John as an achiever, a teacher, a pioneer, a good friend and one of the most gentle and lovable people we are likely to meet. His life was a blessing for us all, and he will be greatly missed.

Risk and safeguarding

There are two kinds of risk that are relevant to work with people with learning difficulties: risk of unnecessary exposure to undesirable events or experiences, and risk of negative consequences when possible benefits and desirable experiences are pursued. For the first of these, a strategy of prevention should be implemented; for the second a strategy of management is required, so that risk and benefit are balanced. There is a concept that has been around in the literature on services for people with learning difficulties for many years (e.g. Perske, 1972) – that of 'the dignity of risk'. Perske argued that we all have a tendency to overprotect people we see as vulnerable, but this can stifle their development, self-esteem and community participation. This is likely to be reinforced if we are surrounded by rules, regulations, inspections and punitive sanctions for transgression that send out a strong message that risk must be avoided at all cost. Overprotection may be as much of a problem for people with learning difficulties as exposure to risk of harm (Titterton, 2004).

Hazards

Most good practices and regulations in health and safety are designed to avoid harm to people from hazards such as fire, electric shock, disease, road traffic, water, heat, cold, dangerous substances, sharp items or falls. Common-sense adherence to accepted health and safety procedures should protect people from such hazards.

However, two points can be made. First, it will be an even greater safeguard of the person's welfare if they can learn to practise safety themselves, and to learn this there must be some exposure to the hazards. For example, we know of a person with learning difficulties who has been taught to safely have an open fire in their home where they live alone with occasional domiciliary support. They know how to lay the fire, light it, guard it if they leave the room, extinguish it at night and dispose of ashes.

A second point is that it is virtually impossible to eliminate entirely the risk associated with some hazards, because the attempt at elimination itself causes other risks. For example, water temperatures may need to be very hot to eliminate risk of water-borne disease like Legionnaire's disease; this in turn creates a risk of scalding which may be tackled by installation of thermostatic mixing valves. However, the people and their supporters may then get out of the habit of also testing the water manually, so that if the thermostat malfunctions people are still at risk, possibly even greater risk than before the controls were fitted. So we can see that total elimination of risk is likely to be elusive, even in relation to major hazards.

In managing this kind of risk it is important that there is a 'no blame' culture so that risk can be identified and where undesired events occur they can be quickly and accurately reported so that action can be taken to remedy harm and learn for the future. The concealment of exposure to hazards is itself a risk for people. For example, if there is an error in the giving of medication to a person, this must be reported and recorded and immediate appropriate action taken. This is more likely to happen if there is an atmosphere of no blame and no sanctions for reporting mistakes. A culture of commitment to the welfare of each person being supported, rather than mere adherence to rules and regulations, is also important to foster, since this will be a more reliable safeguard. It is that which will ensure the bath water is tested by hand, just in case the thermostat isn't working.

CASE STUDY

In July 1972, 30 patients in a hospital for people with learning difficulties – Coldharbour Hospital at Sherborne in Dorset, now closed – died in a fire on one of the wards in the early hours of the morning. The subsequent inquiry found that some of the factors behind the tragedy were as follows.

The newly refurbished ward had been equipped with flammable partitions, decorations and furniture.

Advice on the use of non-flammable materials by fire officers had either not been communicated to architects, designers and planners or had been overruled in order to retain greater homeliness.

The risk of a major fire was considered to be small, since it was assumed by planners that staff would always be present.

CASE STUDY continued

The ward accommodated 40 patients with a wide range of characteristics; some had very limited self-help skills while others had problems of behaviour.

After an argument, a patient stole a lighter from the pocket of a member of staff and while still upset set fire to a curtain in the night.

The ward was staffed by only one member of staff at night, and it was allowed practice for that member to leave the ward unattended for short periods to report to a senior member of the night staff without disturbing the patients on the ward; that was the case when the fire broke out.

The ward was locked and all doors had different keys, a factor that delayed entry to the ward after the fire started.

Staff had no training in fire-fighting or ward evacuation.

No smoke alarms or sprinkler system had been fitted.

ACTIVITY 6.3

What do you think should have been done after the Coldharbour Hospital fire to minimise the risk of such an event happening again?

COMMENT

In a book called Learning from Disasters (Toft and Reynolds, 1997) the Coldharbour Hospital fire is discussed. The authors make the point that such disasters are rare, because they are usually the result of a whole series of unfortunate events coming together in what is sometimes called a 'systems failure'. The interesting corollary of this is that if any one of the many factors involved in the fire had been different, the tragedy might have been prevented. We therefore do not need to go 'overboard' with excessive restrictions, as long as some effective safeguards are in place, in this case any of these:

- smoke alarms and sprinklers;
- staff training in firefighting and evacuation;
- master keys to the doors;
- a rule that the ward would never be left unattended;
- recognition of the needs and feelings of the patient who started the fire;
- greater security by staff over items like lighters;
- smaller numbers accommodated on the ward;
- a rule that taking the advice of fire officers is compulsory.

The Coldharbour Hospital fire did in fact lead to legislation making adherence to the advice of fire officers compulsory in relation to all public buildings.

Discrimination in services

Despite the fact that nearly every individual working in services would say that they want the best for people with learning difficulties, there is strong evidence of widespread discrimination and oppression. This phenomenon is known as 'institutional discrimination', a concept expounded particularly in the Macpherson Report (1999) in relation to failings of the Metropolitan Police following the racist killing of Stephen Lawrence (see also Nzira and Williams, 2009).

In 1993, despite clear evidence of abuse by a care worker, a woman with Down's syndrome was declared by the Crown Prosecution Service to be 'too handicapped' to be a reliable witness and the CPS refused to take the case to court. The woman's parents were so incensed by this that they founded an organisation, Voice UK, to support people with learning difficulties in pursuing their rights to justice following abuse. Eventually, their case was taken to court, and the care worker was found guilty and served a term of imprisonment. The work of Voice UK led to the introduction of special arrangements for vulnerable people to give evidence in court under the Youth Justice and Criminal Evidence Act 1999.

In 1995 a book was published called *Invisible Victims*, in which the author, Chris Williams, recounted numerous ways in which the human and legal rights of people with learning difficulties were often flouted, without any redress for the victims. It reinforced the growing realisation that people with learning difficulties were being denied justice and their vulnerability to abuse was not being taken sufficiently seriously. A number of scandals of serious abuse of people in care homes also emerged in the 1990s, publicised in television programmes or books (see Pring, 2003).

The Disability Rights Commission (2006) provided much evidence of discrimination against people with learning difficulties in the NHS. Mencap also published two reports (2004, 2007) describing discrimination against people with learning difficulties in the NHS. The 2007 report *Death By Indifference* recounted the deaths of six people through health service neglect. This led to the government setting up an independent inquiry which confirmed a high level of discrimination in the NHS (Michael, 2008). In 2006 there was a scandal about the conditions being experienced by people with learning difficulties receiving NHS residential care in Cornwall, leading to a further highly critical report (Healthcare Commission and Commission for Social Care Inspection, 2006).

More recently there has been the case of Winterbourne View, a private hospital for people with learning difficulties near Bristol (Flynn, 2012). After secret filming by the BBC television programme *Panorama*, six members of staff were sent to prison for abuse of residents.

Abuse

As well as within services, unfortunately people with learning difficulties are sometimes at risk of abuse within their families, by their friends, by other people with learning difficulties or by strangers. The extent of such abuse has only been revealed by research during recent years.

The Foundation for People with Learning Disabilities states that 23 per cent of adults with learning difficulties have experienced physical abuse, and 47 per cent have experienced verbal abuse and bullying (*Statistics on Learning Disabilities*, **www.learningdisabilities.org.uk**). The Department of Health survey of adults with learning difficulties (NHS, 2005) found that 43 per cent of respondents had been bullied at school and 32 per cent had experienced rude or offensive remarks towards them in the last year. The Ann Craft Trust states on its website (**www.anncrafttrust.org**) that *recent studies have shown that around 60% of adults with learning disabilities have experienced abuse at some point in their lives.* Lyttelton (2003) gives an annual figure of 1,400 cases of reported sexual abuse of people with learning difficulties and points out that many more cases are likely to be unreported (see also Turk and Brown, 1993).

Safeguarding and vulnerable adults procedures

Following such examples, the Department of Health produced a report in 2000 called *No Secrets*. Its subtitle was *Guidance on Developing and Implementing Multi-agency Policies and Procedures to Protect Vulnerable Adults from Abuse*. It set out a blueprint for the establishment of local procedures for reporting, investigating and taking action on any instances of abuse of vulnerable adults, including people with learning difficulties.

All local authorities now have a safeguarding process for considering any report of abuse. A nominated person within the local authority social services department will be allocated to investigate the incident, and will call in the police or other relevant agencies if necessary. In addition, abuse can be reported directly to the police, to the Care Quality Commission or to organisations concerned with protection from abuse, which include Voice UK, the Ann Craft Trust, Respond (which offers psychodynamic therapy for people with learning difficulties who are either victims or perpetrators of abuse) and Mencap (which operates a helpline that people with learning difficulties can contact direct – 0808 808 1111).

Part of the vulnerable adult protection procedures is a requirement for all staff and volunteers working with people with learning difficulties to have any criminal convictions identified through a Criminal Records Bureau check. There is also a separate Department of Health list of people considered unsuitable to work with vulnerable adults because of previous disciplinary offences or other similar reasons.

The need to safeguard people from abuse has gradually taken greater and greater priority over recent years. Department of Health guidance has been strengthened through its policy documents *Modernising Social Services* (1998), *No Secrets* (2000), *Putting People First: Transformation of Adult Social Care* (2007a), and *Safeguarding Adults* (2009c). The General Social Care Council suggested in 2008 that the role of social workers should concentrate more on safeguarding. In 2012 the issue reached even greater proportions with the Winterbourne View scandal and the allegations against Jimmy Savile. While of course every effort should be made to prevent and address abuse, there are dangers in going 'overboard'. There is a danger that the very necessary task of promoting good relationships for people with learning difficulties is forgotten in the priority given to preventing bad relationships. This issue has been raised by a parent of a person with learning difficulties (Birrell, 2012) in an article with the title 'Killing kindness with red tape' and the sub-caption:

Human warmth is at the heart of relationships between vulnerable people and their carers. But heightened fears about abuse mean simple friendship is increasingly viewed with suspicion.

A key challenge for social workers today is to balance safeguarding with fostering and encouraging all the good and helpful relationships which many people with learning difficulties desperately need. (See the discussion on friendship at the end of Chapter 4.)

Risk to others

There are certain kinds of risk that people with learning difficulties may pose for other people. An important area of risk that social workers are likely to be involved in assessing is that to family carers, usually parents and particularly the mother, but also affecting siblings and possibly members of the wider family such as grandparents, uncles, aunts and cousins. There are two kinds of stress associated with caring for, and caring about, a family member with learning difficulties: physical and emotional. Non-family carers and supporters of people with learning difficulties may also experience similar stresses.

CASE STUDY

Kevin is 60 years old and has always lived with his mother who is now 84. She was widowed 30 years ago when her husband died of lung cancer. Kevin is her only son and there are no other close relatives. Kevin has severe learning difficulties and is totally dependent on his mother for daily living tasks such as dressing, washing and eating. His mother is getting more frail and is deeply worried whether she will be able to care for Kevin much longer.

Sometimes there is a risk to family members, carers and support staff from the behaviour of people with learning difficulties. Perhaps an even more important risk is that to other disabled people who live with or receive services with a person who shows undesirable behaviour, since they are less likely to have chosen to be with the person and are less able to defend themselves. The behaviour of some people with learning difficulties can also be upsetting to members of the public. This can include any behaviour that is unpleasant or transgresses against the expectations of other people in public settings. The risk that we will be upset by the behaviour of some people with learning difficulties in turn increases the risk that we will resist their inclusion and participation in society and that they will suffer the 'wounds' of rejection and ascription of negative social roles. Occasionally, too, some people with learning difficulties may be destructive of their own or other people's property, and this may use up resources as well as upset other people.

A small number of people with learning difficulties are convicted of serious criminal offences or are considered to need conditions of security because of serious behaviour problems. They may be detained under sections of the Mental Health Act and live in secure accommodation, including the special high-security hospitals – Rampton, Ashworth and Broadmoor in England and Carstairs in Scotland. Work with serious offenders with learning difficulties is a specialist area of work and one that may be a special vocation for some social workers.

Managing behaviour problems

It is in their best interests for attempts to be made to minimise undesirable or upsetting behaviour by people with learning difficulties. Much research and guidance is available on this (e.g. Brown, 1998; Emerson, 2001; Emerson et al., 1993; Harris et al., 2001; SCIE, 2011). There are two important factors that should be recognised. First, the behaviour may be the person's way of trying to communicate a need or problem. They may be in pain or discomfort; they may be unhappy with their living situation, their relationships or their activities; they may have been upset by a particular event or person; they may be grieving because of a loss; they may be suffering from any of the 'wounds'; they may be suffering from a recognition that they are perceived by others as a 'problem' or as of low social value. We should always seek to discover the possible communicative function of the person's behaviour. (See the account of 'gentle teaching' in Chapter 1.)

The second consideration is that there is a risk of defining people in terms of their behaviour problems: 'a person with challenging behaviour' is a term that can often be heard. Peter Houts and Robert Scott, the originators of the strengths/needs approach to assessment described in Chapter 7, once wrote a booklet called *How To Get Caught Doing Something Right* (1975b). It was written in the context of services for people who had transgressed social norms in their behaviour, such as convicted offenders in prison. It provided ideas for how the emphasis could be switched from their problem behaviour onto all their behaviours that were acceptable, constructive and helpful. In services for some people with learning difficulties there is a risk that everyone is on the lookout for instances of their problem behaviour, and the many instances there are likely to be of unproblematic behaviour are ignored. This is bad for the perception of the person by others and their own self-esteem. It may also inadvertently encourage problem behaviour by giving it more attention than constructive behaviour.

CASE STUDY

Graham's everyday behaviour includes such things as getting himself up, making his breakfast, tidying his room, doing his washing and ironing, carrying out gardening tasks at the day service, helping to make supper for himself and others, welcoming and conversing with visitors, making cups of tea, going along with others' choice of music or TV programmes, bathing and retiring to bed at a reasonable hour. About once a month he loses his temper, threatens others with violence and destroys some of his clothing. This is indeed a serious problem that needs attempts at understanding its cause and a strategy for tackling it. However, it is also the main topic at all meetings about Graham. Whenever service staff speak of him they express concern about his temper and his destruction of clothes. He is more or less identified in people's minds as 'the person with the temper who destroys clothes'. The fact that he often goes for a month or more engaged in constructive, considerate and helpful behaviour without temper or destructiveness is difficult to discover from the way people speak of him.

One interesting approach to 'challenging behaviour' is to absorb it, in order to demonstrate to the person that your commitment to them is unconditional and in order to break through the issues of power and control involved. This is from an account of L'Arche (see Chapter 2) by Clarke (1974), also quoted by Williams (2002):

> *I began to realise that any resistance to David was a kind of violence that only added another link to the whole chain of violence in which he was a victim. So I adopted an attitude of greater receptivity and non-violence towards him, allowing him to do as he pleased with me. The first thing that I discovered once I stopped resisting him was that a great deal of tension went out of me. I could now adopt a very simple and consistent openness to him. I found myself no longer avoiding his company, but rather seeking him out just for the pleasure of being with him. Although nothing seemed to have changed in his attitude towards me, something had changed quite considerably in me by virtue of the gift I had received to no longer resist his aggressive activity. In the lowering of some of my own barriers of aggression and self-preservation, the two of us came much closer together. With this greater closeness I could see much more of the goodness and beauty of his person, which one could scarcely fail to love.*

(Clarke, 1974: 84–5)

ACTIVITY 6.4

Do you think there is any potential in this approach? Write down some arguments in its favour and some problems that you envisage.

COMMENT

It probably requires a special vocation to adopt such an approach. The advantages might be that you show the person that you are fond of them, you enjoy supporting them, you are resilient to their behaviour towards you and you do not impute malicious motives to them. This may convince them that their problem behaviour serves no function, and it is easier and more pleasant to interact with you without showing that behaviour. The problems lie in the fact that it may not work and you may get hurt. Nowadays, there are duties on employers not to subject their employees to unnecessary risks and the organisation you work for may not be prepared to support such a non-interventionist approach. And even if it works for you, other people may not be able to adopt the same approach and may still be at risk. You may feel that, in work with people with difficult behaviour, you are willing to accept and absorb a certain amount of hurt from the people you support. Or not. You decide.

The balance of benefit and risk

Where risk is associated with benefits, plans can be made to minimise the risk without taking away desirable outcomes too.

Example of a risk assessment and consequent risk management plan
(Based on an example in the Risk Management Manual of the voluntary organisation United Response.)

Activity being considered:
JS lives in a small residential care home. He has expressed a wish to go out more at weekends. His brother and his keyworker at his day service have met with care staff and they have identified gym sessions at a local leisure centre as a potential activity he would enjoy.

Risks:
JS sometimes hits other people, probably through frustration at not being able to do more for himself. On visits to the leisure centre, he may hit out and cause hurt to staff or to other people attending the leisure centre.

Benefits of the activity:
JS will gain stimulation and physical exercise, making him less bored and his behaviour more amenable at home. He will meet new people and gain new skills and interests. Other people attending the leisure centre may befriend him and take an interest in him.

Plan to enable benefits to be retained while minimising risk:
Negotiations will take place for JS to join the gym class at the leisure centre, on Saturday mornings or afternoons (according to his apparent preference). JS will be accompanied by a member of his support staff at all times while at the centre. New staff will not do this until they have received training and experience in the individualised ways of reassuring him to reduce his hitting out, and defusing and managing the situation if he does hit out. The gym teacher at the centre will also be briefed on ways of working with him to reduce hitting and manage it when it occurs. Three preparatory visits to see the gym class will take place before JS actually joins it. If JS does hit out while at the centre he will immediately be taken out by his support member of staff. He will be taken back after three minutes and an apology offered to anyone hurt, with an offer of taking the matter further if they wish. Everything possible will be done to avoid JS being excluded from the activity. He will be praised for going through sessions without hitting. A review will take place six weeks after JS has started the classes, by the care home manager and the staff member who acts as his keyworker. Also invited, if they can come, will be his brother, his keyworker at the day service and the gym instructor from the leisure centre.

Outcome of the six-week review (attended by the home manager, the home keyworker, JS himself and his brother):
JS had successfully attended the gym classes for six weeks. He had been befriended by a young man in the gym class who had bought him drinks and expressed an interest in visiting him at home. JS had not hit out on any occasion in the gym class. It was noticed that JS engaged in tasks better and seemed to enjoy himself more if he went to morning rather than afternoon classes. It was therefore agreed that he would go regularly on Saturday mornings. This was also the time when his new friend attended. The next review would be in another six weeks, but if all was going well future reviews could be less often. His new friend at the centre would be asked if he would be interested in attending.

CHAPTER SUMMARY

This chapter has outlined some of the issues for adults with learning difficulties and their consequent needs. The importance of the concept of valued social roles is emphasised. The chapter has also included an analysis of the concept of risk and outlined some areas of risk relevant to people with learning difficulties. Many situations involving risk also have benefits. The task therefore is to manage risk so that it is at a reasonable level without losing the benefits.

FURTHER READING

Fray (2007) *Caring For Kathleen: A Sister's Story about Down's Syndrome and Dementia* is an informative example of a biography of a person with learning difficulties right up to older age and death.

Department of Health (2000) *No Secrets: Guidance on Developing and Implementing Multi-Agency Policies and Procedures to Protect Vulnerable Adults from Abuse* is essential reading on procedures for preventing and tackling abuse.

Mantell and Scragg (2008) *Safeguarding Adults in Social Work* provides a useful link between issues of protection and those of empowerment.

Priestley (2003) *Disability: A Life Course Approach* covers life stages from the perspective of the social model of disability.

Titterton (2004) *Risk and Risk-Taking in Health and Social Welfare* is a comprehensive book on the benefits of thoughtful risk-taking as well as assessment and planning to avoid harm.

Two recent books in the Learning Matters series are particularly relevant to this chapter: **Bickerton** (2011) on safeguarding, and **Palley** (2012) on promoting positive behaviour.

Chapter 7
Assessment, planning and evaluation

Introduction

This chapter covers a wide range of issues concerning assessment, service planning and service evaluation. The main themes are:

- positive assessment of individuals and families;

- assessment of community resources;

- a critical approach to community care assessments;

- the exchange model and the need to involve people;

- the life-history approach;

- assessing environmental influences on people and their social status;

- evaluating services;

- a critical approach to the concept of 'quality of life';

- person-centred planning;

- story-telling as assessment and evaluation.

Assessment and values

Assessment involves a systematic description for a particular purpose. It can be of an aspect of a person, a family, the environment, a service or a community. The nature and purpose of an assessment is highly related to values. Although assessment of problems is necessary to allocate resources and seek solutions, we can only capitalise on potential if we perceive positive value, and for that purpose positive assessment is required. Table 7.1 gives some idea of this.

Table 7.1 *Problem- v. strengths-orientated assessment*

	Problem-orientated assessment involves describing	Strengths-orientated assessment involves describing
Person	What they cannot do	Their achievements, gifts and capacities
Family	The problems the family has	The skills and achievements of the family
Environment	How the environment exacerbates perceived problems	Positive resources in the environment
Service	How the service fails to reach set standards	The pioneer achievements of the service
Community	Rejection and abuse within the community	The wealth of resources and relationships available in the community

Positive assessment of individuals

This chapter will cover a number of approaches to assessment and allied planning of services or interventions, beginning with an example of positive assessment of an individual person with learning difficulties. Houts and Scott (1975a) developed a framework for assessing strengths and needs. (Note that in identifying areas for possible intervention, they used the term 'needs' rather than the negative term 'weaknesses'.)

A feature of the Houts and Scott framework is that it does not require any pre-printed forms or templates. We often hanker after official-looking proformas and charts to guide our assessments, but in many cases the best tool is a plain sheet of paper on which a flexible amount of space can be devoted to recording information under whatever headings are felt to be necessary. An example of positive headings is given in the following case study.

CASE STUDY

Here is an assessment of the strengths of a 9-year-old girl, Sarah, with a profound degree of learning difficulty; she has multiple physical and sensory impairments and no speech (taken from Atkinson and Williams, P. 1990).

Things she can do

- *Smile*

- *Sit up with support*

- *Discriminate taste*

- *Kick her legs*

CASE STUDY continued

- *Good hearing*
- *Cry*
- *Express displeasure by pulling away*
- *Digest mashed or liquefied food*
- *Turn her head*
- *Spit out food*
- *Respond to water on her legs*
- *Move her arms*
- *Open and close her hands*
- *Move her fingers*

Things or activities she likes

- *Having no clothes on*
- *Having her teeth brushed*
- *Movement of the car or school bus*
- *Lying on her tummy after meals*
- *The noise of other children playing*
- *Rocking on a swing seat*
- *Going out in her wheelchair*
- *Physical contact*
- *Banana, warm milk, ice cream, mousse, yoghurt, blancmange, Weetabix*

People available or helpful

- *Mother*
- *Father*
- *Brother (age 6)*
- *Brother's friends who come in to play and are accepting of Sarah*
- *Neighbours and friends who will look after Sarah for short periods*
- *One neighbour who cuts Sarah's hair sensitively and well*
- *Aunts and grandmothers who knit and sew special clothes for Sarah*
- *Doctors in the local group practice are helpful*
- *The school teachers are helpful*

- *Staff at the hospital providing short-term care are helpful*
- *The driver of the school bus is friendly and helpful*
- *A good dentist has been found to treat Sarah*
- *The local teaching hospital has made a film about Sarah*

Resources

- *Specially made clothes*
- *A car with a special seat is owned by the family and both parents drive*
- *The school is very well staffed*
- *Sarah has a well-adapted wheelchair and a special armchair at home*
- *Short-term care is available at the hospital*
- *Day-care is provided during the school holidays*
- *Liquidiser to enable Sarah to eat the same food as the rest of the family*
- *Good service providing disposable incontinence aids*

Personal appearance

- *Well groomed*
- *Wears pretty dresses*
- *Curly hair*
- *Clean, nice-smelling (with talcum powder)*
- *Short nails*
- *Nice smile*
- *Delicate skin*
- *Wears bracelets and jewellery*
- *Light to lift*

Other

- *Parents do not mind questions about Sarah and they give sensible answers*
- *Parents are healthy and strong*
- *Sarah has a pleasant Victorian-style bedroom*

Such a list as this can give people who might be meeting Sarah for the first time a positive impression of her whereas otherwise they might feel overwhelmed by the degree of her impairments. It can also be used to generate ideas for how to meet any needs she may have. These needs can be reviewed under similar headings: things she might learn to do, opportunities for activities she might enjoy, extending her social network, gaining additional resources, maintaining personal appearance and so on.

ACTIVITY 7.1

Write down a strengths list about yourself, using the headings above or any other headings you think would be useful. When you've completed the list, review it to see if it suggests any ideas for meeting any needs that you might have.

Assessment of community resources

It is often thought that nowadays communities are crumbling and have few resources for self-support. However, a systematic listing of community resources can give a very different picture. For example, in the London Borough of Tower Hamlets, renowned for extensive poverty and social problems, a group called the Community Organisations Forum carried out a survey of self-help or special interest groups in the borough. They found around 700 separate organisations, including 90 for minority ethnic groups, 33 for women, 51 giving advice or information and 72 concerned with recreation (King's Fund Centre, 1988). Kretzmann and McKnight (1993) suggest headings for assembling what they call an 'association map', i.e. a comprehensive list of community organisations that may be helpful in building up contacts for and participation in by people at risk of social exclusion (for example, people with learning difficulties). The list includes:

- artistic organisations (e.g. painting, theatre, writing);
- business organisations (e.g. Chamber of Commerce, trade unions);
- charitable groups and voluntary organisations;
- churches and church groups;
- organisations for civic events (e.g. exhibitions, fairs, carnivals);
- collectors' groups;
- community support groups (e.g. hospital friends);
- groups for older people;
- organisations for minority ethnic groups;
- organisations for other minorities (e.g. gay, lesbian and transgender);
- health and fitness groups;
- special interest groups (e.g. pets, cars, gardening);

- local government agencies;

- local media;

- men's groups;

- women's groups;

- mutual support or self-help groups (e.g. disability organisations or Alcoholics Anonymous);

- neighbourhood groups (e.g. Neighbourhood Watch);

- outdoor groups (e.g. ramblers, bird watching, local tours);

- political parties and groups;

- school groups (e.g. parent–teacher organisations);

- community service groups (e.g. Rotary Clubs, Round Tables, Lions);

- social cause groups (e.g. Greenpeace, rights groups);

- advocacy groups (e.g. citizen advocacy schemes, welfare rights, People First);

- volunteer groups (e.g. Community Service Volunteers);

- sports groups;

- veterans (ex-services) groups;

- youth groups.

Even this is likely to be only a partial list of possible community organisations and resources that could be identified.

A critical approach to community care assessments

A major form of assessment in which social workers are involved is the Community Care Assessment in the context of care management. Here, a person is assessed for their vulnerability to possible threats to their welfare and hence for their eligibility for services provided through the care management process. This process can be very uncomfortable for social workers. They are charged with objectively assessing a person's needs, but this assessment has then to be entered into a system of resource allocation that depends on a number of other factors (Lymbery, 2005). Particularly in the current climate where local authorities are having to cut expenditure quite drastically, there may be considerable pressure on social workers to fit assessments to available resources rather than objectively assessing needs.

The government requires local authorities to operate a method of determining eligibility for services (Department of Health, 2003a). The assessment is used to classify need as critical, substantial, moderate or low. Priority in use of available resources has to be in meeting critical needs first, then substantial needs, and so on. The recommendations of care managers go before a funding panel which acts as an arbiter of expenditure. Many people with needs judged to be low are likely not to get any services at all. In particular, low priority is likely to be given to interventions that may prevent future serious needs arising. An example of this in relation to people with learning difficulties is the low level of resources likely to be devoted to helping adults move out of their parents' home and their parents' care where this situation is currently not presenting severe problems. However, there comes a time when a crisis of care arises, perhaps because of illness or death of a parent, and an urgent and unplanned alternative has to be arranged.

Eligibility criteria can also be changed, and many local authorities have done this in recent years to save money. (See Brand et al., 2010.)

The exchange model

An accurate and maximally helpful assessment is likely to result from what has been called the exchange model (Smale and Tuson, 1993; Coulshed and Orme, 1998). In this model a range of people in the person's life – health, social care and other professionals, the person's family and key members of their social network and, most importantly, the person themselves – exchange information on a basis of equality. The care manager is a coordinator of the process and of the writing down of a combined account.

Smale and Tuson (1993) emphasise that this model helps to provide a holistic picture of the person in their social context and to identify informal resources within that context that might be mobilised in addition to official services. The person themselves, or key advocates for them, have influence over the content of the assessment and who contributes to it. However, care managers may not have the time, or the knowledge of the person and their social network, to operate this model. Sometimes, a care manager will gain information merely by interviewing the person and one or two others, for example a key carer, in order to record information under predetermined headings. This is likely to give a much less satisfactory picture than the exchange model.

Involvement of the person themselves has been aided by application of the Mental Capacity Act (2005). This states that a person must be assumed to have the capacity to make informed decisions about themselves unless there is concrete evidence to the contrary.

Typical suggested headings within a community care assessment are:

- background history;
- senses and communication;
- learning, work and leisure;
- relationships;
- physical health;
- emotional health;
- accommodation;
- looking after self;
- running a home;
- getting around;
- budgeting.

The difference between a routine assessment and an exchange assessment can be illustrated by the contrast between the following accounts of a person with severe learning difficulties in the areas of background history and relationships. These two areas turned out to be key ones in decisions about his care.

CASE STUDY

Michael is 52 years old and is being assessed because his current home, a large local authority hostel for people with learning difficulties, is closing and Michael needs alternative accommodation. He has no speech. The community care assessment is carried out by a care manager interviewing his key worker at the hostel, who has known Michael for a few years. Later, Mr K, a friend of Michael who has known him for 40 years, provides a separate account.

From the Community Care Assessment

Michael was the only child of a single mother who was a teacher. His father is not known. His mother never spoke of any relatives. She died in 1986 and Michael has had no contact with family since then. Michael has lived at one hostel, and then his present one, since 1968. He has friends, Mr and Mrs K, who keep in regular contact with him. Mr and Mrs K visit occasionally and Michael sends them Christmas cards. Michael is vulnerable to aggressive behaviour from other residents around him. Among his peers at the hostel, Michael has known some of them for many years, but he appears to have no close friends. Michael shows affection towards his carers. On rare occasions, usually due to a change in routine, he may become agitated and restless.

Recommendation

Michael needs accommodation where he would not be vulnerable to aggressive behaviour from others. This can be sought anywhere within the local authority area (a large county).

From information provided separately by Mr K

Michael has lived all his life in X (the local town). In the mid-1960s, when Michael transferred from children's services to adult services, a new day service had opened which was oriented towards sheltered work. There was some doubt as to whether this service could cater for people with a severe degree of learning difficulties, but Michael was given a trial there and performed so well that this opened the way to acceptance there of several people with more severe impairments than it had originally been envisaged would be possible. Michael can thus be regarded as a pioneer of adult services in X. He was also a founder member of a club for people with learning difficulties in X, which he attended every week for 35 years. Although Michael does not appear to have what we might call close friendships with anyone, he certainly recognises familiar people and clearly enjoys their company. He is known to a large number of people in X, including staff, former staff and volunteers at the three hostels he has lived in, the day service and the weekly club, and fellow residents of the hostels, attendees at the day service, and members of the club, and many of their family members too. I would estimate that at least 200 people in X know Michael and are well disposed towards him and whom he recognises and enjoys seeing when they meet.

CASE STUDY *continued*

Strong request

That accommodation be found for Michael within X, in the light of his past contribution to services there and the extensive social network he has in the town.

Outcome

Based on the cursory information about history and relationships in the Community Care Assessment, a proposal was made to house Michael in a different town, 20 miles away from the people and places he had known all his life. Only after considerable protest by Mr K was a new assessment done and Michael's need to remain in X acknowledged.

The problem of standardisation and computerisation

As often happens in life, when a good idea emerges there are pressures that operate in the opposite direction. *Valuing People* advocated that assessment should take the form of highly individualised 'person-centred planning' (see later in this chapter). However, in parallel with attempts to implement this policy, the government was also pursuing an agenda for standardised assessment and computerised records that militates against flexibility and individuality. Examples include:

- the Common Assessment Framework for children's services;

- the Single Assessment Process for services for older people;

- a standard method of computerising data from assessments, the Electronic Social Care Record;

- CareFirst, computer software for recording Community Care Assessments;

- CareAssess, the framework for assessment to make it recordable in CareFirst.

You can find out more about these systems through search engines on the internet.

These systems claim to be able to incorporate a wide range of kinds of data in a flexible way. In principle, therefore, such standardised systems should be capable of incorporating person-centred planning approaches. However, in practice it is too complicated and time-consuming to translate the rich, varied and unsystematic data from a person-centred plan into data that a computerised system can cope with. Social workers are often torn between using a flexible, individualised approach to assessment, and using simple standard assessment tools that can be relatively easily computerised. As a consequence, one can often hear it said that 'We have no resources for person-centred planning' or 'We cannot adopt person-centred planning because we have to use CareFirst.'

The life-history approach

Person-centred planning will be covered later in this chapter, as a method that is highly individualised and is much more in tune with the exchange model than standard 'Community Care Assessment' procedures. First, we will discuss further the power and importance of considering the history of a person and using that knowledge to identify needs. This life-history approach to identifying needs owes much to the analysis developed by Wolfensberger (see Chapter 2) as the basis for his framework of 'social role valorisation' (Wolfensberger, 1998; Flynn and Lemay, 1999; Race, 1999).

Wolfensberger's starting point was the insight that people who are at risk of oppression are in that position because of negative perceptions of them in society. He has categorised the main negative perceptions, or 'devalued roles', as:

- non-human;
- menace, object of dread;
- waste, rubbish;
- trivial, unimportant, object of ridicule;
- object of pity;
- object or burden of charity;
- eternal child;
- holy innocent;
- sick, diseased;
- dying, already dead, or associated with death.

(Wolfensberger, 1992; Race, 1999)

An important point made in this analysis is that it is the negative perceptions of people – the negative social roles they are cast into – which result in negative experiences rather than specific service structures. Thus large institutions may reflect negative perceptions and reinforce them in the minds of the public, but they are not the root cause of oppression. People are still at risk of oppression and bad experiences even when all the institutions have disappeared for as long as negative role perceptions remain. A major task for us, says Wolfensberger, is to support people in positively valued social roles, for example as friend, neighbour, citizen, contributor. All services can contribute to this or (however unconsciously or unintentionally) hinder it.

As we described in the last chapter, Wolfensberger (1992; see also Race, 1999) has described the negative experiences resulting from social devaluation as the 'wounds' of the people concerned. Examples of 'wounds' that he identifies are:

- rejection, from family, community, social agencies;
- being assumed to have more impairments than you have (e.g. a person with learning difficulties being assumed also to have mental health problems);
- segregation away from ordinary society and valued people, places and opportunities;
- enforced congregation (with no choice or control) with other people who have difficulties or are likely to be seen in a negative light;
- loss of choice, control, autonomy and freedom;
- discontinuity, being suddenly removed from familiar or loved people or places, with little or no retention of contact;

- enforced idleness and wasting of one's time;
- abuse and exploitation.

ACTIVITY 7.2

Suppose that all large institutions are closed and everyone is living in small groups in their own homes or in small residences in the community. Can you think of ways in which each of the above negative experiences might still happen to people?

COMMENT

Later in this chapter, when we consider Wolfensberger's framework for evaluating services, we will outline features of buildings, groupings, relationships or practices that may result in negative experiences for the people served. Despite great strides in avoiding some of the negative consequences of the old institutions (Horner, 2012), many people are still not offered a choice of who they live with. People are still often housed outside the local community areas where they belong. Sometimes few attempts are made to support people to keep in touch with acquaintances and friends. People still sometimes sit around in day services or at home with little appropriate activity. There are still horrific stories of abuse.

No amount of training, government White Papers or inspection operations seems capable of eliminating these problems.

On the other hand, the variation in services these days is great, and it is possible to find many examples of good, innovative and exemplary practice. And at least the words are there in government policy to set an agenda for many of these things to continue to be tackled and remedied.

For an international perspective on these issues, see Race (2007).

The life-history review

If we can gain a picture of the 'wounds' that have been experienced by a person in the past, this can help us to identify current needs. One way of analysing people's needs from an account of past experiences is to carry out a 'life-history review'. As with other kinds of assessment, this may best be done in an open-ended way, with plain paper and headings tailored to the individual. To give an indication of the areas of life that can usefully be covered, these questions can be suggested;

- What has been the person's experience of family?
- What has been the person's experience of community and society's behaviour towards them?
- What has been the person's economic status, in terms of resources, possessions and disposable income?
- What has been the practical and emotional impact on the person of their impairments?
- What has been the person's experience of choice and control?

- What has been the person's experience of key life events – birth, going to school, leaving school, close personal relationships, work, marriage, having children?

- What future has the person had to look forward to?

Experiences in these areas can be wounding or they can be good. In assessing an individual person, therefore, we need to have a way of turning both negative and positive experiences into statements of need. This is done as follows.

- If a person's experiences in an area of life have always been generally good, the need is for that situation to be maintained and safeguarded.

- If a person's experiences have been generally good but have recently or temporarily worsened, then the need is to restore the previous situation as far as possible.

- If a person's experiences have been persistently bad, the need is for positive compensation for their disadvantage and oppression in that area of life; services need to bend over backwards to provide particularly valued and good experiences for the person.

Here are two case studies illustrating the process of reviewing past experiences, deriving a consequent statement of needs and planning action to meet those needs. The first relates to the area of family relationships, the second to choice.

CASE STUDY

Past experience

Barry's parents were divorced when he was a young child. Both have subsequently remarried, but both have kept in touch with Barry, though they have only rarely visited him.

Barry attended a residential school and has lived apart from his family for the past 20 years. He is now 25 years old. In the past, when members of his family did meet him they tended to treat him as still a young child.

Statement of needs

As far as possible, with the agreement of Barry and his family, for family contact to be increased, and for Barry to develop an adult role in his family.

Meeting the needs

Following agreement by Barry and his family, a regular pattern of telephone calls, visits to and visits from both parents and other family members has been facilitated. When his family members visit, Barry is supported in offering meals and refreshments. He can meet with family members in privacy. If necessary, family members are offered transport to visit. A diary is kept of family birthdays and other celebrations, and cards and presents are exchanged between Barry and his family. Barry has been invited to, and attended, family events including a christening, a marriage and a funeral. With Barry's consent, his parents are informed of his activities and achievements, and are invited to reviews and meetings concerning him. Barry was supported to have a 25th birthday party to which both sides of his family were invited and to which many of them came, some of them meeting each other for the first time for many years. With Barry's help, and with the cooperation of his family, a list was drawn up of presents he would like, avoiding inappropriately child-like items.

Past experience

Martha had virtually no experience of choice for the first 25 years of her life. She is now 27. During her childhood and early adulthood she lived in a large number of different institutional residences, with no choice of who she spent her time with and no choice over her environment or activities.

Statement of needs

Martha to have lots of choice; her choices to be respected; Martha to learn about alternatives and how to make choices.

Meeting the needs

Martha now lives in a small house with three other people, where she has her own bedroom, opening up choices of decor and furnishing. She has been taken shopping to personally choose wallpaper, curtains and bedroom furniture. She has been taken on a wide variety of outings and holidays to discover which she prefers, those she dislikes being terminated and those she prefers being repeated. Martha has been introduced to a wide range of people and activities, again to identify preferences which can be maintained. Martha has shown a particular enjoyment of church, and she has been supported in going regularly and in joining a church women's group. The range of Martha's clothing has been increased so that she can exercise more choice; she has been offered a choice of hairstyles at the hairdressers, and her choice followed. Choice of food is offered at mealtimes and Martha has learned to ask for what she prefers. She is often able to choose what she would like on television and is encouraged to make choices of programme to watch.

Environmental influences and experiences

Another kind of assessment is the discovery and description of environmental influences on a person. This can be done at a 'micro' level: assessing the ways in which factors in a person's daily environment affect their detailed behaviour. This can be especially important in discovering 'triggers' for difficult behaviour, or the ways in which behaviours are influenced by their consequences. The assessment involves discovering the function of behaviour in meeting needs or desires of the person, or in communicating wishes or feelings. The process of discovering and describing this is called 'functional analysis' and it can lead to programmes in which environmental factors – in particular the responses of other people to the person – are structured to help the person learn new skills or develop helpful behaviour. Such an approach is sometimes called 'behavioural' (Emerson et al., 1993; Harris et al., 2001). (See also the discussion of 'gentle teaching' in Chapter 1.)

Other assessments of environmental influences are at a more 'macro' level. Based on his concept of 'social role valorisation', Wolfensberger devised an instrument, called PASSING, for assessing or evaluating the extent to which a service helps or hinders the achievement and maintenance of valued social roles and a high social status for the people served. The latest version is Wolfensberger and Thomas (2007). Within social role valorisation it is posited that there are two main factors influencing people's social status and reputation: the messages that are sent out about people through the images that surround them, and the competencies they are able to develop to present themselves well to others. Some of the aspects of a service which are investigated by the PASSING instrument are presented below:

Aspects of the building and physical setting that may primarily influence image

- How well the building fits in with neighbouring buildings

- How well the nature of the service fits in with the nature of the neighbourhood

- The external and internal aesthetics of the building

Aspects of the building and physical setting that may primarily influence the development and maintenance of competence

- Availability of relevant community resources in the neighbourhood

- Physical comfort

- Individualisation of personal spaces in the building

Aspects of groupings and relationships that may primarily influence image

- The presence of different services with different functions in the same building or in close proximity (e.g. an advisory service for disabled people and a probation office for offenders in the same building)

- The number of people congregated together in the service

- The identity, skills and characteristics of staff of the service

Aspects of groupings and relationships that may primarily influence the development and maintenance of competence

- The competencies of other people that service users come in contact with

- The quality of personal relationships and interactions within the service

- Individualisation of support given to people

Aspects of activities that may primarily influence image

- Appropriate distinction in time and place between functions such as home life, education, work, health care, leisure

- The nature of activities

- The timing of activities

Aspects of activities that may primarily influence the development and maintenance of competence

- How well the service addresses the relevant needs of the people served

- The efficiency of use of time within the service

- The provision of relevant possessions for people

Review a service known to you, using some of the above categories. In any of the areas you choose, do you think the service is fully supporting people to have a good reputation and status in society, or do you think there may be aspects that, however unconsciously or unintentionally, may be damaging people's social image or ability to portray themselves well to others?

The Care Standards

A rather different approach to the evaluation of services can be seen in the Care Standards devised to accompany the Care Standards Act 2000. This established a system of regular inspection of care services by independent inspectors, using sets of specific criteria for different kinds of service and for different client groups. These criteria were devised, not from a theoretical framework like social role valorisation from which PASSING was derived, but from suggestions and recommendations made by a range of people through a consultation process.

As an example of the areas covered by Care Standards, here are some from the National Minimum Standards for Care Homes for Younger Adults, which are relevant to many residential services for people with learning difficulties.

- The registered person ensures that there is a clear and effective complaints procedure, which includes the stages of, and time scales for, the process, and that service users know how and to whom to complain.

- The registered person ensures that service users are safeguarded from physical, financial or material, psychological or sexual abuse, neglect, discriminatory abuse or self-harm or inhuman or degrading treatment, through deliberate intent, negligence or ignorance, in accordance with written policy.

- The home's premises are suitable for its stated purpose; accessible, safe and well maintained; meet service users' individual and collective needs in a comfortable and homely way; and have been designed with reference to relevant guidance.

- The registered person provides each service user with a bedroom which has useable floor space sufficient to meet individual needs and lifestyles.

These are just four of almost 50 areas in which minimum standards are specified and regularly inspected. This may be felt to be admirable and a much-needed safeguard for the welfare of the people served. However, the Care Standards and their inspection have been described as 'draconian' (Ridout, 2003), especially since they are backed up by legal sanctions. There have been criticisms that they are bureaucratic and unhelpful (Williams, 2005a). Inspections focusing merely on records can miss serious abuse, as has actually happened in a number of instances.

RESEARCH SUMMARY

A research study at the Tizard Centre, a specialist research unit on services for people with learning difficulties, part of the University of Kent, looked at the scores given by Care Standards inspectors to 52 registered homes serving 299 people with learning difficulties, compared to scores on measures of service quality which had been shown to have scientific validity. The study found no relation between the inspectors' judgements and the other established measures. Its authors say:

There were few relationships between care standards ratings and the other measures of service quality and service user outcome. There [was] no relationship between care standards ratings and ... homelikeness. It seems implausible that the standards could be measuring important outcomes which were not reflected at all in the lived experience of residential care, as assessed by measures of engagement, activity and choice. These are outcomes of central importance in the day-to-day lives of people, and to have a national system of quality assurance which fails to capture them may be difficult to defend.

(Beadle-Brown et al., 2005)

Other measures of service quality

PASSING looks at service processes that are likely to be affecting the public status of the people served, and the Care Standards look at service practices that are thought to affect the welfare, safety and well-being of people. Neither of them measure specific outcomes for the individual people served. Some of the measures that do do this are:

- the Index of Participation in Domestic Life (Raynes et al., 1994);
- Momentary Time Sampling of service user engagement in meaningful activity and staff contact (Beasley, et al., 1989);
- the Choice-Making Scale (Conroy and Feinstein, 1986);
- the Active Support Measure (Mansell and Elliott, 1996);
- the Choice Questionnaire (Stancliffe, 1995);
- the Comprehensive Quality of Life Scale (Cummins, 1997).

A very useful resource for reviewing the quality of supported living services is Paradigm (2008).

A critical approach to the concept of 'quality of life'

Global measures of experiences and satisfaction are often called 'Quality of Life' measures. There are some arguments against use of the term 'Quality of Life'. The term is used in a health services context for evaluation of the benefit of medical treatment for people who have terminal illnesses (see the concept of the 'Quality-Adjusted Life Year' or QALY: Phillips and Thompson, 2001). A poor quality of life is associated with withdrawal of treatment rather than with renewed efforts to improve experience. We believe, therefore, that the term should be avoided when we are talking of the day-to-day experiences of people. We much prefer the term 'quality of experience'. We should not see ourselves as judging the quality of their lives, which may ultimately put them at risk of death, but rather as judging the quality of their daily experiences.

The concept of quality of life or quality of experience has attracted much attention from researchers, service planners and philosophers, and discussions around the issue are of considerable interest and relevance to social work. The following sources of further information are recommended: Brown and Brown (2003), Rapley (2003), Schalock et al. (2002), Seed and Lloyd (1997), Brown (1997), Schalock (1996, 1997), Goode (1994).

Methods of assessing quality of life or quality of experience rest on the principle that we can evaluate a person's experiences in a range of areas where there are universally agreed notions of what constitute 'good' experiences, but we should also supplement these judgements with information about each individual person's own evaluation of their experiences. Each of these tasks is attempted in relation to various 'domains' of experience. Schalock et al. (2002) list eight domains as being particularly important for people with learning difficulties (as they are likely to be for everyone). These are:

- emotional well-being;
- interpersonal relations;
- material well-being;
- personal development;
- physical well-being;
- self-determination;
- social inclusion;
- rights.

Person-centred planning

The principle that we should consult people themselves about their satisfaction with their experiences, in order to determine their needs and the quality required of services designed to help meet those needs, leads on to consideration of the development of ways of making the person being served central in the process of assessment and planning. As part of the concept of 'person-centred planning', which we will discuss below, some very interesting and powerful methods have been devised for assessment.

Two frameworks for identifying the needs of a person and turning them into a plan to meet the needs are MAPS (Making Action Plans: Forest and Lusthaus, 1989) and PATH (Planning Alternative Tomorrows with Hope: Pearpoint et al., 1992). These are not instruments for professionals or researchers to use. They depend on a 'circle of support' being organised around the person, consisting of key people interested and willing to assist the person. This is likely to include family members, friends, neighbours, advocates, as well as professionals willing to enter into the spirit of the exercise, and of course the person themselves. Because of the informality of the process and the presence of people with a close relationship with the person, they are much more likely to feel comfortable than in a more formal assessment or planning context.

MAPS is primarily about collecting information about the person, their history, their wishes, their difficulties and the resources that might be mobilised to help them. PATH extends this process into plans for the medium and long term. Because the process is not service-driven or service-oriented, possibilities, resources and actions can be considered that involve ordinary community networks and activities. The aim is to mobilise as many resources as possible to help the person meet their needs and achieve their wishes. The tools required for MAPS and PATH are not formal questionnaires or checklists, but plain pieces of paper. Indeed, the process is facilitated by the use of very large pieces of paper pinned on the wall, with information and suggestions being recorded with large felt-tipped pens using creative graphics as appropriate. The result is often visually stimulating as well as practically useful. The plan is for as far ahead as people wish to work: it can be for a short period or for as long as ten years. The process is unique to the person and depends on close relationships with the person.

There are some other closely related methods of gaining highly individualised information involving the person themselves and a close circle of involved people, for example 'Shared Action Planning' (Brechin and Swain, 1986), 'Essential Lifestyle Planning' (Smull and Sanderson, 2005) and 'Personal Futures Planning' (Mount, 2000).

One feature of a MAPS or PATH exercise is the very different terminology used from that likely to be found in more formal and conventional methods: terms like 'vision', 'dreams', 'gifts', 'passion', 'discovery', 'meaning', 'belonging', 'commitment'. The process initiated by MAPS and PATH and similar methods is called 'person-centred planning' and much work has been done to share advice and experience on how to pursue this method and practice (O'Brien and Lovett, 1992; Sanderson et al., 1997; O'Brien and Lyle O'Brien, 1998, 2002; Holburn and Vietze, 2002; Department of Health, 2002).

One of the most useful sources of information and resources on person-centred planning is Helen Sanderson Associates (**www.helensandersonassociates.co.uk**). They provide training and tools for the process, based on wide experience of its development and use. The following list describes some of the elements in the person-centred planning process for which particular tools or processes have been devised.

One-page profiles

Introducing the person and thinking about what makes really good support for them.

Timeline

Learning about the person's history, how they got where they are today.

What is important to and important for the person

Finding out the things that really matter to the person, and ways to keep them healthy and safe.

Communication chart

Learning what the person is telling us with different words and behaviours.

What do we like and admire about the person (positive reputations)

Thinking about the person's gifts and skills, what the person has to offer.

Achievement tool

Recording and celebrating the person's achievements – and learning from them.

Matching

Linking the person with people who have the right skills, personality characteristics and interests to give them the best support.

Relationship circles

Thinking about who the important people are in the person's life, and about how to maintain relationships and make them closer.

What is working or not working

Thinking about what is working and not working in the person's life.

Good day and bad day

Thinking about what makes a good day and what makes a bad day so as to find out what makes good quality of experience for the person.

Routines and rituals

Thinking about the important rituals and routines in the person's life.

Dreams and nightmares

Thinking with the person and their circle about how to move towards the person's dreams and avoid their nightmares.

Questions

What's been tried, what's been learned, what we're pleased about, what we're concerned about.

Contribution

Ways of helping the person to contribute to activities.

Decision-making agreement

Thinking with the person and their circle about how they will be involved in different decisions in their life – big or small.

CASE STUDY

Lynette Hunt (her real name, since she is proud of her achievements and has kindly given permission for this information to be included here) is a person with learning difficulties who has always lived in care, for the last 20 years in an ordinary house with three others, supported by the same service throughout her life. This case study describes just two elements in a comprehensive review process with Lynette, based on person-centred planning. Before the review a booklet is sent out to people who support Lynette or know her well, covering some of the questions in the list of tools and processes above. The booklet was developed by Niki Marshall, Diane Staniforth and Ruth Mathieson, and is available through Helen Sanderson Associates. Here are the answers that were given by ten of her supporters and friends to the question: What do you like and admire most about Lynette?

- *Her inner beauty; her wonderful caring nature; her sense of humour; her kindness; her love of life*

- *Her kind and caring nature; always happy and cheerful; loves to talk and share her thoughts; a joy to be with*

- *Very caring and loving; always willing to help out; always enthusiastic*

- *Caring; kind; spiritual; loves music*

- *I admire Lynette's patience; she will try until she gets where she needs to go*

- *Kind; loving; never lets anything get her down*

- *I admire the way Lynette has grown inwardly; a beautiful person*

- *Speaking up for herself; saying what she wants; so caring about other people; her ability to pick up on when you're feeling down, and wanting to help put it right*

- *Loves to go out and enjoy herself, dancing, singing or listening to music*

- *Amazing and loving person*

At the review meeting itself were Lynette herself and five others: the manager of her support service, two support workers and two friends. They had known Lynette for periods from 8 years to 30 years. Here are the lists of things that were recorded as important to Lynette now and in the future.

Important to Lynette now

- *Cookery*

- *Performing arts*

- *Her day programme*

- *Ironing*

- *Hoovering*

- *Washing*

- *Making beds*

- *Making tea*
- *Music*
- *Church*
- *Writing notes*
- *TV*
- *Chatting*
- *Her bedroom*
- *Availability of car to take her to church*
- *Instruments to play*
- *Pub*
- *Yoga*
- *Shows*
- *Holidays*
- *Parties*
- *'Big Brother'*
- *Laughing at jokes*
- *Movement exercises*
- *Beadwork*
- *Riding*
- *Singing*
- *Food and drink*
- *Massage*
- *Visiting friends*
- *Going by bus to college*
- *Tea breaks*
- *Relaxation*
- *Art*
- *Swimming*
- *Making speeches*
- *Knowing people's birthdays*

CASE STUDY continued

- *Discos*

- *Time with Sarah*

- *Body care products*

- *Praying and worship*

- *Having her poems written down*

- *Toast and Marmite*

Important to Lynette for the future

- *A partner to love*

- *Involvement in 'Big Brother'*

- *Help to clean the kitchen*

- *Church and reading the Bible*

- *Support from other people*

- *Day activities*

- *Continue her role in training support workers*

- *Good care*

- *Enjoying life*

- *Continuing to live in her home*

- *Being an advocate for others*

- *Maintaining relationships*

- *Having varied choices*

- *Maintenance of health and well-being*

- *Achieving secure tenancy of her home*

- *Continuing to stay over at her friend's house*

These and other pieces of information are used to draw up an action plan for support of Lynette.

Valuing People (Department of Health, 2001) strongly endorsed and recommended person-centred planning as the way forward for the improvement of services for people with learning difficulties. It said:

> *A person-centred approach to planning means that planning should start with the individual (not with services), and take account of their wishes and aspirations. Person-*

centred planning is a mechanism for reflecting the needs and preferences of a person with a learning disability and covers such issues as housing, education, employment and leisure ... The government will ... help local councils develop a person-centred approach and put people with learning disabilities and their families at the centre of the process of planning services for and with them.

(2001: 49)

This was not, however, an open-ended commitment. It was also said that:

Person-centred frameworks will need to be fully compatible with the locally agreed joint eligibility criteria which councils and local health bodies will be asked to develop.

(2001: 51)

Whether person-centred planning is compatible with care management has been a topic of debate and uncertainty since *Valuing People* was published. Several resources have emerged giving ideas on how to achieve compatability. The Valuing People Support Team, set up to guide implementation, produced a *Workbook on Person-Centred Care Management* (2004). This identified seven themes in working towards a model of care management capable of incorporating person-centred planning. These were:

- individualised design of services;
- individualised funding, such as direct payments;
- direct support to people to take decisions, e.g. through advocacy;
- empowerment of people to design their own plans;
- clarity and openness in entitlements to funding;
- sharing information and experience to ensure quality;
- working in partnership with the wider community.

The consultancy organisation Paradigm (**www.paradigm-uk.org**) promotes and advises on the implementation of person-centred planning and on supported living as a concept for helping people to have their own homes. Simon Duffy from Paradigm has written a stimulating book giving practical advice on achievement of these things (2003), called *Keys to Citizenship*. Six 'keys' are covered in depth, namely:

- self-determination (through empowerment);
- direction (through person-centred planning);
- money (with control by the person or on their behalf);
- a true home of one's own;
- individualised support;
- a full community life and a network of relationships.

Recently, Paul Cambridge and Steven Carnaby of the Tizard Centre at the University of Kent have edited a book called *Person-Centred Planning and Care Management with People with Learning Disabilities* (2005) which discusses in depth whether the two are compatible. In a chapter entitled 'Managing the tensions between the interests of organisations and service users', Tony Osgood (2005) questions whether care management processes can ever meet the requirements of person-centred planning, either in time-scale or commitment to deliver. Social work with people with learning difficulties is likely to be a long-term undertaking requiring commitment to each person to help them to achieve their dreams and visions for themselves throughout their lives. This is one reason why people with learning difficulties often like to see social workers and other professionals as their friends. Good friends make long-term commitments to you.

Stories

Formal assessment or evaluation, planned in advance, often involves asking people to tell partial stories about aspects of their lives, but what these stories are about is predetermined by the assessor or evaluator. Open-ended or informal storytelling leaves control of the story to the storyteller; it is therefore a user-friendly, non-oppressive and empowering method of gaining information. Formal assessments with predetermined categories of data have the advantage that comparisons can easily be made between the situations or characteristics of different people, families, environments, services or communities at a point in time, or between the same people, families, environments, services or communities at different times. They provide frameworks for standard descriptions of need and for evaluation of change.

Stories are much messier, though it is possible to use frameworks for analysis after the story has been told rather than before. For example, to evaluate services one might ask for open-ended stories of people or events that informants think are important, and then see the extent to which they reflect or illustrate the 'accomplishments' delineated by John O'Brien (1987): community presence, development of competence, choice, respect and dignity, and community participation. This might enable useful comparisons or aggregates to be made from a number of different stories.

However, any framework of analysis is likely to leave out much of the detail that makes stories so rich in information. Here, for example, is a powerful story which clearly evaluates a service and identifies a need:

> *I have a son who has just reached eighteen. He will be leaving school in September of this year. He has Down's syndrome. I have spent the last two years looking to see what is on offer for when he leaves school. I cannot believe that the school has no contact with businesses for work placements, nor links with colleges, and yet it is right next door to a college. I have done my own research with Connexions and have asked them directly: how many adults with learning disabilities have they been able to place in the working environment? The answer is 'nil', and yet they glorify how much they*

help people when they leave school. I go to supermarkets and explain the situation: could they try my son out for a few hours? They ask me what he can do. I explain that he has Down's syndrome. They then change the subject, and say they will give me an application form. I explain my son cannot write, and they then tell me he cannot get an interview without an application form. Is this a way of eliminating the disabled? Where are their rights? Just because someone cannot write it does not mean they cannot work. My son has never had a social worker. I have tried, but this area is short-staffed. I have received letters to say they are unable to help me. Children's Services say Adult Services should help him, but when I contact Adult Services they won't do anything until my son actually leaves school. I just don't want my son to stay at home and have nothing to do; he will be going from a full day to absolutely nothing.

(Anonymous contribution to the Choice Forum on the Internet, **www.choiceforum.org**, run by the Foundation for People with Learning Disabilities, January 2006)

In contrast, stories can give positive accounts of achievement of a service in supporting people. Taylor (2003), in a biography of a group of people with learning difficulties which tells the story of their move out of an institution and their lives in a community setting over more than 20 years, describes an occasion when one of the people nominated the staff of the local post office for a newspaper 'Good Citizen' award for helping her. The post office was awarded the prize and she and the post office staff were pictured together in the newspaper following the presentation.

John O'Brien is a frequent visitor to Britain from his home in Georgia, USA. He gives inspirational presentations consisting mainly of stories of the achievements of people with learning difficulties when they are well supported. With his wife Connie and other colleagues, he has also produced compilations of stories, designed to motivate and sustain the energies and commitment of staff of support services, under such titles as *Cultivating Thinking Hearts* (Zipperlen and O'Brien, 1994), *Remembering the Soul of Our Work* (O'Brien and Lyle O'Brien, 1992) and *Celebrating the Ordinary* (O'Brien et al., 1998).

In Britain, many stories of people with learning difficulties have been published, particularly by the British Institute for Learning Disabilities (e.g. Atkinson et al., 2000; Johnston and Hatton, 2003). In Chapter 6 we recommended the biography by Margaret Fray (2007) of her sister Kathleen, which tells in a powerful way of the emotional turmoil and practical issues when a person with learning difficulties develops Alzheimer's disease.

ACTIVITY 7.4

Write a brief story about yourself and an event or experience or situation that has been important for you. If you know a person with learning difficulties well, try writing a similar story about them. What did you learn from the stories? To what extent do you think they can be called 'assessment' and are useful for identifying needs, planning to meet needs and evaluating results?

CHAPTER SUMMARY

This chapter has reviewed a range of approaches to assessment of individual people, their families, the environment the person experiences, the services they receive and the communities they belong to. The value of an emphasis on the positive was stressed. Formal and informal methods of discovering and recording information were considered. Approaches to defining needs and planning ways of meeting those needs were explored. The benefits of a life-history perspective and the open-ended telling and recording of stories were outlined.

FURTHER READING

Atkinson et al. (eds) (2000) *Good Times, Bad Times: Women with Learning Difficulties Telling Their Stories* is an example of the power of storytelling.

Beresford et al. (2011) *Supporting People: Towards a Person-Centred Approach* gives a comprehensive account of the concept of person-centred thinking in social work and social care generally.

Cambridge and Carnaby (eds) (2005) *Person-Centred Planning and Care Management with People with Learning Disabilities* discusses the possibilities of incorporating person-centred planning within the structures of care management, and is therefore particularly relevant to current social work practice.

Duffy (2003) *Keys To Citizenship* is a stimulating account of the potential of person-centred planning.

Parker and Bradley (2010) *Social Work Practice: Assessment, Planning, Intervention and Review* gives a general background to the topic of this chapter.

Tilley (2011) *Person-centred Approaches when Supporting People with a Learning Disability* is a useful guide to the practice of person-centredness.

Whittington (2007) *Assessment in Social Work: A Guide for Learning and Teaching* is a useful source of information and discussion of relevant issues.

WEBSITE

www.helensandersonassociates.co.uk is an essential resource on person-centred planning.

Chapter 8

Communication and sensory needs

ACHIEVING A SOCIAL WORK DEGREE

This chapter will help develop the following capabilities, to the appropriate level, from the **Professional Capabilities Framework**:

- **Professionalism**, Identify and behave as a professional social worker committed to professional development
- **Values and Ethics**, Apply social work ethical principles to guide professional practice
- **Diversity**, Recognise diversity and apply anti-discriminatory and anti-oppressive principles in practice.

It will also introduce you to the following standards as set out in the 2008 social work subject benchmark statement.

5.1.5 The nature of social work practice
5.6 Communication skills
5.7 Skills in working with others
7.3 Knowledge and understanding

Introduction

The College of Social Work highlights that *effective communication, building trust and maintaining strong relationships with people who use services and carers are the crucial attributes of a social worker and will help to enable change in people's lives. Social work is practised, whenever possible, in partnership with children, adults, families and communities and tries to improve the personal, practical, psychological and social aspects of people's lives* (**www.collegeofsocialwork.org**). In order to build such relationships it is essential that communicative methods be considered in conjunction with the effectiveness of communication through empowerment and person-centredness. In this chapter we will explore these factors, including how sensory need can impact on communication for a person with a learning difficulty, and describe tips and techniques to enhance the communicative relationship.

As identified in the Department of Health document *Better Communication: Improving Services for Children and Young People with Speech, Language and Communication Needs* (Department of Health, 2008), speech, language and communication are crucial to every child's ability to access and get the most out of education and life. However, when a child has speech, language and communication needs due to a learning difficulty, effective communication and support need to be provided in order for the child to reach their full potential. This also applies to adults. However, before exploring the range of communication methods and their application in practice it is essential to understand the meaning of communication.

Communication defined

Write down how you would define communication and consider what communication means to and for you personally and professionally.

COMMENT

Fiske defines communication as social interaction through messages (Fiske, 1990: 2). Use of the word 'social' is significant because communication can be described as a social activity and without social interaction, especially when addressing speech, language and communication needs, individuals could become isolated (Evans and Whittaker, 2010). Additionally, from a professional perspective communication is essential to be able to support effectively and advocate for the person with whom you are working, e.g. in articulation of needs to family, carers, peers or other professionals or agencies, or in support for people to plan their future and achieve their aspirations and goals. In this chapter we will be exploring a range of alternative communication methods to contribute to ensuring a positive communicative relationship.

Alternative communication

As we have seen from earlier chapters, there is a very wide range of characteristics, strengths and needs among people who may be described as 'people with learning difficulties'. There are people so described who have written poetry and books, become accomplished artists and performers, given talks at conferences, have played a valuable role in teaching professionals, have acted as consultants on government policy and so on. However, difficulties in speech, language and communication are often an accompaniment of learning difficulties. The publication *Fundamental Facts* from the Foundation for People with Learning Disabilities (Emerson et al., 2001) estimates that between 50 per cent and 90 per cent of people with learning difficulties have communication difficulties, according to the definitions used and the sample surveyed.

In this context, we should remember the notion of 'our mutual handicap' (Chapter 1). The other side of what we may describe as a person's 'difficulty in communicating' is our difficulty in understanding. Communication difficulty is not a possession of a person, but an issue for relationships between that person and others, with needs on both sides. We should therefore regard actions to help people to communicate as also being actions to help us to understand (SCOPE, 2002). Tragically, it is almost certainly the case that some people with learning difficulties spend a lifetime trying to communicate with us, but we lack the means to understand. However, being aware, and understanding that the communicative needs of people with learning difficulties are as diverse as people's personalities, can assist in enhancing the communicative relationship.

Intensive interaction

Intensive interaction is a method of responding to the behaviour of a person with profound or multiple impairments in a way that treats the behaviour as communication that can be the basis for mutual interaction (British Institute of Learning Disabilities, 2005). The method was first systematically developed by Gary Ephraim, a psychologist at one of the old large institutions for people with learning difficulties, Harperbury Hospital near London (now closed). Literature and training on the methods were later provided by Nind and Hewett (1994, 2001) and others (e.g. Caldwell, 2005a, b). The method involves close observation of a person's use of their body to create their 'inner world' of communication with themselves. This may involve making sounds, moving their eyes, touching or moving their hands or feet: it will be highly individual to each person. A carer or supporter then enters this world of communication by using the same sounds, touches or movements to begin a conversation with the person. The video by Caldwell (2005a) shows impressive examples of the pleasurable reaction of people as they are brought out of their internal world into shared communication with another person. This very simple but powerful technique is probably used naturally by many carers, family members and friends of people with very severe impairments. It illustrates how communication is possible with everyone, no matter how severely impaired, if we can only master effective ways of sharing in and understanding their behaviours.

Makaton and Signalong

Some people with communication and learning difficulties can learn systems of communication that are alternatives to speech. In practice they are often most effectively used in combination with speech. There are two systems, Makaton and Signalong, which are based on simplified signs. The signs for Makaton are used in conjunction with speech, with words and signs complimenting each other. Signs are used in speech order unlike British Sign Language which is a language in its own right with its own linguistic and grammatical structure and is used by people who are seen as a cultural minority group (Campbell and Oliver, 1996).

Of course, making signs in Makaton or Signalong will only be helpful for a person if the other person to whom they are trying to communicate also knows the signs, and thus this limits their use for communication with the general public (see **www.makaton.org** and **www.signalong.org.uk**). Makaton is increasingly being taught and used for non-disabled children in schools to aid communication, an example of a development in the field of learning difficulty becoming of more general benefit.

Symbols

There are some systems of symbols that have been developed to help people to understand written text or to communicate. There are symbolic representations of Makaton signs that can be used. The 'widgit' symbols system (**www.widgit.co.uk**) includes software to enable translations to be made of text into symbols. The symbols can be printed onto paper or a board so that the person can point to them with their hand, a pointer attached to hand, head, mouth or foot, or eye movement. This can be especially useful for people with physical impairments combined with speech difficulties. Again such aids are only useful if the person has learned the symbols and genuinely finds them helpful to understanding or communication. Jones (2001) makes the following point: *Because alternative ways of representing meaning using, for example, pictures or symbols, have proved effective for some people with learning disabilities, the assumption is all too easily made that these means must be effective for all … This has led, for example, to organisations producing information in symbols, often translated directly from complex language using available software, when the intended recipient may have had no opportunity to learn or understand what the symbols represent* (Jones, 2001: **www.learningdisabilities.org.uk**). This highlights the essentiality of person-centredness and individualisation when considering communication and communicative methods.

Communication boards can be low-technology, using letters, symbols, pictures, photographs or words, or high-technology, using electronic software and interactive speech programmes. (For more information see **www.speechdisorder.co.uk/communication-boards.html**.)

TEACCH

The letters TEACCH are an acronym for Treatment and Education of Autistic and Related Communication Handicapped Children (Talbot et al., 2010). The primary aim of TEACCH is to provide a structured visual learning style to support and prepare children, young people and adults with autism to live or work more independently at home, at school, in college, at work or in the community. Visual information is used to create daily schedules. For example, the day is put at the top of the board and pictures of the daily schedule are arranged underneath the day in the sequence of events and order of activities. For example, a picture of teeth brushing, a picture of washing, a picture of going to school, a picture of being at school and so on. This can be created as a weekly visual aid; however, depending on the level of understanding it may be better to take one day at a time. The daily schedule not only encourages independence but can also alleviate anxiety or worry, enabling order and sequence in the adult, young person or child's life (**www.autism.org.uk/living-with-autism/strategies-and-approaches/teacch.aspx**).

Pictorial Exchange Communication System (PECS)

PECS is an expressive symbol communication using prompting and reinforcement which encourages opportunities, independence and choice. It has been a positive form of communication for children and adults who are on the autistic spectrum (Talbot et al., 2010). People can communicate their wants and this is an inexpensive/creative method of communication available to all. PECS can be used in conjunction with various media, from creating your own sticker board (see Figure 8.1) to exploring the latest technology such as iphone, ipad and ipod. Two useful programmes are available through itunes: PictureCanTalk (**itunes.apple.com/us/app/picturecantalk/id434989881?mt=8**) and Proloquo2Go (**itunes.apple.com/gb/app/proloquo2go/id308368164?mt=8**).

Figure 8.1

Communication passports

Communication passports enable people with learning difficulties to build relationships, convey information and support independence and control in their lives. A communication passport contains personal information about the adult's or child's needs, such as their medical conditions, likes and dislikes. The passport is owned by the adult or child and helps new people understand their personal needs. It is useful if parents or carers can create a communication passport, so that their child's wishes and feelings can be conveyed to new people, e.g. health visitors, social workers, nurses or short-break care centre staff, as required by the Children Act 1989 (see **www.sense.org.uk**).

A communication passport might contain:

- key things you need to know;
- special people;
- my family;
- my friends;
- how I communicate;
- how you can help me with communication;
- things I like to talk about;
- places;
- my work;
- my past;
- special moments and events in my life;
- things that cheer me up;
- things that upset me;

- things that make me cross;

- things I need help with;

- food and drink;

- my sight and hearing.

Total communication

The best advice on helping people with learning difficulties to understand materials and to communicate is probably to use as many different means as possible. This approach is sometimes called 'total communication'. It might involve using manual signs, pictures, photographs, simplified text, audio or visual recordings on tape or DVD, the taking of photographs or videos by the people themselves, computers, the telling of stories, painting and drawing, music, dancing, play, etc. – anything that might possibly help a person to understand others and to communicate their views and needs.

Good practice also is to involve a speech and language therapist for advice. They are experts in communication and are familiar with a wide range of aids to good understanding and communication (Lloyd et al., 1997; Royal College of Speech and Language Therapists, 2003).

Under the name of Storytracks, Nicola Grove and Keith Park run workshops to help people with severe learning difficulties to tell stories, in particular stories about themselves that can help them communicate important information to others (see Grove and Park, 1996, 2001). A personal portfolio of materials that aid communication for an individual can be built up. This might take the form of a story book or personal history, or it might be a resource of useful pictures, symbols, images or written words. The use of PowerPoint on a computer can be a particularly useful way of combining text, pictures, photographs, videos and sound to aid understanding and communication.

Facilitated communication

Attempting to help people to communicate is not without its dangers. Great controversy has raged around a method known as facilitated communication. This was developed following the discovery by Rosemary Crossley that a child she cared for in an Australian institution could communicate with physical help to point to words or pictures. That dramatic story was told in a book (Crossley and McDonald, 1980) and a popular film, *Coming Out*. In facilitated communication, the facilitator supports a client's hand, wrist or arm while that person uses a communicator to spell out words, phrases or sentences (National Autistic Society, 2005). The obvious risk is that the facilitator, consciously or unconsciously, guides the person's hand for them, so that the resulting communication reflects the facilitator's views or needs instead of those of the person themselves. A father was cleared of sexual abuse of his son, who had no speech but appeared to allege abuse through a facilitator using facilitated communication. After the case, the judge, Dame Elizabeth Butler-Sloss, described facilitated communication as dangerous and declared that it should not be used in the courts to support or reject allegations of abuse (Rumbelow, 2000).

Mostert (2001), in a comprehensive review of research studies of facilitated communication, concluded that claims for its success were largely unsubstantiated and that its use could not be recommended. Nevertheless, some people have achieved extraordinary things through facilitated communication. Perhaps best known are the works of Christopher Nolan, a young man with cerebral palsy whose speech is very difficult to understand. He was enabled to type on a typewriter with a pointer attached to his head, with his mother holding his head to keep it steady. He has written a book of poetry, *Dam-Burst of Dreams*, an autobiography of his schooldays, *Under the Eye of the Clock*, and a novel, *The Banyan Tree* (Nolan, 1981, 1987, 2000).

Kochmeister writes: *Because of an extremely controversial process called Facilitated Communication, I have been freed from a life of silence and anonymity ... I have gone from classes in special schools where little was expected of me ... to a world of higher education where expectations run high* (1995: 11). She describes how she cannot perform well when strangers are around trying to test the authenticity of what she types. She says she needs facilitators she can trust and who trust her. If this is true of many people who use facilitated communication, it may explain why research studies have failed to demonstrate its efficacy.

Accessible written material

Much work has taken place in recent years to help people with learning difficulties to understand written material. The White Paper *Valuing People* (Department of Health, 2001) included the statement: *The Government expects organisations working with learning disabled people to develop communication policies and produce and disseminate information in accessible formats*. The Equality and Human Rights Commission (established in 2007) has strongly backed up this expectation, and the Care Quality Commission includes in its requirements that care providers produce information in accessible form.

'Accessible' usually means in simplified language accompanied by pictures. The organisation Inspired Services (**www.inspiredservices.org.uk**) provides a service to help agencies produce accessible versions of documents, and many materials from government, local government, service providers and other bodies have been made available in accessible form. A similar service is provided by Working with Words (**www.mcch.org.uk/workingwithwords/index.aspx**). The Social Care Institute of Excellence has guidance on its website on 'How to produce information in an accessible way' (SCIE, 2005).

The organisation Change, which includes people with learning difficulties themselves, has produced a 'picture bank' – specially designed pictures to illustrate a wide range of themes and concepts of relevance. The following is from their website: **www.changepeople.co.uk**.

> *CHANGE believes that accessible information gives people with learning disabilities more power, control and choice in our lives ... Our accessible information team of people with learning disabilities works closely with our in-house illustrators to make information accessible. We do this by changing hard words into easy words, adding pictures and changing the layout and design of documents.*

Change has published some very useful information material of its own, using the pictures from its bank, including one on the parenting of babies, designed specifically for people with learning difficulties (Affleck, 2005). There is some evidence that the most useful pictures to aid understanding of written materials are photographs, especially if the person actually using the material is pictured. For example, a person may be able to follow a cooking recipe if it is accompanied by photographs of themselves performing the various stages in the process. There is an organisation that specialises in producing photographic images for use in making written documents or instructions accessible to people with learning difficulties: **www.photosymbols.com**.

Difficult or challenging behaviours as a form of communication

What are difficult or challenging behaviours? The term 'difficult' is defined as *needing much effort or skill … troublesome or perplexing* (Thompson, 1996: 273); whereas challenging is defined as *demanding … difficult* (Thompson, 1996: 156). You may have heard the term 'challenging behaviour' used by parents, families, carers, support workers and professionals; however in this section the terminology 'difficult behaviours' will be used. The reason for this is that whilst the behaviour may present as a challenge for parents, carers and professionals working with the person, the terminology 'difficult' identifies that much effort and skill is needed to work in partnership effectively with the person exhibiting the behaviours. Thus in this context 'difficult behaviours' is more appropriate.

ACTIVITY 8.2

Write down how 'difficult behaviours' could be exhibited.

COMMENT

The difficult behaviour you identify might involve aggression, tantrums, destructiveness to self, others or property, or self-injury. However, the point we make here is that such behaviour might well be being used as a form of communication. Thus, rather than the behaviour being considered as purely demanding or difficult, when it is explored and analysed a better understanding of it can contribute to more effective and acceptable communication.

RESEARCH SUMMARY

Chiang (2008) 'Expressive communication of children with autism: the use of challenging behaviour'

Autism is described as being characterised by qualitative impairment in social interaction and communication, as well as restricted repetitive and stereotyped patterns of behaviour. The study set out to investigate challenging behaviour among Australian and Taiwanese children with autism who were non-verbal or had limited speech. A total of 32 children were studied.

The results showed that challenging behaviour was directed to adults significantly more than to peers and was exhibited more in the classroom than at free time. Instances of self-injury, tantrums, aggression and destructiveness were shown to relate to gaining attention, seeking access to an item or escaping demands. In other words challenging behaviour was used as a form of communication. This explained why the behaviour was more prevalent towards adults and in the classroom environment. The study concluded: A high proportion of children with autism with severe speech impairments (16 out of the 32) used challenging behaviour as a form of expressive communication in their school environment. *How a teacher dealt with the behaviour had an impact on the communicative outcome. Therefore whilst difficult behaviours can be a challenge, recognising they are a form of expressive communication and combining appropriate responses and interactions can contribute to a positive communicative relationship.*

Sensory needs

ACTIVITY *8.3*

Identify what you would consider to be a sensory need. Think of it in the context of children and adults.

COMMENT

Sensory is defined as sensation of the senses *(Thompson 1996: 930). Evans and Whittaker highlight that this term is based on the Latin* sentire sens *which literally means 'to feel' (2010: 2). Furthermore Thompson defines need as* circumstances requiring some form of action *(1996: 172). Thus is could be proffered that sensory needs are sensory related circumstances that arise and require action (Evans and Whittaker, 2010). Whilst the term 'sensory' could refer to taste, touch and smell, for the purpose of this section we will be considering sensory in terms of deafness, deafblindness and visual impairment. However, it should be borne in mind that children with learning difficulties and people with dementia may communicate through touch and smell especially where the adult or child is non-verbal and does not use a form of symbol or sign language to communicate. Non-verbal communication should never be under-estimated as it is sometimes the case that people with learning difficulties may use non-verbal communication due to developmental linguistic impediment. Furthermore, Kadushin and Kadushin claim that* non-verbal vocabulary includes 5000 distinctly different hand gestures and 1000 different body postures *(Kadushin and Kadushin, 1997: 315).*

ACTIVITY *8.4*

List as many communication methods you can think of that could be used when communicating with a person who has a sensory need. Think specifically of a person who is deaf or Deaf (see definition below), hard of hearing, deafened, deafblind, partially sighted or blind.

COMMENT

You may have considered Makaton, PECS and Signalong (as considered earlier), British Sign Language (BSL), Sign Supported English (SSE), Hands on Signing, Deafblind manual alphabet, Objects of reference, Block, Braille, Moon, Bold Print Format, Tadoma, Lipspeaking, Lipreading, Clear Speech, Cued Articulation (often used in education), Paget Gorman, Cued Speech or indeed others not mentioned here (see the glossary at the end of this chapter for explanations of these communication methods).

Referral to deafness and deaf people is sometimes made with a small 'd' and sometimes with a capital 'D'. Small 'd' deafness often refers to people who are likely to have been a previously hearing person or one who was born deaf and grew up in a hearing family with oral communication being the primary means of communication. Persons who have previously experienced hearing may regard themselves as disabled after the loss. However, a capital 'D' Deaf person would most likely be a profoundly Deaf person who considers themself to be part of a minority group with its own culture, history and linguistics. This was highlighted by the British Deaf Association (BDA) when British Sign Language attained official language status on 18 March 2003. Deaf people who are part of this community often consider themselves proud to be Deaf and would most likely not consider themselves to be disabled (Evans and Whittaker, 2010).

People who are profoundly Deaf often use British Sign Language (BSL) as their first language. People who use BSL may require an interpreter to translate from one language to BSL and vice versa. It essential that you as a social worker ensure an interpreter is present for an assessment or intervention, and that you book early to ensure interpreter availability. It is essential when working with someone who is Deaf not to use the term 'deaf and dumb' to avoid offensive vocabulary.

Interpreters can be used for any individual with a sensory need. For example a hard of hearing person may use a lipspeaker or a deafblind person may use a deafblind manual alphabet interpreter.

> The interpreter's role is to communicate everything that is being said and to 'voice over' in English everything the person with the sensory need communicates. Interpreters are usually trained professionals and work to a Code of Ethics, which includes impartiality, respect for diversity and confidentiality. An interpreter is not a social worker and will only communicate information spoken. The social worker should always speak 'directly' to the service user, addressing them in the first person, e.g. 'It is nice to meet

you', rather than 'Can you tell her it is nice to meet her?' It is important when using an interpreter in a group setting such as a Child in Need Meeting (in child protection and safeguarding) or Adult Protection (Safeguarding) Meeting for only one person to speak at a time. This allows the interpreter to convey all information accurately which is extremely important especially if the case involves going to court.

(Evans and Whittaker, 2010: 32)

Communication tips and practical guidance

Sensory needs are often hidden needs, similar to that of autism. It may not be visually apparent that a person has additional requirements. For example unless a person who experiences visual difficulties has glasses, a white cane or a guide dog, it may not be visible that that person experiences sight loss. The same with someone who is Deaf, deaf, deafened or hard of hearing: unless a person has a hearing aid, hearing dog for the Deaf or you see a visual form of communication being used, e.g. BSL, you may not realise someone has a sensory need.

When communicating with someone who has a sensory need you may find the following communication tips useful.

General sensory tips

- Attract the person's attention.
- Check their preferred method of communication.
- Ensure there is no background noise. Switch off ambient noise, e.g. the television or radio.
- Be clear in your introduction.
- Rephrase and paraphrase as necessary.
- Be on time.
- Check you have been understood.
- Sit or stand at the same level as the person with the sensory need.
- Allow enough time to carry out the assessment – you may need more time when there is a sensory need.
- Use clear straightforward speech.
- Avoid distractions – focus on the person you are communicating with.
- Provide an appropriate interpreter.

Sensory tips for a person who is Deaf, deaf, hard of hearing or deafened

- Think of where you are seated. If you sit opposite a window the light will shine on your face and make your lips easier to read. Make sure you are not sitting in shadow.

- If they have a hearing aid, ensure it is on, the batteries are working, the tubing is clean and it is adjusted properly.

- Avoid shouting – use clear speech.

- Avoid bold patterns on your clothing, dangly earrings, bright lipstick, graded lenses or sun glasses, especially if using sign language.

- Choose a quiet environment as other noises may affect existing residual hearing.

- When talking, be face to face. Avoid looking down or side to side, e.g. retrieving items from your bag.

- Keep facial hair trimmed, e.g. beards and moustaches.

- Avoid putting your hand over your mouth.

- If using sign language – remember it is unique to the individual. Some Deaf people may use Sign Supported English, others British Sign Language, others may mix the two or use an alternative or simplified version. Sign language is regional – avoid assuming every Deaf person will sign the same.

- Where possible try to produce information in DVD format using BSL.

- Children with a learning need may use Makaton or PECS. Often the school will have a 'communication passport' for the child outlining how to communicate effectively.

- Ensure there is a loop system if required (equipment with microphone, an amplifier and a loop wire which is installed around the area in which the person sits – this maximises sound for persons with a hearing aid).

- Use pen, paper, play, painting or drawing.

Sensory tips for a person who is blind or partially sighted

- Use clear speech.

- Does the person need to change their glasses? Is a magnifying glass or screen needed?

- Consider producing information in Braille, Moon or audio.

- Use tactile forms of communication such as manual alphabet or Block.

- Use Hands on Signing.

- Produce information in clear large bold print, e.g. font 16 bold Arial.

Sensory tips for a person who is deafblind

- Use combinations of Deaf, deaf, hard of hearing and visually impaired methods.

- If a person has 'Usher syndrome' they may need time for their eyes to adjust to the light and time to focus into what they see (**www.sense.org.uk/content/usher-syndrome**).

- Use Hands on Signing, deafblind manual or Block tactile communication.

- Use objects of reference, e.g. a cup may be used by a person to indicate whether they want a drink.

For more information see Evans and Whittaker (2010), pp25–6, 32–3.

Other aspects to consider in facilitating effective communication with people with sensory needs are working with interpreters and human aids to communication, e.g. Communicator Guides, who provide regular human contact and support to deafblind people, Communication Support Workers, who support an individual with regard to communication needs, and Intervenors, who support children 0–19 years who are deafblind with communication, empowerment and 'interpreting the world' (Evans and Whittaker, 2010: 13).

Supporting communication

Aids to communication have to be highly individualised to suit the needs of the person. This usually requires getting to know the person really well before communication beyond a basic level is possible. Interaction with the public may require a supporter or advocate to act as interpreter for the person, or to explain the person's individual method of communication. In view of the importance of fostering a wide range of relationships for people, this is likely to be a particularly necessary and valuable task.

Empowerment

Empowerment is an essential element within the context of communication. As will be discussed in Chapter 9, 'empowerment' is a deeper and more sophisticated concept than just always acceding to a person's apparent wants and choices. This richer concept concerns enabling the person to participate in and contribute to relationships and community life and could be described as shifting power over to the service user at key stages whilst ensuring risk is balanced with need (Gardner, 2011). Therefore, it is essential to listen to the voice of people with learning difficulties and to support their own personal or joint ways of surviving the oppression they may experience. In addition families and carers need to be empowered in their pursuit of the best interests of their sons and daughters or people they are supporting.

Glossary

Block: Communication is conveyed by drawing capital letters onto the palm of the hand of the visually impaired or deafblind person. As with the deafblind manual alphabet there is a pause in between words.

Bold print format: Bold outline and/or large font size. This is personalised to each individual. A guideline may be bold font Arial16.

Braille: A tactile system of writing in which patterns of raised dots represent letters and numerals.

British Sign Language (BSL): A visual means of communication using signs. BSL has its own grammatical structure and syntax and is recognised as an official language in its own right. BSL is regional and thus signs will vary. BSL is not used the world over and each country will have their own sign language. For example, American Sign Language (ASL) is primarily conveyed using one hand.

Clear speech: Use of clear speech; light and environment can enhance the sound quality of the speech.

Cued articulation: Used in education. This is a set of hand cues for teaching the individual sounds in a word. It is not sign language. However, each hand movement represents one sound and the cue gives clues as to how and where sound is produced.

Cued speech: Uses eight hand shapes in four different positions near the mouth to clarify the lip patterns of normal speech.

Deafblind manual alphabet: The alphabet is similar to that of BSL but is communicated directly onto the hand of the visually impaired or deafblind person. Each letter is placed over the top of the last. There is a brief pause in between words to indicate a new word has started.

Hands-on signing: A communication method based on BSL enabling a person to feel the signs. With this form of communication the deafblind person follows the sings by placing his or her hands over those of the signer and feeling the signs produced.

Lipspeaking: A lipspeaker is a hearing person who is clearly visible to the lipreader and silently and accurately repeats the spoken message. This form of communicative method is often used in large conference or meeting settings where the speaker's lips are not easily read.

Lipreading: The Deaf, deaf or hard of hearing person uses a lipspeaker as an interpreter and reads the lips to receive information.

Makaton: A simplified sign system using simple hand signs. This is not to be confused with BSL which is a language in its own right. Signs are used in conjunction with the spoken word and they support each other to improve speech and language acquisition and facilitate communication.

Moon: A code of raised shapes which enables people who are visually impaired or deafblind to read tactilely.

Objects of reference: This method of communication is often used by persons who are deafblind and refers to association of the object with what is required. This could be a picture, drawing, photograph or the actual object, e.g. a cup representing a drink. Objects can be used for leisure, personal care needs, school timetabling, etc. It is important that whatever method is used it is consistent between home, school and other places the person goes.

Paget Gorman: A grammatical sign system which reflects normal patterns of English.

Pictorial Exchange Communication System (PECS): PECS is an expressive symbol system of communication using prompting and reinforcement which encourages opportunities, independence and choice.

Signalong: A sign-supporting system based on BSL. It is often used to support individuals with communication difficulties as part of a total communication approach.

Sign Supported English (SSE): A visual means of communication using signs in English word structure.

Tadoma: Used primarily by people who are deafblind. The deafblind person places their thumb on the speaker's lips and their fingers along the speaker's jaw line. The middle three fingers often fall along the speaker's cheeks with the little finger picking up the vibrations of the speakers throat.

For a more detailed sensory glossary see Evans and Whittaker (2010: 125–7).

CHAPTER SUMMARY

This chapter has given accounts of a wide range of approaches to the empowerment of people with learning difficulties and explored an array of alternative communication methods including those used by people with sensory needs. However, this chapter has also highlighted that it is essential to remember that communicating with each other is just as important as communicating with the person using alternative communication and language. This includes parents, care givers, students on placements, charitable and specialist organisations, professionals, social workers and care managers, support workers, speech therapists, teachers, etc. Thus, in order to support, empower and facilitate change in the lives of people with learning difficulties the communicative relationship consists of partnership working. Building trust and maintaining strong relationships with people who use services and their carers and supporters are crucial components of effective social work.

Evans and Whittaker (2010) *Sensory Awareness and Social Work*.

This book is full of practical tips, case studies and activities to raise sensory awareness for social work students, practitioners, carers and other professionals. Understanding sensory needs is fundamental to effective social work/care management and is an important aspect of anti-oppressive practice. This book outlines different sensory needs relating to Deafness, deafness, hearing impairment, deafblindness and visual impairment, and imparts skills and tips to address these needs in practice.

Koprowska (2005) *Communication and Interpersonal Skills in Social Work*.

This book is part of the Transforming Social Work Practice series written specifically to support students on social work degree courses. The honours degree in social work requires all students to learn communication skills with children, adults and those with communication difficulties, and to have these skills assessed. This book is an interactive source and is very practical in approach, with activities and case studies throughout the text. The case study summaries of contemporary research and theory illustrate and draw out key points to aid and reinforce learning.

Chapter 9
Advocacy and empowerment

Introduction

This chapter introduces the concept of advocacy as a powerful means of protecting and
empowering people. Leading on from the exciting phenomenon of self-advocacy by people
with learning difficulties themselves, various other contexts for empowerment are discussed,
including discussion of the Mental Capacity Act. Empowerment of families is also touched
on. The chapter ends with some direct quotes from people with learning difficulties.

Advocacy

Advocacy is standing up for a person, standing by them (Williams, 1998) in times of trou-
ble, offering friendship, sympathy and support, celebrating their achievements, sharing
enjoyment and – in John O'Brien's words (see below) – *bringing their gifts and concerns
into the circles of ordinary community life*. Advocacy can be a better way of ensuring
protection from harm than the imposition of ever-increasing bureaucratic rules and regulations. It is also a way of supporting empowerment.

There are many different kinds of advocacy, and any of them can be useful in particular circumstances. Because of the vulnerability and powerlessness of people with learning difficulties, it is probably best if all forms of advocacy can work together. Advocacy by people with learning difficulties themselves, known as 'self-advocacy', will be covered later in this chapter. As will be seen, the development of self-advocacy demonstrates that people with learning difficulties are not helpless victims. They can, and do, make a major contribution themselves to the pursuit of their rights, wishes and best interests. However, this is made even more effective if there is also support in the form of other kinds of advocacy.

Each form of advocacy has its strengths and limitations, as indicated in Table 9.1.

Table 9.1 *Strengths and limitations of types of advocacy*

Type of advocacy	Example	Strengths	Limitations
Paid advocacy	Solicitor	Expertise, especially on legal rights Powerful representation	Costly Often an unnecessarily 'heavy' response
Advocacy as part of a professional role	Social worker Nurse	Influence within services Time allocated as part of job Experience and knowledge of needs	Usually working with more than one person, so attention limited that can be given to individuals Bound by conditions of employment Possible conflict of interest, for example if a person needs help to complain about one's colleagues or employers
Advocacy by an organisation on behalf of a group	Mencap Royal National Institute for the Deaf Age Concern	Expertise Power deriving from membership Influence on national policy	Usually concerned with general rather than individual issues
'Formal' problem-oriented advocacy	Ombudsman Citizens Advice Bureau Local councillor MP Patient advice (PALS)	Formal or legal basis Independence Authority by virtue of role	Often oriented towards complaints or specific problems
Statutory advocacy	Independent Mental Capacity Advocate (IMCA)	Represents an individual person Independent of services Statutory availability and power Expertise	Requires formal training Role constrained by Mental Capacity Act Limited in scope
'Informal' single-issue unpaid advocacy	Crisis or instrumental outcome-oriented citizen advocacy	Flexible Informal Expression of citizenship and social capital Minimises conflict of interest since unpaid and voluntary	Concerned with single issues rather than long-term needs

Type of advocacy	Example	Strengths	Limitations
'Informal' long-term unpaid advocacy	Relationship-based citizen advocacy partnerships Advocacy by family and friends	Same as single-issue unpaid advocacy, plus: Long-term relationship-based Protective as well as empowering	Great trust required that the relationship will pursue the person's best interests
Self-advocacy by individuals on their own behalf	Creative arts Taking part in own reviews Expressing wishes Involvement in person-centred planning	Empowering Ensures relevance Participatory Enhances self-esteem	Lacks power Depends on adequate support
Self-advocacy by a group on behalf of its members	People First National Pensioners Convention British Council of Disabled People	Gives a voice to the otherwise unheard Expression of basic rights Supportive to members	Likely to be concerned with general rather than individual issues Depends on financial and advisory support for success
Advocacy by individuals on behalf of a group	Elected representatives Partnership Board Advisory panels	Contribution of relevant views Expression of democratic participation and rights	Individuals may not be representative Views expressed may not be those of the group as a whole

The advocacy role of a social worker has been generally accepted and is described in many general textbooks on social work (e.g. Payne, 1997; Coulshed and Orme, 1998), in texts specifically on advocacy in social work (e.g. Bateman, 2000; Brandon and Brandon, 2001; United Nations, 1994), and in writings on advocacy with disabled people (e.g. Brandon, 1995; Gray and Jackson, 2002).

Advocacy requires effort and commitment over and above the ordinary requirements of a job or of friendship. It involves standing up for the rights of a person, working to protect them from harm, helping them to have a voice, and arguing for resources to meet their needs. It involves working to prevent discrimination and oppression, and tackling them when they occur. Brandon and Brandon (2001) identify risks to social workers associated with their advocacy role. They may antagonise colleagues and other professionals, incur the displeasure of managers and employers, put their job and career prospects at risk, lose promotion opportunities or be subject to complaints or disciplinary procedures. Advocacy may involve anxiety and stress, and devotion of extra time and energy, possibly incurring objections from family. 'Whistleblowing' may damage one's reputation and earn a label of 'troublemaker'.

Nevertheless, advocacy on behalf of people supported is an important aspect of social work, and it is to be hoped that organisations employing social workers have robust policies to respect and protect this aspect of their role. The risks do create a 'conflict of interest', however, and this is why it is important to support other forms of advocacy that can be more powerful and successful in particular instances.

Citizen advocacy

One of the most powerful forms of advocacy is informal advocacy by unpaid volunteers. The vast majority of this form of advocacy is performed by family members, friends, neighbours or others just in the course of everyday life, without any organisation, regulations or bureaucracy.

ACTIVITY 9.1

Think of an act of advocacy that you have performed, or that someone has performed for you, just as a family member, friend or neighbour. Would the advocacy have benefited from some more professional, perhaps paid, advocacy?

Correspondingly, think of an act of advocacy for a person with learning difficulties or their family that might be performed by a social worker as part of their job. In what ways could that advocacy be helpfully supported by unpaid, volunteer advocacy?

Citizen advocacy schemes recruit unpaid volunteer advocates and match them up with vulnerable people in need. The advocate may serve a short-term, specific function, such as helping a person to have their views listened to at a time of moving house, or helping a person to open a bank account, or supporting a person being interviewed by the police, or helping someone make a complaint. The major achievement, however, of citizen advocacy is when the advocate undertakes to support a person in the long term. This requires getting to know the person and forming a relationship of partnership with them in pursuing rights and needs with an unspecified timetable into the future. Here is a definition of such advocacy, given originally by John O'Brien and quoted in much of the citizen advocacy literature (e.g. Wertheimer, 1998):

> *A person connected to the networks of community life, unpaid and independent, creates a relationship with a person at risk of social exclusion. The advocate seeks to understand, respond to and represent their partner's interests as if they were the advocate's own. Thus, the partner's gifts and concerns are brought into the circles of ordinary community life.*

(O'Brien, quoted in Wertheimer, 1998: 1)

The context of community in this definition covers the dual function of advocacy – protection and empowerment. The person is protected from social exclusion (the root of many of the 'wounds' and of loneliness), and is empowered to participate in and contribute to community life. The latter concept of 'empowerment' goes beyond merely according choice; it seeks to extend the control a person has over their life in a social, not just an autonomous personal, context.

Citizen advocates cannot be controlled by threats to job, status, etc. because they are just ordinary citizens doing it out of love, friendship, community spirit and social responsibility. This reduces conflict of interest and gives advocates great potential power to speak out and act without being hidebound by the requirements of job and official role. It can also be seen that citizen advocacy, at least in its long-term, relationship-based form, is not a 'service' that can be bought or commissioned from some agency. A citizen advocacy scheme will recruit advocates, give them some training, link them with people in need and keep an eye on basic standards of behaviour. However, it cannot determine the content of the advocacy or the nature of the relationship; it cannot set goals and 'evaluate' outcomes. The advocacy can only come from the freely developing relationship between two people.

ACTIVITY *9.2*

A major controversy in the field of citizen advocacy is between these two views:

- *An advocate for a person should always pursue what they judge to be in the person's best interests, even if this goes against the person's apparent wishes.*

- *An advocate for a person should always respect the person's wishes and help the person to achieve what they want, even if this goes against the advocate's judgement of the person's best interests.*

Look back at the examples of Peter in Chapter 6 being best man at his brother's wedding and of JS in the risk management example also in Chapter 6. What might be the issues of choice versus best interest in these examples?

Can you think of any examples from your own experience where there might be a conflict between choice and best interest? What would you decide to do, and why, in that situation?

Write down some arguments in favour of each of the views above.

COMMENT

Many people with learning difficulties have had very little experience of choice and very little power or control over many aspects of their lives. It may appear clear that a major part of their oppression has been their subjection to control by others all their lives. It is natural to adopt the position that advocacy must at all costs support autonomy and choice, to give back freedom and control and give maximum respect to the person.

In practice, things are more complicated. If a person's only experience has been of exclusion, lack of opportunity, time-wasting and being thought of in negative terms, they may have very low expectations of themselves, they may fear any change or challenge and they may be very distrustful of other people. Their apparent choices may not be in their best interests. When an advocate reaches an understanding of the 'wounds' their partner may have suffered in the past, their resources, networks and contacts can be used to help redress those wounds. There may be instances where pursuing needs in important areas of experience of the person may require overruling apparent choice. 'Best interest' advocacy might include at least strong persuasion, if not actual coercion, in areas such as family relationships, community presence and participation, constructive activity, presentation of self, health and respect for oneself and others.

However, many commentators challenge this view. For example, Brandon and Brandon (2001: 75) write:

> We don't know how others ought to live, what ways of behaving are mature and immature, what are 'personality disorders' and what are not. It is no part of the role of being an advocate to 'know what is best' for clients. We don't even know what is best for us.

Self-advocacy

There are two kinds of self-advocacy: individual and group. Individual self-advocacy is where a person has been given the confidence and the support to represent their own views and pursue their own interests. Education in confidence-building and assertiveness, and any aids to understanding and communication as outlined in Chapter 8, can help people to achieve this. Many schools and colleges of further education include activities in their curriculum designed to help people with learning difficulties in this respect.

The beginning of the modern self-advocacy movement of people with learning difficulties is usually taken as the organising of some conferences of people with learning difficulties in Scandinavia in the 1960s to discuss leisure activities (Nirje, 1972). In Britain, the organisation Campaign for the Mentally Handicapped (later called Values Into Action) organised some more general conferences in the early 1970s, and the proceedings of these were written up and published (Shearer, 1972, 1973; Williams, 1974). The idea spread to Canada and the USA, and several conferences were held there during the 1970s. At one conference a name was coined for the self-advocacy movement: People First; one delegate had said, *We are people first and handicapped second* (Williams and Shoultz, 1982; Dybwad and Bersani, 1996; Goodley, 2000).

Alongside these conferences, local groups of people with learning difficulties had begun to be established. In America these were usually independent of services; they were set up in a locality, perhaps supported by a local voluntary organisation such as a branch of The Arc (the US equivalent of Mencap in England and Wales). In Britain, the groups were more often associated with a service, for example a group of people attending a particular day service, or a group of residents in a residential care service. Such groups need the support of non-disabled people, and they usually have one or more such people in the role of 'adviser'. This role involves a delicate balance between helping the group and not controlling it.

ACTIVITY **9.3**

What do you envisage the components of your role would be if you were an adviser to a self-advocacy group of people with learning difficulties? If you were able to perform this role as part of your job as a social worker, might this create any possible conflicts of interest?

> ### COMMENT
>
> *The sorts of tasks that advisers perform are:*
>
> - *helping the group to raise money for their activities;*
> - *helping to arrange transport to and from meetings;*
> - *helping to find suitable places for meetings;*
> - *helping with writing letters;*
> - *helping with recruitment of new members;*
> - *helping the group to develop 'ground rules' for meetings;*
> - *helping with voting procedures (but not voting themselves);*
> - *helping the group to gain information about options and choices;*
> - *accompanying and supporting people on visits or speaking engagements;*
> - *helping people to claim payment for work they do as self-advocates;*
> - *helping people to prepare presentations;*
> - *helping to produce a newsletter.*

There may indeed be pressures on social workers if this is part of their job to limit the time spent on the role, not to get involved in anything controversial the group might wish to do or say, not to support any complaints about services and so on. Many social workers are in fact involved in support of self-advocacy. They may just try to manage any conflicts of interest that arise, they may be involved in a purely voluntary capacity outside their job, or in a few cases they may actually be employed by the self-advocacy group if the group has been able to attract sufficient funding.

In 1984, a group of people with learning difficulties from Britain were supported to attend an international conference in the USA. They were not only inspired to establish one of the first completely independent self-advocacy groups in Britain – People First London and Thames – but they were determined to mount the next international conference in the UK. This was held in 1988 at St Mary's College, Twickenham, and was attended by 300 people from Australia, Canada, Switzerland and the US, as well as from all parts of the UK (Wertheimer, 1988). Around the same time, a national conference of self-advocacy groups in Scotland was held, organised by the self-advocacy group called the Lothian Rights Group, and a videotape of the conference was made and widely distributed. Values Into Action and other organisations also began to produce instructional material to help groups develop and to clarify the role of adviser. These and other similar developments gave a great boost to the establishment of independent groups in many parts of Britain.

There are now many strong and impressive self-advocacy groups of people with learning difficulties all over the world, especially in the USA and Britain. There are five main kinds of activity that the groups may engage in. These are:

- the support of members, through solidarity, friendship, empathy, shared experience, teaching or advice;

- the pursuit of rights and needs, through meetings, negotiations, requests and demands, and linkage with other rights groups;

- enjoyment and fun, through parties, social events, celebrations, outings and sharing common interests;

- information exchange and mass communication, through conferences, newsletters and publicity;

- providing specialist information and advice to others, for example service providers, government policy-makers or training courses for professionals.

ACTIVITY 9.4

Find the internet sites of some self-advocacy groups by typing 'People First' into a search engine, to gain a picture of their aims, activities, achievements and resources. Through the internet, your local library or other contacts, find out your nearest self-advocacy group and how to make contact with it. If you are able to, visit the group to see first hand how it operates and what it achieves. Many self-advocacy groups are involved in social work courses, contributing to selection, teaching, research or other activities. If this is not yet the case on your course, you might perhaps take the initiative to suggest involvement of your local group.

Statements of rights

One function of self-advocacy groups is to press for rights to be acknowledged and pro-tected for people with learning difficulties. Many groups have a constitution or other document which states the rights that members feel they do have or that they would like to have. A pioneer British self-advocacy group in the 1970s, the Avro Adult Training Centre Students' Council, based in Southend, Essex, included the following statement of rights in its Constitution.

- *To be treated like any other human being without being labelled.*

- *To go into the community when we please and do the same things as other people do.*

- *To vote in elections.*

- *To choose where we want to live and who we want to live with.*

- *To love and be with the person we love.*

- *To receive education and training that will help us to become more independent.*

- *To work.*

- *To say 'no' to something we don't want to do.*

- *To stand up for ourselves, or speak out for others, if we are abused or treated in a degrading way.*

- *To have our point of view listened to.*

(Williams and Shoultz, 1982: 241–2)

The White Paper *Valuing People* uses the language of 'rights' in its intentions for developing better services for people with learning difficulties. There is also a United Nations *Declaration on the Rights of Mentally Retarded Persons* (1971) which lays down basic rights of people with learning difficulties. It is primarily concerned with rights to health, education, economic security, community living, guardianship and protection from abuse. Rather more powerful in its intent and provisions is the *UN Convention on the Rights of Disabled People*, ratified by the UK government in 2009. People with learning difficulties are firmly included in the Convention, following the work of several advocacy organisations (see Mittler, 2010).

It is of course the case that people with learning difficulties have the same rights as anyone else – there is nothing inherent in a label of 'person with learning difficulties' that takes away any rights at all. The United Nations Declaration starts off with the sentence: *The mentally retarded person has, to the maximum degree of feasibility, the same rights as other human beings.* The first step in protecting the rights of people with learning difficulties is thus to ensure that rights that we all take for granted – to choice, to relationships, to housing, to education, to financial security, to health care, to political enfranchisement, for example – are not denied to people with learning difficulties.

The Mental Capacity Act

This Act came into force in 2005. We will not cover it in detail here, since other resources are available (e.g. Brown et al., 2009). However, it is a very important piece of legislation for people with learning difficulties, for good and bad reasons. The basic principle behind the Act is that there should be an assumption of capacity to make decisions unless there is concrete proof that a person is not capable. In principle, this should enable many people with learning difficulties to have a greater say in decisions affecting them. However, as often with good ideas, drawbacks have emerged in practice. The Act has sensitised many people to the issue of capacity to consent, and this capacity is being explored or questioned in more instances than might have been the case previously. For example, some authorities have delayed agreeing to anyone with learning difficulties becoming a tenant of their housing until their capacity to enter into a contract is established (Young, 2008).

Bureaucracy surrounding implementation of the Act has also been greatly increased by the 'Bournewood' judgement of the European Court of Human Rights in 2004. A man with learning difficulties was kept in a hospital (called Bournewood) against the wishes of his carers, who took the matter to the European Court. The Court decreed that there should be rules and procedures governing any loss of liberty of a person where that person's capacity to agree may be in doubt. As a result, attached to the Mental Capacity Act are procedures called DOLS (Deprivation of Liberty Safeguards) requiring those caring for or working with people with learning difficulties to document in detail the justification for any restriction on the movements or opportunities of those they support. Information can be accessed by typing 'MCA DOLS' into an internet search engine. However, there is a view that practice formerly guided by common sense and best-interest judgements has been bureaucratised, diverting people into yet more paperwork instead of direct support of people.

Where very important decisions, for example about detention or withdrawal of medical treatment, need to be taken for a person judged not capable of consenting, there is a statutory advocacy service providing support independent of services: the Independent Mental Capacity Advocate (see **www.justice.gov.uk/downloads/protecting-the-vulnerable/mca/making-decisions-opg606-1207.pdf**).

Voting and political involvement

A key democratic right of all of us, including people with learning difficulties, is to vote in local and national elections. The Elfrida Society, a voluntary organisation advocating for the rights and needs of people with a mild or moderate degree of learning difficulties, has a 'Community Development Project' which seeks to support people with learning difficulties in registering to vote, in finding out about political issues and the policies of political parties, and in actually voting. For the 2001 General Election, the project tried to persuade the main political parties to produce information in an accessible 'easy read with pictures' format. The Liberal Democrats and the Green Party did so; the Labour Party merely produced an audiotape and charged for it; the Conservative Party did nothing. Some years previously Mencap had carried out a survey which showed that only 5 per cent of people with learning difficulties voted. The Elfrida Society project found that 28 per cent of people they contacted were not even registered. As a result of their work to support registration and increase awareness, the proportion of the people with learning difficulties involved who voted went up to 44 per cent (Tilley and Bright, 2003).

Some people with learning difficulties take a great interest in politics. Simone Aspis, who describes herself as a 'person with learning difficulties' and has received services under that label all her life, has canvassed for, spoken at meetings for and appeared on television for the Green Party. She was chosen as parliamentary candidate for the Green Party in the London Borough of Brent at the 2001 election, standing against Ken Livingstone, Labour, and received a highly respectable 5,000 votes.

Involvement in service and policy development

A central principle in the White Paper *Valuing People* is that people with learning difficulties must be involved in decisions that affect them. This should happen at all levels, from everyday decisions affecting individuals to major issues of national policy. There was an advisory group of people with learning difficulties that played a central role in drawing up *Valuing People*. The White Paper proposed a structure for ensuring ongoing input into government policy directly from people with learning difficulties themselves. At local authority level there were to be Partnership Boards involving equal membership by people with learning difficulties, families, service providers and policy-makers. There would also be a National Forum of people with learning difficulties themselves, with a regional structure feeding into it. The National Forum would provide representatives to the main body responsible for advising on and monitoring the implementation of the White Paper, the Learning Disability Taskforce. This Taskforce operated at the Department of Health up until 2011, led by a National Director for Learning Disabilities and a Co-director who was a person with learning difficulties. This has now been disbanded and replaced with a National Learning Disability Programme Board. The National Forum still feeds information into this group and has members on the Board.

The National Forum

The National Forum is a group of about 25 people. They come together for a two-day meeting every four months. The Forum is just for people with learning difficulties; most people will have support to prepare for meetings, to get there and to take part, but all discussions and decisions are among the members only. There are subgroups for Planning, Finance, Communication and Political Policy. There are nine regional forums, each of which elects two representatives to the National Forum. The representatives bring regional issues to the National Forum and report information back to the regional forums. Members of the forums are not paid, since the government did not want to be seen as paying for people's views, which might be seen as paying for what they want to hear rather than people being free to say what they want. Work outside Forum meetings, e.g. collecting information for subgroups, speaking on behalf of the Forum, being on the Programme Board, etc., is remunerated (**www.nationalforum.co.uk**).

Partnership boards

Partnership Boards operate at individual local authority level. They bring together local councillors, senior officers of local health, education, leisure, housing, employment and social services, representatives of provider services, family carers and people with learning difficulties themselves. People are members by invitation, though often the local self-advocacy group will be asked to nominate the members who have learning difficulties. The Partnership Boards have financial support and power to influence decisions. For an excellent website illustrating the work of a local partnership board (Oxfordshire), see **www. easywords.co.uk**.

In Control

Some approaches to determining needs and planning services mentioned previously in this book have built-in ways of involving and empowering the person. These include person-centred planning and direct payments, both of which give greater control over the process to the person.

The voluntary organisation In Control, originally concerned with people with learning difficulties but now with a wider remit covering other groups too, has run a number of pilot projects that have tested how direct payments and person-centred planning together can greatly increase the choice and empowerment of people, even with severe degrees of learning difficulty (**www.in-control.org.uk**). The organisation was influential in developing the governments 'personalisation' agenda, set out in the Green Paper on Adult Social Care, *Independence, Well-Being and Choice* (Department of Health, 2005), and the subsequent White Paper, *Our Health, Our Care, Our Say* (Department of Health, 2006). This is an example of how pioneer work in learning difficulty services can influence government social policy over a much wider area.

Other sources of empowerment

People with learning difficulties can be involved in evaluating services. Whittaker et al. (1991) describe an evaluation of day services in a London borough by people with learning difficulties, and a more recent evaluation of direct payments by members of Swindon People First self-advocacy group is described by Gramlich et al. (2002).

Employment can greatly increase the confidence and self-esteem of people, and if it is paid employment then the extra resources available to the person increase their choice and power.

Creative activities, such as painting, music, dancing, drama, photography, writing, can give greater confidence and allow people to express their feelings, views, interests and needs (Goodley and Moore, 2002). Several self-advocacy groups have newsletters to which members can contribute. The Down's Syndrome Association publishes a magazine called *Down2Earth*, which is edited and contributed to entirely by people with Down's syndrome.

One area in which people with learning difficulties have been supported in recent years to make a major contribution to literature is that of the history of services. Several books have been published giving first-hand accounts by people with learning difficulties of their experiences (for example, Potts and Fido, 1991; Atkinson et al., 1997; Atkinson et al., 2000; Mitchell et al., 2006). Many of the more recent of these accounts have been generated through the work of a Learning Disability History Research Group at the Open University (**www.open.ac.uk/hsc/ldsite**).

Computers

ACTIVITY 9.5

Using a search engine, try to find some websites designed for use by people with learning difficulties. What do you think of them? Could they be designed better? How easy was it for you to find them? Can you suggest additional topics on which useful websites for people with learning difficulties might be developed?

COMMENT

If you had difficulty finding sites, try accessing the following sample directly:

www.heartandsoul.co.uk

www.wildbunchclub.com

www.oneforus.com

www.carousel.org.uk

www.disabled-world.com/editorials/heavy-load.php

You can find more by using the 'Links' button on these websites.

In the future there will probably be many more interactive websites where people with learning difficulties can communicate with others using voice, symbols or pictures as well as written words. It is also possible, of course, for a person to have their own website, and there are several people with learning difficulties who do. See if you can find any on the internet.

Empowerment of families

Parents and families – even if we may consider their behaviour to be in some ways unhelpful to their son or daughter – are the best long-term safeguard against the two devastating 'wounds' of loneliness and abandonment. Families often act as vociferous advocates for their son or daughter and their right to good services. Families, therefore, need empowerment if they are to be effective in this role.

There are several organisations helping parents and families to develop more confidence and skill in advocacy and negotiation. Mencap has a network of local groups consisting mainly of parent and family members.

During the last ten years, a project to increase the skills of parents in negotiations, advocacy and contributing to policy has run in this country. It is called Partners in Policymaking, described as *a leadership development course for disabled adults and parents of disabled children ... Partners provides information, training and skill-building to participants so that they may gain the knowledge, skills and confidence they need to campaign and advocate for better treatment and social justice for disabled people in our society* (see **www.partnersinpolicymaking.co.uk**). A typical course would last for about 16 days, spread over a year.

Merseyside Partners

Merseyside Partners supports families and makes sure that family voices are heard by people who make decisions and run services. Before this, parents did not get on very well with people providing services. Their experience and knowledge were often ignored and a lot of time and resources went on disputes between providers and families. In 1999 ... a group of parents and self-advocates [went] on a family leadership course called 'Partners in Policymaking'. They came back and started Merseyside Partners. Parents are often very angry with service providers who haven't listened to them or treated them as equal partners. The Partners course listens to parents, and helps them understand why this has happened. They are then able to get the skills, information and confidence to work in more harmonious and effective partnerships.

Confident and well-informed parents mean they are no longer seen as 'off the wall' parents by professionals. By working with parent leaders, policy makers, planners and providers can find useful, positive and practical solutions to the difficult tasks and decisions they have to deal with.

(Valuing People Support Team, 2005)

The Open University Learning Disability History Group has begun to record the experiences of families as well as those of people with learning difficulties themselves (Rolph et al., 2005).

The voice of the people

To end this book we give just a few examples of the recorded words or writings of people with learning difficulties themselves. Such authentic, first-hand voices can communicate a wide range of interests, ideas, understanding and experience.

Anya Souza

In a book entitled *Empowerment in Everyday Life*, edited by Ramcharan et al. (1997), is a chapter called 'Everything You Ever Wanted to Know About Down's Syndrome But Never Bothered to Ask'. It was written by Paul Ramcharan from a tape-recorded account of her life by a woman with Down's syndrome, Anya Souza. The account was checked out with Anya and she confirmed the accuracy of what she said.

[My mother] could have hidden me in my pram, lost her friends because I was different. It would have been all too easy for her to take the easy way out of being subjected to society's prejudices. Don't forget this was 32 years ago when the idea of community care was only very young.

But my mother did not do any of these things. She took the nurse's advice and looked for the good in me, she treated me as any other child would be treated. She got joy out of me as she did with all her other children. And when there were stories in the family they were all about the good things that we remembered. My mum had prevented the first separation of myself from society. But she had gone beyond this. She had made a commitment to place me in society where I belonged just like everybody else and she had found in me another individual with their strengths, likes, dislikes and weaknesses.

Knowing what I now know about things, it could all have been so very different and I think it often is for other people who are labelled in the way the doctor labelled me at birth. I know that each person has different needs, and just because those needs may be different from another child does not mean they have to be all negative. If they are made into a negative thing then they will be. But it really does not have to be like that.

Jason Kingsley and Mitchell Levitz

The book *Count Us In: Growing Up with Down Syndrome* by Jason Kingsley and Mitchell Levitz (1994) takes the form of a dialogue between two young men with Down's syndrome. It uses their verbatim words, written down by their parents as they conversed.

Mitchell: The important thing about having a disability is that you should think about this disability and it can encourage you a lot. It's an encouragement knowing who you are. You're an individual, an adult with disability, who can handle any issue, tackle any issue. It's part of being an adult, knowing who you are, understanding who you are. Because we are people who understand, knowing about our disability.

People can change, people can realise you are an individual and an identity is important to you, to your family, even to your community. People consider you an individual with rights. People respect you for who you are. Not just your disability. The person who you are makes it. That's what counts. That's why we call this book Count Us In. We are individuals and they are counting us in.

Jason: After people read this book, strangers will become our friends.

Mitchell: Count Us In means that everyone together are helping each other out, by reaching out, by helping each other, which what it means is we want to be included. Count Us In makes the future better for people with disabilities.

Every single one counts because we are an important asset in the community and they need our voice.

Elizabeth

Throughout the first half of the twentieth century there was an official category of learning difficulty called 'moral defect'. This particularly applied to young unmarried women who became pregnant. Many women came to live in the old large institutions for this reason, some for the whole of their lives. The book *A Fit Person to Be Removed: Personal Accounts of Life in a Mental Deficiency Institution* by Potts and Fido (1991) opens with this recollection by Elizabeth of when she was 17 in 1927, transcribed verbatim from an interview with her after she had lived in the institution for over 60 years.

> When I left school I worked at Freeman's. It's going back since I was seventeen. I worked up until I got into trouble. I didn't go home 'cos they knew I was in trouble – they knew what had come. When I did go home, she (mother) said, 'If you are having a child,' she says, 'I won't have neither the child nor you near me doorstep!'

> I was out all night and then I went home. Door was locked so I went down 'cellar. And in those days with coal, you know coal fires, I slipped down 'wall grate and got in that way. And just as I got to 'top o' steps me brother and uncle were on 'step wi' belt. Gave me such a good hiding cross 'back, sent me out and locked 'door again.

> And then I were out all night. Executive Officer went to Freeman's to see if they'd have me till it were born. Then when it were me last day, he came and said I were going home. Instead of taking me home, he took me to another hospital and I never saw me mother and father.

> Well, me elder sister went down and took her from me when I were in hospital. I didn't know me sister was going to come for it. I thought I was going to get it all over, meself better and when it were time to go home I was going to take her with me. I didn't know nothing – anything about it. She brought her up as hers, had her name changed and everything. To think I've never had her, with her bringing her up, 'cos that hurt me more than anything. Well I cried and cried – I couldn't help it. And there's been hours I've been in bed at The Park (the institution) on Villa 4, cried me eyes out.

Sue Virgin

The book *Know Me As I Am: An Anthology of Prose, Poetry and Art by People with Learning Difficulties* (Atkinson and Williams, F. 1990) was produced to accompany a course on learning difficulties at the Open University. It is a marvellous book, containing hundreds of contributions from people with learning difficulties themselves on a very wide range of topics and experiences. Here are extracts from an account by Sue Virgin of her wedding, transcribed from a tape recording:

> I'd always wanted to get married but I thought nobody would have me! I was as calm as anything right up to getting to the Church. I had two lovely bridesmaids, Kerry-Ann and Angela, who I went to school with. I had sequins, flowers, a veil. The dress was beautiful. Coming down the aisle there were all those people. I didn't expect so many. My father took me up the aisle. That was really nice. I went in as Miss Susan Hirons and came out as Mrs Susan Virgin.

Mrs Dixon did all our flowers. They were gorgeous. Uncle Terry drove the cars and helped with the disco. My dad done the disco and all the music. We had to start the dancing off, so people could follow us onto the floor. Linda and Bridget did a lovely reception. Mum and Dad paid for everything! I'll never forget it. Sausage rolls, chicken legs, cheese and pineapple, peanuts. We cut the wedding cake between us. That was most important. People were taking a lot of photos of us. Cameras everywhere.

After the wedding we were tired, exhausted. Chris woke up at five o'clock on our wedding night and made a cup of tea. He said, 'I can't sleep! I'm too in love!' It's nice to be married. I would say to anyone else – try it!

Alison Kerridge

Alison lives by herself in a flat supported by her family and a Supported Living scheme. Among her many interests is writing poetry, and here are three examples.

Autumn leaves

September, October and November
Are autumn months of the year.
The trees are changing colour
From green to yellow, red, orange
And different kinds of browns.
When they have fallen from the trees
They are crisp and curvy and curled up;
Wrinkled and dry like an old person's skin
They lie on the ground discarded and dying.
The wind lifts the leaves up into the air:
They land together in heaps on the grass.
When we walk through the leaves
They crunch, crumpled and crackly at our feet.

Blustery days

The trees were swaying madly,
It was pouring cats and dogs.
A wild and dangerous day!
Creaking, rattling tiles like old bones
The wind was wailing everywhere
Becoming a howling gale.
It went on and on and on
All day and all night.
Perhaps it will never stop!

The view from my window
There are lots of trees in different shades of green;
They wave in the breeze as I look out of the window.
I'm above the rooftops looking down on the quilt

Of browns, yellows, pinks, greys, oranges among the greens.
The hills look grey in the distant clouds;
The birds are flying backwards and forwards feeding their young.
I hear them singing even when the window is closed,
Especially early in the morning!
There is lots of movement in the street below:
Cars, lorries, milk van, dustman, cyclists too,
Busy people walking by, children going off to school.
All this I can see from the window.

John-Paul Gower

John-Paul is a young man with Down's syndrome who lives with his adoptive parents. He wrote this 'Millennium Prayer' in 1999 when he was 14.

A Millennium Prayer
Thank you God
For making me like I am.
I don't mind having Down's Syndrome.
Thank you
For my family who love and spoil me.
Thank you
For helping me to beat most people at Nintendo, especially Dad.
Thank you
For all the exciting things I do, like going to the cinema, theatre, concerts, Alton Towers and McDonald's.
In the new Millennium, please help all people with handicaps to be as happy as me.
Amen.

CHAPTER SUMMARY

This chapter began with an account of different forms of advocacy on behalf of people with learning difficulties, with an emphasis on the value of unpaid voluntary citizen advocacy. Advocacy has a protective function which is likely to be at least as effective as policies, rules and regulations. It also has the function of empowerment, and further exploration of this need was introduced with an account of the exciting phenomenon of self-advocacy. Various strategies for increasing the ability of people with learning difficulties to take a full part in community life and relationships were presented. Support can be given to people to help them understand and take part in debates and decision-making. The skills and confidence and opportunities for individual and group self-advocacy can be supported. Rights can be delineated and respected. Opportunities and structures can be provided to enable people to participate as equals in service and policy developments. Service planning can be individualised, and funding can be made flexible and more in the control of the person. People can be involved in service evaluation, creative activities, employment and the documenting of history. All these ways contribute to people having more power and influence, and to the avoidance of oppression and disempowerment. Families can be empowered in similar ways. Finally, we should see it as our task to seek out, encourage, listen to, learn from and act on the authentic voices of the people themselves.

FURTHER READING

Brandon and Brandon (2001) *Advocacy in Social Work* is a very readable, interesting and challenging introduction to advocacy.

Brown et al. (2009) *The Mental Capacity Act: A Guide for Practice* is a comprehensive account of the requirements and impact of this important legislation.

Department of Health (2006) *Our Health, Our Care, Our Say* is a White Paper outlining the government's latest thinking and policy on involvement of people in service development.

Goodley (2000) *Self-Advocacy in the Lives of People with Learning Difficulties* gives a comprehensive account of the development of group self-advocacy in Britain, placing it in the context of political rights movements.

Gramlich et al. (2002) *Journey to Independence* reports on a research project by people with learning difficulties on the value and use of direct payments.

Rolph et al. (eds) (2005) *Witnesses to Change* is a book of contributions by families of people with learning difficulties to the documentation of history.

Conclusion

This book has ranged widely over the field of work with people with learning difficulties. Chapter 1 considered definitions and perceptions of who the people are. Chapter 2 emphasised the importance of values by giving illustrations from history and from current social policy. Chapter 3 covered important policy and legislation. Chapter 4 showed how social work skills and knowledge can be applied to support people and their families in a wide range of situations. Chapters 5 and 6 looked at issues and needs at different life stages, and included coverage of protection and safeguarding. Chapter 7 discussed approaches to assessment of individuals, services and community resources. Chapter 8 covered communication and sensory needs, and Chapter 9 introduced the concept of advocacy and discussed various means of empowerment of people, with quotations from the people themselves.

The book has focused on areas of work with people with learning difficulties that social workers might find themselves involved in. It has not concentrated on current organisational structures that may in practice constrain the social worker's role. The social worker has been presented as someone with particular knowledge, skills and values that can be of relevance in a wide variety of contexts and circumstances, rather than as someone who works in a particular organisational role.

We hope that the book may have stimulated you to consider applying your knowledge, skills and values to work in this field. We hope we have conveyed some of the interest, stimulation, excitement and satisfaction that can be derived from supporting people with learning difficulties and their families. In particular, we have emphasised the possibility of long-term work and of strong and lasting relationships that may be more available in this field than in other areas of social work.

If you have read the whole book, turn back to the Introduction and review the list of aims stated there. Do you think they have been met?

Internet resources

Social workers have to develop skills of finding information and the internet is an excellent resource for this. The following list of sites relating to people with learning difficulties is not exhaustive, but represents a sample of useful sources of information. Further relevant sites can be found by following the 'Links' sections of these sites.

disabilitystudies.syr.edu/resources/reports.aspx (note this address does not begin with **www.**)
Publications on service innovations and community inclusion.

www.advocacyresource.org.uk
Site of Advocacy Resource Exchange, Britain's leading source of information on advocacy.

www.anncrafttrust.org
Support for people with learning difficulties who have experienced abuse.

www.autism.org.uk
Site of the National Autistic Society, with information on autism and Asperger's syndrome.

www.bild.org.uk
Site of the British Institute of Learning Disability, a major source of information and resources on all aspects of learning difficulty.

www.changepeople.co.uk
Site of Change, an organisation involving people with learning difficulties themselves in providing accessible information and advice.

www.dimagine.com
Imaginative articles and resources by David Pitonyak, an inspirational writer about people with learning difficulties.

www.downs-syndrome.org.uk
Site of the Down's Syndrome Association, with information, advice and publications on people with Down's syndrome.

www.learningcommunity.us
Home of the Learning Community for Person-Centred Practices: resources and support for the implementation of person-centred planning.

www.enable.org.uk
Site of Enable Scotland, the Scottish equivalent of Mencap.

www.helensandersonassociates.co.uk
A key resource of articles, tools and examples for person-centred planning.

www.in-control.org.uk
An organisation promoting control by people themselves over services they need.

www.inclusiononline.co.uk
Catalogue of publications and resources for person-centred planning and community inclusion.

www.inspiredservices.org.uk
Support to make information accessible to people with learning difficulties.

www.intellectualdisability.info
Much information about people with learning difficulties, with an emphasis on health.

www.jkp.com
Jessica Kingsley Publishers have an extensive catalogue of books relating to learning difficulty and to autism.

www.learningdisabilities.org.uk
Site of the Foundation for People with Learning Disabilities, a major source of advice and information on all aspects of learning difficulty.

www.learningdisabilitycoalition.org.uk
Site of a coalition of leading voluntary organisations working with people with learning difficulties, giving news and information.

www.lifetimecaring.org.uk
Resources concerning older family carers for people with learning difficulties.

www.makaton.org
Site of the Makaton sign and symbol language designed to help communication for people with learning difficulties.

www.mencap.org.uk
Site of the main voluntary organisation providing advice, information and support for people with learning difficulties and their families.

www.nationalforum.co.uk
The National Forum for people with learning difficulties to advise the government.

www.open.ac.uk/hsc/ldsite
Open University site on their emancipatory research projects involving people with learning difficulties as contributors rather than subjects.

www.paradigm-uk.org
Resources on person-centred planning, supported living and community inclusion.

www.pcpld.org
Palliative care for people with learning disabilities: an organisation providing support and information for those involved in care of people with life-limiting illnesses.

www.peoplefirst.org.uk
Site of Central England People First, with links to many self-advocacy groups and resources.

www.peoplefirstltd.com
Site of a London-based self-advocacy group.

www.pmldnetwork.org
The profound and multiple learning disability network: information, advice and support relating to people with a severe degree of learning difficulty.

www.respond.org.uk
Support for people with learning difficulties who have experienced abuse.

www.sense.org.uk
Information and support on deafblindness.

www.speakup.org.uk
Site of a self-advocacy group based in Rotherham.

www.voiceuk.org.uk
Support for people with learning difficulties who have experienced crime or abuse.

Appendix 1 Professional capabilities framework

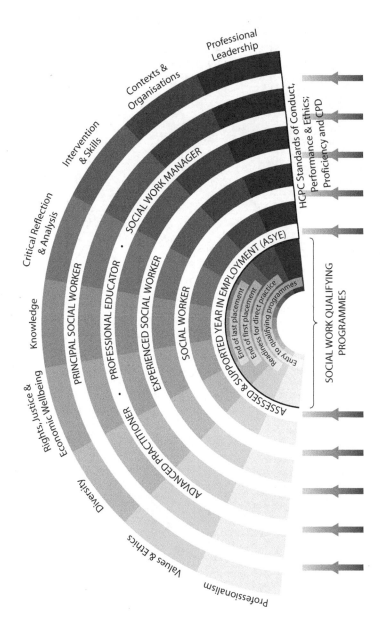

Professional Capabilities Framework diagram reproduced with permission of The College of Social Work

See page x for the full list of standards.

Appendix 2 Subject benchmark for social work

Subject benchmark for social work

4 Defining principles

4.1 As an applied academic subject, social work is characterised by a distinctive focus on practice in complex social situations to promote and protect individual and collective well-being. This underscores the importance of partnerships between HEIs and service providers to ensure the full involvement of practitioners, managers, tutors, service users and carers with students in both academic and practice learning and assessment.

4.2 At honours level, the study of social work involves the integrated study of subject-specific knowledge, skills and values and the critical application of research knowledge from the social and human sciences, and from social work (and closely related domains) to inform understanding and to underpin action, reflection and evaluation. Honours degree programmes should be designed to help foster this integration of contextual, analytic, critical, explanatory and practical understanding.

4.3 Contemporary definitions of social work as a degree subject reflect its origins in a range of different academic and practice traditions. The precise nature and scope of the subject is itself a matter for legitimate study and critical debate. Three main issues are relevant to this.

- Social work is located within different social welfare contexts. Within the UK there are different traditions of social welfare (influenced by legislation, historical development and social attitudes) and these have shaped both social work education and practice in community-based settings including residential, day care and substitute care. In an international context, distinctive national approaches to social welfare policy, provision and practice have greatly influenced the focus and content of social work degree programmes.

- There are competing views in society at large on the nature of social work and on its place and purpose. Social work practice and education inevitably reflect these differing perspectives on the role of social work in relation to social justice, social care and social order.

- Social work, both as occupational practice and as an academic subject, evolves, adapts and changes in response to the social, political and economic challenges and demands of contemporary social welfare policy, practice and legislation.

4.4 Honours graduates in social work should therefore be equipped both to understand, and to work within, this context of contested debate about nature, scope and purpose, and be enabled to analyse, adapt to, manage and eventually to lead the processes of change.

4.5 The applied nature of social work as an academic subject means that practice is an essential and core element of learning. The following points clarify the use of the term 'practice' in the statement.

- The term 'practice' in this statement is used to encompass learning that not only takes place in professional practice placements, but also in a variety of other experiential learning situations. All learning opportunities that bear academic credit must be subject to methods of assessment appropriate to their academic level and be assessed by competent assessors. Where they form part of the curriculum leading to integrated academic and professional awards, practice learning opportunities will also be subject to regulations that further define learning requirements, standards and modes of assessment.

- In honours degree programmes covered by this statement, practice as an activity refers to experiential, action-based learning. In this sense, practice provides opportunities for students to improve and demonstrate their understanding and competence through the application and testing of knowledge and skills.

- Practice activity is also a source of transferable learning in its own right. Such learning can transfer both from a practice setting to the 'classroom' and vice versa. Thus practice can be as much a source of intellectual and cognitive learning as other modes of study. For this reason, learning through practice attracts full academic credit.

- Learning in practice can include activities such as observation, shadowing, analysis and research, as well as intervention within social work and related organisations. Practice-learning on honours degrees involves active engagement with service users and others in practice settings outside the university, and may involve for example virtual/simulated practice, observational and research activities.

4.6 Social work is a moral activity that requires practitioners to recognise the dignity of the individual, but also to make and implement difficult decisions (including restriction of liberty) in human situations that involve the potential for benefit or harm. Honours degree programmes in social work therefore involve the study, application of, and critical reflection upon, ethical principles and dilemmas. As reflected by the four care councils' codes of practice, this involves showing respect for persons, honouring the diverse and distinctive organisations and communities that make up contemporary society, promoting social justice and combating processes that lead to discrimination, marginalisation and social exclusion. This means that honours undergraduates must learn to:

- recognise and work with the powerful links between intrapersonal and interpersonal factors and the wider social, legal, economic, political and cultural context of people's lives;

- understand the impact of injustice, social inequalities and oppressive social relations;

- challenge constructively individual, institutional and structural discrimination;

- practise in ways that maximise safety and effectiveness in situations of uncertainty and incomplete information;

- help people to gain, regain or maintain control of their own affairs, insofar as this is compatible with their own or others' safety, well-being and rights;

- work in partnership with service users and carers and other professionals to foster dignity, choice and independence, and effect change.

4.7 The expectation that social workers will be able to act effectively in such complex circumstances requires that honours degree programmes in social work should be designed to help students learn to become accountable, reflective, critical and evaluative. This involves learning to:

- think critically about the complex social, legal, economic, political and cultural contexts in which social work practice is located;

- work in a transparent and responsible way, balancing autonomy with complex, multiple and sometimes contradictory accountabilities (for example, to different service users, employing agencies, professional bodies and the wider society);

- exercise authority within complex frameworks of accountability and ethical and legal boundaries;

- acquire and apply the habits of critical reflection, self-evaluation and consultation, and make appropriate use of research in decision-making about practice and in the evaluation of outcomes.

5 Subject knowledge, understanding and skills

Subject knowledge and understanding

5.1 During their degree studies in social work, honours graduates should acquire, critically evaluate, apply and integrate knowledge and understanding in the following five core areas of study.

5.1.1 **Social work services, service users and carers**, which include:

- the social processes (associated with, for example, poverty, migration, unemployment, poor health, disablement, lack of education and other sources of disadvantage) that lead to marginalisation, isolation and exclusion, and their impact on the demand for social work services;

- explanations of the links between definitional processes contributing to social differences (for example, social class, gender, ethnic differences, age, sexuality and religious belief) to the problems of inequality and differential need faced by service users;

- the nature of social work services in a diverse society (with particular reference to concepts such as prejudice, interpersonal, institutional and structural discrimination, empowerment and anti-discriminatory practices);

- the nature and validity of different definitions of, and explanations for, the characteristics and circumstances of service users and the services required by them, drawing on knowledge from research, practice experience, and from service users and carers;

- the focus on outcomes, such as promoting the well-being of young people and their families, and promoting dignity, choice and independence for adults receiving services;

- the relationship between agency policies, legal requirements and professional boundaries in shaping the nature of services provided in interdisciplinary contexts and the issues associated with working across professional boundaries and within different disciplinary groups.

5.1.2 **The service delivery context**, which includes:

- the location of contemporary social work within historical, comparative and global perspectives, including European and international contexts;

- the changing demography and cultures of communities in which social workers will be practising;

- the complex relationships between public, social and political philosophies, policies and priorities and the organisation and practice of social work, including the contested nature of these;

- the issues and trends in modern public and social policy and their relationship to contemporary practice and service delivery in social work;

- the significance of legislative and legal frameworks and service delivery standards (including the nature of legal authority, the application of legislation in practice, statutory accountability and tensions between statute, policy and practice);

- the current range and appropriateness of statutory, voluntary and private agencies providing community-based, day-care, residential and other services and the organisational systems inherent within these;

- the significance of interrelationships with other related services, including housing, health, income maintenance and criminal justice (where not an integral social service);

- the contribution of different approaches to management, leadership and quality in public and independent human services;

- the development of personalised services, individual budgets and direct payments;

- the implications of modern information and communications technology (ICT) for both the provision and receipt of services.

5.1.3 **Values and ethics**, which include:

- the nature, historical evolution and application of social work values;

- the moral concepts of rights, responsibility, freedom, authority and power inherent in the practice of social workers as moral and statutory agents;

- the complex relationships between justice, care and control in social welfare and the practical and ethical implications of these, including roles as statutory agents and in upholding the law in respect of discrimination;

- aspects of philosophical ethics relevant to the understanding and resolution of value dilemmas and conflicts in both interpersonal and professional contexts;

- the conceptual links between codes defining ethical practice, the regulation of professional conduct and the management of potential conflicts generated by the codes held by different professional groups.

5.1.4 **Social work theory**, which includes:

- research-based concepts and critical explanations from social work theory and other disciplines that contribute to the knowledge base of social work, including their distinctive epistemological status and application to practice;

- the relevance of sociological perspectives to understanding societal and structural influences on human behaviour at individual, group and community levels;

- the relevance of psychological, physical and physiological perspectives to understanding personal and social development and functioning;

- social science theories explaining group and organisational behaviour, adaptation and change;

- models and methods of assessment, including factors underpinning the selection and testing of relevant information, the nature of professional judgement and the processes of risk assessment and decision-making;

- approaches and methods of intervention in a range of settings, including factors guiding the choice and evaluation of these;

- user-led perspectives;

- knowledge and critical appraisal of relevant social research and evaluation methodologies, and the evidence base for social work.

5.1.5 **The nature of social work practice**, which includes:

- the characteristics of practice in a range of community-based and organisational settings within statutory, voluntary and private sectors, and the factors influencing changes and developments in practice within these contexts;

- the nature and characteristics of skills associated with effective practice, both direct and indirect, with a range of service-users and in a variety of settings;

- the processes that facilitate and support service user choice and independence;

- the factors and processes that facilitate effective interdisciplinary, interprofessional and interagency collaboration and partnership;

- the place of theoretical perspectives and evidence from international research in assessment and decision-making processes in social work practice;

- the integration of theoretical perspectives and evidence from international research into the design and implementation of effective social work intervention, with a wide range of service users, carers and others;

- the processes of reflection and evaluation, including familiarity with the range of approaches for evaluating service and welfare outcomes, and their significance for the development of practice and the practitioner.

Subject-specific skills and other skills

5.2 As an applied subject at honours degree level, social work necessarily involves the development of skills that may be of value in many situations (for example, analytical thinking, building relationships, working as a member of an organisation, intervention, evaluation and reflection). Some of these skills are specific to social work but many are also widely transferable. What helps to define the specific nature of these skills in a social work context are:

- the context in which they are applied and assessed (e.g., communication skills in practice with people with sensory impairments or assessment skills in an interprofessional setting);

- the relative weighting given to such skills within social work practice (e.g., the central importance of problem-solving skills within complex human situations);

- the specific purpose of skill development (e.g., the acquisition of research skills in order to build a repertoire of research-based practice);

- a requirement to integrate a range of skills (i.e., not simply to demonstrate these in an isolated and incremental manner).

5.3 All social work honours graduates should show the ability to reflect on and learn from the exercise of their skills. They should understand the significance of the concepts of continuing professional development and lifelong learning, and accept responsibility for their own continuing development.

5.4 Social work honours graduates should acquire and integrate skills in the following five core areas.

Problem-solving skills

5.5 These are sub-divided into four areas.

5.5.1 **Managing problem-solving activities**: honours graduates in social work should be able to plan problem-solving activities, i.e. to:

- think logically, systematically, critically and reflectively;

- apply ethical principles and practices critically in planning problem-solving activities;

- plan a sequence of actions to achieve specified objectives, making use of research, theory and other forms of evidence;

- manage processes of change, drawing on research, theory and other forms of evidence.

5.5.2 **Gathering information**: honours graduates in social work should be able to:

- gather information from a wide range of sources and by a variety of methods, for a range of purposes. These methods should include electronic searches, reviews of relevant literature, policy and procedures, face-to-face interviews, written and telephone contact with individuals and groups;

- take into account differences of viewpoint in gathering information and critically assess the reliability and relevance of the information gathered;

- assimilate and disseminate relevant information in reports and case records.

5.5.3 **Analysis and synthesis**: honours graduates in social work should be able to analyse and synthesise knowledge gathered for problem-solving purposes, i.e. to:

- assess human situations, taking into account a variety of factors (including the views of participants, theoretical concepts, research evidence, legislation and organisational policies and procedures);

- analyse information gathered, weighing competing evidence and modifying their viewpoint in light of new information, then relate this information to a particular task, situation or problem;

- consider specific factors relevant to social work practice (such as risk, rights, cultural differences and linguistic sensitivities, responsibilities to protect vulnerable individuals and legal obligations);

- assess the merits of contrasting theories, explanations, research, policies and procedures;

- synthesise knowledge and sustain reasoned argument;

- employ a critical understanding of human agency at the macro (societal), mezzo (organisational and community) and micro (inter and intrapersonal) levels;

- critically analyse and take account of the impact of inequality and discrimination in work with people in particular contexts and problem situations.

5.5.4 **Intervention and evaluation**: honours graduates in social work should be able to use their knowledge of a range of interventions and evaluation processes selectively to:

- build and sustain purposeful relationships with people and organisations in community-based, and interprofessional contexts;

- make decisions, set goals and construct specific plans to achieve these, taking into account relevant factors including ethical guidelines;

- negotiate goals and plans with others, analysing and addressing in a creative manner human, organisational and structural impediments to change;

- implement plans through a variety of systematic processes that include working in partnership;

- undertake practice in a manner that promotes the well-being and protects the safety of all parties;

- engage effectively in conflict resolution;

- support service users to take decisions and access services, with the social worker as navigator, advocate and supporter;

- manage the complex dynamics of dependency and, in some settings, provide direct care and personal support in everyday living situations;

- meet deadlines and comply with external definitions of a task;

- plan, implement and critically review processes and outcomes;

- bring work to an effective conclusion, taking into account the implications for all involved;

- monitor situations, review processes and evaluate outcomes;

- use and evaluate methods of intervention critically and reflectively.

Communication skills

5.6 Honours graduates in social work should be able to communicate clearly, accurately and precisely (in an appropriate medium) with individuals and groups in a range of formal and informal situations, i.e. to:

- make effective contact with individuals and organisations for a range of objectives, by verbal, paper-based and electronic means;

- clarify and negotiate the purpose of such contacts and the boundaries of their involvement;

- listen actively to others, engage appropriately with the life experiences of service users, understand accurately their viewpoint and overcome personal prejudices to respond appropriately to a range of complex personal and interpersonal situations;

- use both verbal and non-verbal cues to guide interpretation;

- identify and use opportunities for purposeful and supportive communication with service users within their everyday living situations;

- follow and develop an argument and evaluate the viewpoints of, and evidence presented by, others;

- write accurately and clearly in styles adapted to the audience, purpose and context of the communication;

- use advocacy skills to promote others' rights, interests and needs;

- present conclusions verbally and on paper, in a structured form, appropriate to the audience for which these have been prepared;

- make effective preparation for, and lead meetings in a productive way;

- communicate effectively across potential barriers resulting from differences (for example, in culture, language and age).

Skills in working with others

5.7 Honours graduates in social work should be able to work effectively with others, i.e. to:

- involve users of social work services in ways that increase their resources, capacity and power to influence factors affecting their lives;

- consult actively with others, including service users and carers, who hold relevant information or expertise;

- act cooperatively with others, liaising and negotiating across differences such as organisational and professional boundaries and differences of identity or language;

- develop effective helping relationships and partnerships with other individuals, groups and organisations that facilitate change;

- act with others to increase social justice by identifying and responding to prejudice, institutional discrimination and structural inequality;

- act within a framework of multiple accountability (for example, to agencies, the public, service users, carers and others);

- challenge others when necessary, in ways that are most likely to produce positive outcomes.

Skills in personal and professional development
5.8 Honours graduates in social work should be able to:

- advance their own learning and understanding with a degree of independence;

- reflect on and modify their behaviour in the light of experience;

- identify and keep under review their own personal and professional boundaries;

- manage uncertainty, change and stress in work situations;

- handle inter and intrapersonal conflict constructively;

- understand and manage changing situations and respond in a flexible manner;

- challenge unacceptable practices in a responsible manner;

- take responsibility for their own further and continuing acquisition and use of knowledge and skills;

- use research critically and effectively to sustain and develop their practice.

ICT and numerical skills
5.9 Honours graduates in social work should be able to use ICT methods and techniques to support their learning and their practice. In particular, they should demonstrate the ability to:

- use ICT effectively for professional communication, data storage and retrieval and information searching;

- use ICT in working with people who use services;

- demonstrate sufficient familiarity with statistical techniques to enable effective use of research in practice;

- integrate appropriate use of ICT to enhance skills in problem-solving in the four areas set out in paragraph 6.2;

- apply numerical skills to financial and budgetary responsibilities;

- have a critical understanding of the social impact of ICT, including an awareness of the impact of the 'digital divide'.

6 Teaching, learning and assessment

6.1 At honours degree level, social work programmes explicitly recognise and maximise the use of students' prior learning and experience. Acquisition and development of the required knowledge and skills, capable of transfer to new situations and of further enhancement, mark important staging posts in the process of lifelong learning. Social work models of learning are characteristically developmental and incremental (ie, students are expected to assume increasing responsibility for identifying their own learning needs and making use of available resources for learning). The context of learning should take account of the impact of the Bologna Process and transnational learning. The overall aims and expected final outcomes of the honours degree, together with the specific requirements of particular topics, modules or practice experiences, should inform the choice of both learning and teaching strategies and aligned formative and summative assessment methods.

6.2 The learning processes in social work at honours degree level can be expressed interms of four inter-related themes.

- **Awareness raising, skills and knowledge acquisition** – a process in which the student becomes more aware of aspects of knowledge and expertise, learns how to systematically engage with and acquire new areas of knowledge, recognises their potential and becomes motivated to engage in new ways of thinking and acting.

- **Conceptual understanding** – a process in which a student acquires, examines critically and deepens understanding (measured and tested against existing knowledge and adjustments made in attitudes and goals).

- **Practice skills and experience** – processes in which a student learns practice skills in the contexts identified in paragraph 4.4 and applies theoretical models and research evidence together with new understanding to relevant activities, and receives feedback from various sources on performance, enhancing openness to critical self-evaluation.

- **Reflection on performance** – a process in which a student reflects critically and evaluatively on past experience, recent performance, and feedback, and applies this information to the process of integrating awareness (including awareness of the impact of self on others) and new understanding, leading to improved performance.

6.3 Honours degree programmes in social work acknowledge that students learn at different rates and in diverse ways, and learn best when there is consistent and timely guidance and a variety of learning opportunities. Programmes should provide clear and accessible information about learning approaches, methods and outcomes that enable students to engage with diverse learning and teaching methods in learning settings across academic and practice environments.

6.4 Approaches to support blended learning should include the use of ICT to access data, literature and resources, as well as engagement with technologies to support communication and reflection and sharing of learning across academic and practice learning settings.

6.5 Learning methods may include:

- learner-focused approaches that encourage active participation and staged, progressive learning throughout the degree

- the establishment of initial learning needs and the formulation of learning plans

- the development of learning networks, enabling students to learn from each other

- the involvement of practitioners and service user and carer educators.

6.6 Students should engage in a broad range of activities, including with other professionals and with service users and carers, to facilitate critical reflection. These include reading, self-directed study, research, a variety of forms of writing, lectures, discussion, seminars/tutorials, individual and group work, role plays, presentations, projects, simulations and practice experience.

6.7 Assessment strategies should show alignment between, and relevance to, social work practice, theory and assessment tasks. They should also be matched with learning outcomes and learning and teaching methods. The purpose of assessment is to:

- provide a means whereby students receive feedback regularly on their achievement and development needs

- provide tasks that promote learning, and develop and test cognitive skills, drawing on a range of sources including the contexts of practice

- promote self-evaluation, and appraisal of their progress and learning strategies

- enable judgements to be made in relation to progress and to ensure fitness for practice, and the award, in line with professional standards.

6.8 Assessment strategies should be chosen to enhance students' abilities to conceptualise, compare and analyse issues, in order to be able to apply this in making professional judgements.

6.9 Assessment methods normally include case-based assessments, presentations and analyses, practice-focused assignments, essays, project reports, role plays/simulations, e-assessment and examinations. The requirements of honours degree programmes in social work frequently include an extended piece of written work, which may be practice-based, and is typically undertaken in the final year. This may involve independent study for either a dissertation or a project, based upon systematic enquiry and investigation. However, the requirements of research governance may restrict opportunities available to students for research involving human subjects. Where practice competences have to be assessed, as identified through national occupational standards or equivalent, opportunities should be provided for demonstration of these, together with systematic means of development, support and assessment. Assessment methods may include those listed above, in addition to observed practice, reflective logs and interview records.

6.10 Honours degree programmes in social work assess practice not as a series of discrete practical tasks, but as an integration of skills and knowledge with relevant conceptual understanding. This assessment should, therefore, contain elements that test students' critical and analytical reflective analysis. As the honours degree is an integrated academic and professional award, the failure of any core element, including assessed practice, will mean failure of the programme.

7 Benchmark standards

7.1 Given the essentially applied nature of social work and the co-terminosity of the degree and the professional award, students must demonstrate that they have met the standards specified in relation to both academic and practice capabilities. These standards relate to subject-specific knowledge, understanding and skills (including key skills inherent in the concept of 'graduateness'). Qualifying students will be expected to meet each of these standards in accordance with the specific standards set by the relevant country (see section 2).

Typical graduate
7.2 Levels of attainment will vary along a continuum from the threshold to excellence. This level represents that of typical students graduating with an honours degree in social work.

Knowledge and understanding
7.3 On graduating with an honours degree in social work, students should be able to demonstrate:

- a sound understanding of the five core areas of knowledge and understanding relevant to social work, as detailed in paragraph 5.1, including their application to practice and service delivery;

- an ability to use this knowledge and understanding in an integrated way, in specific practice contexts;

- an ability to use this knowledge and understanding to engage in effective relationships with service users and carers;

- appraisal of previous learning and experience and ability to incorporate this into their future learning and practice;

- acknowledgement and understanding of the potential and limitations of social work as a practice-based discipline to effect individual and social change;

- an ability to use research and enquiry techniques with reflective awareness, to collect, analyse and interpret relevant information;

- a developed capacity for the critical evaluation of knowledge and evidence from a range of sources.

Subject-specific and other skills

7.4 On graduating with an honours degree in social work, students should be able to demonstrate a developed capacity to:

- apply creatively a repertoire of core skills as detailed in section 5;

- communicate effectively with service users and carers, and with other professionals;

- integrate clear understanding of ethical issues and codes of values, and practice with their interventions in specific situations;

- consistently exercise an appropriate level of autonomy and initiative in individual decision-making within the context of supervisory, collaborative, ethical and organisational requirements;

- demonstrate habits of critical reflection on their performance and take responsibility for modifying action in light of this.

References

Affleck, F (2005) *You and Your Baby, 0–1*. Leeds: Change.

Anderson, B (2003) *Sally: Face Like a Flower*. North Yorkshire: Dent Dale Publishing.

Atherton, H and Crickmore, D (eds) (2011) *Learning Disabilities: Towards Inclusion*. London: Churchill Livingstone.

Atkinson, D (1989) *Someone To Turn To: The Social Worker's Role and the Role of Front Line Staff in Relation to People with Mental Handicaps*. Kidderminster: BIMH Publications (now BILD).

Atkinson, D and Williams, F (eds) (1990) *'Know Me As I Am': An Anthology of Prose, Poetry and Art by People with Learning Difficulties*. London: Hodder & Stoughton, in association with the Open University.

Atkinson, D and Williams, P (1990) *Mental Handicap: Changing Perspectives – Workbook 2: Networks*. Buckingham: Open University Press.

Atkinson, D, Jackson, M and Walmsley, J (eds) (1997) *Forgotten Lives: Exploring the History of Learning Disability*. Kidderminster: BILD Publications.

Atkinson, D, McCarthy, M and Walmsley, J (eds) (2000) *Good Times, Bad Times: Women with Learning Difficulties Telling Their Stories*. Kidderminster: BILD Publications.

Attwood, T (2008) *The Complete Guide to Asperger's Syndrome*. London: Jessica Kingsley.

Baldwin, H (2005) *Can Enthusiasm for Adult Placement be Justified?* MA Dissertation. Reading: University of Reading.

Barber, P, Brown, R and Martin, D (2012) *Mental Health Law in England and Wales*. London: Sage/Learning Matters.

Barnes, C and Mercer, G (2010) *Exploring Disability*, 2nd edition. Cambridge: Polity Press.

Baron-Cohen, S (2008) *Autism and Asperger Syndrome – the Facts*. Oxford: Oxford University Press.

Bateman, N (2000) *Advocacy Skills for Health and Social Care Professionals*. London: Jessica Kingsley.

Bayley, M (1997) *What Price Friendship?* Minehead: Hexagon Publishing.

Beadle-Brown, J, Hutchinson, A and Mansell, J (2005) *Care Standards in Homes for People with Intellectual Disabilities*. Canterbury: Tizard Centre, University of Kent.

Beasley, F, Hewson, S and Mansell, J (1989) *Momentary Time Sampling: Handbook for Observers*. Canterbury: Centre for Applied Psychology of Social Care, University of Kent.

Beresford, P, Fleming, J, Glynn, M, Bewley, C, Croft, S, Banfield, F and Postle, K (2011) *Supporting People: Towards a Person-Centred Approach*. Bristol: Policy Press.

Bernard, C (1999) Child sexual abuse and the black disabled child. *Disability and Society*, 14: 325–329.

Bewley, C and Holman, A (2002) *Pointers to Control*. London: Values Into Action.

Beyer, S and Kaehne, A (2008) The transition of young people with learning disabilities to employment: what works? *Journal on Developmental Disabilities*, 14: 85–94.

Bickerton, S (2011) *Principles of Safeguarding and Protection for Learning Disability Workers*. Exeter: Sage/Learning Matters.

Birrell, I (2012) Killing kindness with red tape. *The Independent*, 9th October.

Blackman, N and Todd, S (2005) *Caring for People with Learning Disabilities Who Are Dying*. London: Worth Publishing.

Bond, R and Hurst, J (2009) How adults with learning disabilities view living independently. *British Journal of Learning Disabilities*, 38: 286–292.

Booth, T and Booth, W (1994) *Parenting Under Pressure: Mothers and Fathers with Learning Difficulties*. Buckingham: Open University Press.

Booth, T and Booth, W (1998) *Growing Up with Parents Who Have Learning Difficulties*. London: Taylor & Francis.

Booth, T and Booth, W (2005) Parents with learning difficulties in the child protection system: experiences and perspectives. *Journal of Intellectual Disabilities*, 9: 109–29

Booth, W and Booth, T (1998) *Advocacy for Parents with Learning Difficulties: Developing Advocacy Support*. Brighton: Pavilion Publishing, in association with the Joseph Rowntree Foundation.

Bouza, F (1996) *Locos, Enanos y Hombre de Placer en la Corte de los Austrias*. Madrid: Temas de Hoy.

Bradley, K (2009) *Review of People with Mental Health Problems or Learning Disabilities in the Criminal Justice System*. London: Department of Health.

Brand, D, Green, L and Statham, D (2010) *Facts about FACS: a Guide to Fair Access to Care Services*. London: Social Care Institute of Excellence.

Brandon, D (1995) *Advocacy: Power to People with Disabilities*. Birmingham: Venture Press.

Brandon, D and Brandon, T (2001) *Advocacy in Social Work*. Birmingham: Venture Press.

Brandon, D and Towe, N (1989) *Free to Choose: An Introduction to Service Brokerage*. London: Good Impressions.

Brayne, H and Broadbent, G (2002) *Legal Material for Social Workers*. Oxford: Oxford University Press.

Brayne, H and Carr, H (2012) *Law for Social Workers*, 12th edition. Oxford: Oxford University Press.

Brechin, A and Swain, J (1986) *Changing Relationships: Shared Action Planning with People with a Mental Handicap*. Cheltenham: Nelson Thornes.

British Institute of Learning Disabilities (2005) *Factsheet on Intensive Interaction*. Available at: www.bild.org.uk.

Brown, H, Burns, S and Flynn, M (2005) *Dying Matters: A Workbook on Caring for People with Learning Disabilities Who Are Terminally Ill*. London: Foundation for People with Learning Disabilities.

Brown, I and Brown, R (2003) *Quality of Life and Disability: An Approach for Community Practitioners*. London: Jessica Kingsley.

Brown, K and Rutter, L (2008) *Critical Thinking for Social Work*. Exeter: Learning Matters.

Brown, L (1998) *Challenging and Inappropriate Sexual Behaviour in People with Learning Disabilities: A Literature Review*. London: The Stationery Office, on behalf of the Scottish Office Central Research Unit.

Brown, R (ed.) (1997) *Quality of Life for People with Disabilities*. Cheltenham: Stanley Thornes.

Brown, R, Barber, P and Martin, D (2009) *The Mental Capacity Act 2005: A Guide for Practice*. Exeter: Learning Matters.

Bruce, E and Schultz, C (2001) *Non-finite Loss and Grief*. London: Jessica Kingsley.

Caldwell, P (2005a) *Creative Conversations*. Videotape and accompanying notes. Brighton: Pavilion Publishing.

Caldwell, P (2005b) *Finding You, Finding Me: Using Intensive Interaction to Get In Touch with People Whose Severe Learning Disabilities are Combined with Autistic Spectrum Disorder*. London: Jessica Kingsley.

Cambridge, P and Carnaby, S (eds) (2005) *Person-Centred Planning and Care Management with People with Learning Disabilities*. London: Jessica Kingsley.

Campaign for the Mentally Handicapped (1971) *Even Better Services*. London: CMH.

Campbell, J and Oliver, M (1996) *Disability Politics*. Abingdon: Routledge.

Carr, J. (1995) *Down's Syndrome: Children Growing Up*. Cambridge: Cambridge University Press.

Charlton, J (1998) *Nothing About Us Without Us: Disability Oppression and Empowerment*. Berkeley, CA: University of California Press.

Chiang, H (2008) Expressive communication of children with autism: the use of challenging behaviour. *Journal of Intellectual Disability Research*, 52: 966–972.

Clarke, AM and Clarke, ADB (eds) (1974) *Mental Deficiency: The Changing Outlook*, 3rd edition. London: Methuen.

Clarke, B (1974) *Enough Room For Joy: Jean Vanier's L'Arche, A Message for Our Time*. London: Darton, Longman & Todd.

Collins, C (2008) That's not my child any more! Parental grief after acquired brain injury. *British Journal of Social Work*, 38: 1499–1517.

Congdon, D (2008) *Mencap Response to 'Valuing People Now'*. London: Mencap. Available at www.mencap.org.uk/document.asp?id=2105.

Conroy, J and Feinstein, C (1986) *The Choice-Making Scale*. Philadelphia, PA: Conroy & Feinstein Associates.

Coulshed, V and Orme, J (1998) *Social Work Practice: An Introduction*, 3rd edition. Basingstoke: Macmillan.

Crawford, K and Walker, J (2008) *Social Work with Older People*, 2nd edition. Exeter: Learning Matters.

Crossley, R and McDonald, A (1980) *Annie's Coming Out*. London: Penguin Books.

Cummins, R (1997) *The Comprehensive Quality of Life Scales: Intellectual Disability*. Melbourne: Deakin University.

Davy, J (2005) *Rudolf Steiner: A Sketch of His Life and Work*. Ann Arbor, MI: Anthroposophical Society in America.

Dean, J and Goodlad, R (1998) *Supporting Community Participation: The Role and Impact of Befriending*. Brighton: Pavilion Publishing, in association with the Joseph Rowntree Foundation.

Department for Business, Innovation and Skills (2011) *Review of Informal Adult and Community Learning*. London: BIS.

Department for Children, Schools and Families (2008) *Special Educational Needs in England*. London: DCSF.

Department for Children, Schools and Families (2010) *Working Together to Safeguard Children: A Guide to Inter-Agency Working.* London: DCSF.

Department for Education and Skills (2004) *Every Child Matters: Change for Children.* London: DfES.

Department of Health (1998) *Modernising Social Services.* London: DoH.

Department of Health (2000) *No Secrets: Guidance on Developing and Implementing Multi-Agency Policies and Procedures to Protect Vulnerable Adults from Abuse.* London: DoH.

Department of Health (2001) *Valuing People: A New Strategy for Learning Disability for the 21st Century*, White Paper. London: Stationery Office.

Department of Health (2002) *Planning with People Towards Person-Centred Approaches: Guidance for Partnership Boards.* London: DoH.

Department of Health (2003a) *Fair Access to Care Services: Guidance on Eligibility Criteria for Adult Social Care.* London: DoH.

Department of Health (2003b) *What to Do if You Are Worried a Child is Being Abused: Children's Services Guidance.* London: DoH.

Department of Health (2005) *Independence, Well-Being and Choice*, Green Paper. London: Stationery Office.

Department of Health (2006) *Our Health, Our Care, Our Say*, White Paper. London: Stationery Office.

Department of Health (2007a) *Putting People First: Transformation of Adult Social Care.* London: DoH.

Department of Health (2007b) *Valuing People Now: From Progress to Transformation.* London: DoH.

Department of Health (2008) *Better Communication: Improving Services for Children and Young People with Speech, Language and Communication Needs.* London: DoH.

Department of Health (2009a) *Building a Safe and Confident Future: Final Report of the Social Work Task Force.* London: DoH.

Department of Health (2009b) *Guidance on Direct Payments for Community Care, Services for Carers, and Children's Services.* London: DoH.

Department of Health (2009c) *Safeguarding Adults: Report on the Consultation on the Review of No Secrets.* London: DoH.

Department of Health (2009d) *Valuing People Now: A New 3-year Strategy for People with Learning Disabilities.* London: DoH.

Disability Rights Commission (2006) *Equal Treatment: Closing the Gap. Interim Report of a Formal Investigation into Health Inequalities.* London: DRC.

Doran, M and Williams, B (2005) Review of training pack 'Epilepsy and Learning Disabilities' from Pavilion Publishing. *Community Living*, 18(4): 28.

Down's Syndrome Association (2008) Simon Beresford: the story continues. *Down's Syndrome Association Journal*, 118: 5.

Duffy, S (2003) *Keys to Citizenship: A Guide to Getting Good Support Services for People with Learning Difficulties.* Birkenhead: Paradigm.

Dybwad, G and Bersani, H (eds) (1996) *New Voices: Self-advocacy by People with Disabilities.* Cambridge, MA: Brookline Books.

Emerson, E (2001) *Challenging Behaviour: Analysis and Intervention in People with Severe Intellectual Disabilities.* Cambridge: Cambridge University Press.

Emerson, E and Hatton, C (2008) *People with Learning Disability in England.* Lancaster: Centre for Disability Research, Lancaster University.

Emerson, E, Hatton, C, Felce, D and Murphy, G (2001) *Learning Disabilities: The Fundamental Facts.* London: Foundation for People with Learning Disabilities.

Emerson, E, Malam, S, Davies, I and Spencer, K (2005) *Adults with Learning Difficulties in England.* NHS Health and Social Care Information Centre. Available at **www.icservices.nhs.uk/documents/LearningDifficultiesSurveyMainReport.pdf**.

Emerson, E, McGill, P and Mansell, J (eds) (1993) *Severe Learning Disabilities and Challenging Behaviours: Designing High Quality Services.* Cheltenham: Nelson Thornes.

Evans, C (2005) *Poems.* Norwich: Assist Trust.

Evans, M and Whittaker, A (2010) *Sensory Awareness and Social Work.* Exeter: Learning Matters.

Fanstone, C and Katrak, Z (2009) *Learning Disabilities, Sex and the Law.* London: Family Planning Association.

Fiedler, B and Lockwood, S (2004) *Person-Centred Approaches and Adult Placement.* London: Social Care Institute of Excellence.

Firth, H and Rapley, M (1990) *From Acquaintance to Friendship: Issues for People with Learning Disabilities.* Kidderminster: BILD Publications.

Fiske, J (1990) *Introduction to Communication Studies,* 2nd edition. London: Routledge.

Florides, T (2012) *Running a Befriending Project for Adults with Learning Disabilities.* London: Circle Support.

Flynn, M (2012) *Winterbourne View Hospital: a Serious Case Review.* Bristol: South Gloucestershire Council.

Flynn, R and Lemay, R (eds) (1999) *A Quarter-Century of Normalisation and Social Role Valorisation: Evolution and Impact.* Ottawa: University of Ottawa Press.

Forest, M and Lusthaus, E (1989) Promoting educational equality for all students: Circles and Maps. In S Stainback, W Stainback and M Forest (eds), *Educating All Students in the Mainstream of Regular Education.* Baltimore, MD: Paul H Brookes.

Fray, M (2007) *Caring for Kathleen: A Sister's Story about Down's Syndrome and Dementia.* Kidderminster: BILD Publications.

Gardner, A (2011) *Personalisation in Social Work.* Exeter: Sage/Learning Matters.

Goleman, D (1996) *Emotional Intelligence: Why It Can Matter More Than IQ.* London: Bloomsbury.

Goode, D (ed.) (1994) *Quality of Life for Persons with Disabilities: International Perspectives and Issues.* Cambridge, MA: Brookline Books.

Goodley, D (2000) *Self-Advocacy in the Lives of People with Learning Difficulties: The Politics of Resilience.* Buckingham: Open University Press.

Goodley, D and Moore, M (2002) *Disability Arts Against Exclusion: People with Learning Difficulties and Their Performing Arts.* Kidderminster: BILD Publications.

Gottshall, J (1995) *The Cutting Edge: Sterilization and Eugenics in California, 1909–1945.* Available at: **www.gottshall.com/thesis/article.htm**.

Gramlich, S, McBride, G, Snelham, N and Myers, B (2002) *Journey to Independence: What Self-Advocates Tell Us about Direct Payments*. Kidderminster: BILD Publications.

Grant, G, Ramcharan, P, Flynn, M and Richardson, M (2010) *Learning Disability: A Life Cycle Approach*, Second edition. Buckingham: Open University Press.

Gray, B and Jackson, R (eds) (2002) *Advocacy and Learning Disability*. London: Jessica Kingsley.

Grove, N and Park, K (1996) *Odyssey Now*. London: Jessica Kingsley.

Grove, N and Park, K (2001) *Social Cognition through Drama and Literature for People with Learning Disabilities*. London: Jessica Kingsley.

Gunzburg, H (1958) Psychotherapy with the feebleminded. In A M Clarke and A D B Clarke (eds), *Mental Deficiency: The Changing Outlook*. London: Methuen.

Haddon, M (2003) *The Curious Incident of the Dog in the Night-time*. London: Jonathan Cape.

Hames, A and McCaffrey, M (eds) (2005) *Special Brothers and Sisters: Stories and Tips for Siblings of Children with Special Needs, Disability or Serious Illness*. London: Jessica Kingsley.

Harbridge, E (2001) Gentle teaching. In National Autistic Society, *Approaches to Autism*. London: National Autistic Society.

Harris, J, Hewitt, D and Hogg, J (2001) *Positive Approaches to Challenging Behaviour*, Course of 6 Workbooks. Kidderminster: BILD Publications.

Hartrey, L and Wells, J (2003) The meaning of respite care to mothers of children with learning disabilities: two Irish case studies. *Journal of Psychiatric and Mental Health Nursing*, 10: 335–42.

Healthcare Commission and Commission for Social Care Inspection (2006) *Joint Investigation into the Provision of Services for People with Learning Disabilities at Cornwall Partnership NHS Trust*. London: Healthcare Commission.

Hellenbach, M (2012) Learning disabilities and criminal justice: custody sergeants' perceptions of alleged offenders with learning disabilities. *British Journal of Learning Disabilities*, 40: 15–22.

Hermelin, B (2001) *Bright Splinters of the Mind: A Personal Story of Research with Autistic Savants*. London: Jessica Kingsley.

Heslop, P, Mallett, R, Simons, K and Ward, L (2001) *Bridging the Divide: The Experiences of Young People with Learning Difficulties and Their Families at Transition*. Bristol: Norah Fry Research Centre, University of Bristol.

Holburn, C and Vietze, P (eds) (2002) *Person-Centered Planning: Research, Practice and Future Directions*. Baltimore, MD: Paul H Brookes.

Holland, T and Benton, M (2005) *Ageing and its Consequences for People with Down's Syndrome*. London: Down's Syndrome Association.

Hollins, S and Sireling, L (2004a) *When Dad Died*. London: Royal College of Psychiatrists.

Hollins, S and Sireling, L (2004b) *When Mum Died*. London: Royal College of Psychiatrists.

Hollins, S, Dowling, S and Blackman, N (2003) *When Somebody Dies*. London: Royal College of Psychiatrists.

Holt, G, Hardy, S and Bouras, N (eds) (2006a) *Mental Health in Learning Disabilities: A Reader*, 3rd edition. Brighton: Pavilion Publishing.

Holt, G, Hardy, S and Bouras, N (2006b) *Mental Health in Learning Disabilities: A Training Resource*. Brighton: Pavilion Publishing.

Horner, N (2003) *What Is Social Work? Context and Perspectives*. Exeter: Learning Matters.

Horner, N (2012) *What Is Social Work?* 4th edition. London: Sage/Learning Matters.

Hothersall, S and Maas-Lowitt, M (2011) *Need, Risk and Protection in Social Work Practice*. Exeter: Sage/Learning Matters.

House of Lords and House of Commons Joint Committee on Human Rights (2008) *A Life Like Any Other? Human Rights of Adults with Learning Disabilities*. London: Stationery Office.

Houts, P and Scott, R (1975a) *Goal Planning with Developmentally Disabled Persons: Procedures for Developing an Individualized Client Plan*. Hershey, PA: Pennsylvania State University College of Medicine.

Houts, P and Scott, R (1975b) *How To Get Caught Doing Something Right*. Hershey, PA: Pennsylvania State University College of Medicine.

Hunt, N (1967) *The World of Nigel Hunt*. Beaconsfield: Darwen Finlayson.

Itard, J (1801) English translation (1972) *L'Enfant Sauvage*. In L Malson and J Itard, *Wolf Children and The Wild Boy of Aveyron*, trans. E Fawcett, P Ayrton and J White. London: NLB.

Jenner, P and Gale, T (2006) A relationship support service for people with learning disabilities. *Tizard Learning Disability Review*, 11(2): 18–25.

Johns, R (2011) *Using the Law in Social Work*. Exeter: Sage/Learning Matters.

Johnson, S and Moorhead, B (2011) Social eugenics practices with children in Hitler's Nazi Germany and the role of social work: lessons for current practice. *Journal of Social Work Values and Ethics*, 8(1). Online journal at **www.socialworker.com/jswve**.

Johnston, P and Hatton, S (2003) *Conversations in Autism: From Insight to Good Practice*. Kidderminster: BILD Publications.

Jones, C (2009) *A Short History of Parliament*. Woodbridge: Boydell Press.

Jones, J (2001) *Topic Paper 4: The Communication Gap*. London: Foundation for People with Learning Disabilities.

Jones, K and Fowles, A (1984) *Ideas on Institutions: Analysing the Literature on Long-term Care and Custody*. Abingdon: Routledge & Kegan Paul.

Josephson, G (1997) *Bus Girl: Poems*. Cambridge, MA: Brookline Books.

Kadushin, A and Kadushin, G (1997) *The Social Work Interview*, 4th edition. New York: Columbia University Press.

Kamen, H (1980) *Spain in the Later Seventeenth Century, 1665–1700*. Harlow: Longman.

Katrak, Z and Fanstone, C (2003) *Sexuality and Learning Disability*. London: Family Planning Association.

Kerr, D and Wilkinson, H (2005) *In the Know: Information and Tools for Supporting People with a Learning Disability and Dementia*. Brighton: Pavilion Publishing.

King's Fund Centre (1980) *An Ordinary Life: Comprehensive Locally-based Residential Services for Mentally Handicapped People*. London: King Edward's Hospital Fund for London.

King's Fund Centre (1988) *Ties and Connections: An Ordinary Community Life for People with Learning Difficulties*. London: King's Fund Centre.

Kingsley, J and Levitz, M (1994) *Count Us In: Growing Up with Down Syndrome*. San Diego, CA: Harcourt Brace.

Kochmeister, S (1995) Facilitated communication and me. *Facilitated Communication Digest*, 3(2): 11–12.

Koprowska, J (2005) *Communication and Interpersonal Skills in Social Work*. Exeter: Learning Matters.

Kretzmann, J and McKnight, J (1993) *Building Communities from the Inside Out*. Chicago, IL: ACTA Publications.

Kunstreich, T (2003) Social welfare in Nazi Germany: selection and exclusion. *Journal of Progressive Human Services*, 14(2): 23–52.

Kushlick, A and Blunden, R (1974) The epidemiology of mental subnormality. In A M Clarke and A D B Clarke (eds), *Mental Deficiency: The Changing Outlook*, 3rd edition. London: Methuen.

Laming, H (2003) *The Victoria Climbie Inquiry Report*. London: Stationery Office.

Laurance, J (2005) NHS 'bias' against mentally ill linked to high death rate. *Independent*, 24 January.

Lifetime of Caring (2005) *Growing Older Together: Supporting People Through Transitions*. Available at: **www.lifetimecaring.org.uk**.

Lloyd, L, Fuller, D and Arvidson, H (1997) *Augmentative and Alternative Communication: A Handbook of Principles and Practices*. Boston, MA: Allyn & Bacon.

Lopez, A (1973) Charles II of Spain. *In The McGraw-Hill Encyclopaedia of World Biography*, Volume 2. New York: McGraw-Hill.

Lyle, J (1960) The effect of an institution environment upon the verbal development of institutional children: the Brooklands Family Unit. *Journal of Mental Deficiency Research*, 4: 14–23.

Lymbery, M (2005) *Social Work with Older People: Context, Policy and Practice*. London: Sage.

Lyttelton, D (2003) Abuse: an all too common experience. *Community Living*, 17(2): 15–17.

McGee, J, Menolascino, F, Hobbs, D and Menousek, P (1987) *Gentle Teaching: A Non-aversive Approach to Helping Persons with Mental Retardation*. New York: Human Sciences Press.

McGill, P, Cooper, V and Honeyman, G (2010) *Developing Better Commissioning for Individuals with Behaviour that Challenges Services*. Canterbury: Tizard Centre, University of Kent, and the Challenging Behaviour Foundation. Available at **www.bit.ly/frPUAT**.

Mackay, N (2002) Nieces abandoned in state-run mental asylum and declared dead to avoid public shame. *Sunday Herald*, 7 April.

McKnight, J (1995) *The Careless Society: Community and Its Counterfeits*. New York: Basic Books.

McNally, S, Ben-Shlomo, Y and Newman, S (1999) The effects of respite care on informal carers' well-being: a systematic review. *Disability and Rehabilitation*, 21(1): 1–14.

Macpherson, Lord (1999) *The Stephen Lawrence Inquiry*. London: Stationery Office.

Maland, D (1966) *Europe in the Seventeenth Century*. Basingstoke: Macmillan Education.

Mallett, R, Power, M, Heslop, P and Lewis, J (2003) *All Change: Transition into Adult Life*. Brighton: Pavilion Publishing.

Mansell, J, Beadle-Brown, J, Ashman, B and Ockendon, J (2005) *Person-Centred Active Support: A Multi-Media Training Resource for Staff to Enable Participation, Inclusion and Choice for People with Learning Disabilities*. Brighton: Pavilion Publishing.

Mansell, J and Elliott, T (1996) *The Active Support Measure*. Canterbury: Tizard Centre, University of Kent.

Mantell, A and Scragg, T (2008) *Safeguarding Adults in Social Work*. Exeter: Learning Matters.

Mason, J and Scior, K (2004) 'Diagnostic overshadowing' amongst clinicians working with people with intellectual disabilities in the UK. *Journal of Applied Research in Intellectual Disabilities*, 17: 85–90.

Mattinson, J (1970) *Marriage and Mental Handicap*. London: Duckworth.

Mayes, R and Llewellyn, G (2009) What happens to parents with intellectual disability following removal of their child in child protection proceedings? *Journal of Intellectual and Developmental Disability*, 34: 92–95.

Mazumdar, P (1992) *Eugenics, Human Genetics and Human Failings: The Eugenics Society, Its Sources and Its Critics in Britain*. Abingdon: Routledge.

Mencap (2004) *Treat Me Right! Better Healthcare for People with a Learning Disability*. London: Mencap.

Mencap (2007) *Death by Indifference*. London: Mencap.

Mencap (2008) *Changing Attitudes*. Available at **www.mencap.org.uk**.

Mencap (2012) *Death by Indifference, 5 years on*. London: Mencap.

Merriman, A (2007) *Tales of Normansfield: The Langdon Down Legacy*. London: Down's Syndrome Association.

Michael, J (2008) *Healthcare for All: Report of the Independent Inquiry into Access to Healthcare for People with Learning Disabilities*. Available at **www.iahpld.org.uk**.

Mickel, A (2011) Using multi-media advocacy to empower people with learning disabilities. *Community Care*, January. Available at **www.communitycare.co.uk/Articles/19/01/2011/116128/ using-multi-media-advocacy-to-empower-people-with-learning-disabilities.htm**.

Mitchell, D, Traustadottir, R, Chapman, R, Townson, L, Ingham, N and Ledger, S (eds) (2006) *Exploring Experiences of Advocacy by People with Learning Disabilities: Testimonies of Resistance*. London: Jessica Kingsley.

Mittler, P (2010) *Thinking Globally, Acting Locally*. Milton Keynes: AuthorHouse.

Moreno-Villa, J (1939) *Locos, Enanos, Negros y Niños Palaciegos: Gente de Placer que Tuvieron los Austrias en la Corte Española desde 1563 a 1700*. Mexico: La Casa de España en México.

Morris, J (1995) *Gone Missing? A Research and Policy Review of Disabled Children Living Away from Their Families*. London: Who Cares? Trust.

Morris, J (2002) *Young Disabled People Moving into Adulthood*, Foundations, ref. 512. York: Joseph Rowntree Foundation. Available at: **www.jrf.org.uk/knowledge/findings/foundations**.

Morris, P (1969) *Put Away: A Sociological Study of Institutions for the Mentally Retarded*. Abingdon: Routledge & Kegan Paul.

Mostert, M (2001) Facilitated communication since 1995: a review of published studies. *Journal of Autism and Developmental Disorders*, 31: 287–313.

Mount, B (2000) *Person-Centered Planning. Finding Directions for Change using Personal Futures Planning*. Amenia, NY: Capacity Works.

Münch, A (1998) *I Am a Woman: Why Call Me Handicapped?* London: Archer.

Munro, E (2011) *The Munro Review of Child Protection: Final Report*. London: Department for Education.

Munro, E (2012) *Progress Report: Moving Towards a Child Centred System*. Available at **www.education.gov.uk**.

Nada, J (1962) *Carlos The Bewitched*. London: Jonathan Cape.

Nash, M and Williams, A (2010) *Handbook of Public Protection*. Abingdon: Willan Publishing.

National Audit Office (2012) *Progress in Implementing the 2010 Adult Autism Strategy*.
London: NAO.

National Autistic Society (2005) *Information Sheet on Facilitated Communication*. Available at:
www.nas.org.uk.

National Council for Civil Liberties (1952) *50,000 Outside the Law*. London: NCCL (now Liberty).

NHS (2005) *National Statistics: Adults with Learning Difficulties in England*. London: Health and Social
Care Information Centre.

Nind, M and Hewitt, D (1994) *Access to Communication: Developing the Basics of Communication
with People with Severe Learning Difficulties through Intensive Interaction*. London: David Fulton.

Nind, M and Hewitt, D (2001) *A Practical Guide to Intensive Interaction*. Kidderminster:
BILD Publications.

Nirje, B (1969) The normalisation principle and its human management implications. In R. Kugel
and W. Wolfensberger (eds), *Changing Patterns in Residential Services for the Mentally Retarded*.
Washington, DC: President's Committee on Mental Retardation.

Nirje, B (1972) *The right to self-determination*. In W Wolfensberger (ed.), *The Principle of Normalisation
in Human Services*. Toronto: National Institute on Mental Retardation.

Nirje, B (1980) The normalisation principle. In R Flynn and K Nitsch (eds), *Normalisation,
Social Integration and Community Services*. Baltimore, MD: University Park Press.

Nolan, C (1981) *Dam-Burst of Dreams*. London: Weidenfeld & Nicolson.

Nolan, C (1987) *Under the Eye of the Clock*. London: Weidenfeld & Nicolson.

Nolan, C (2000) *The Banyan Tree*. London: Phoenix.

Nzira, V and Williams, P (2009) *Anti-Oppressive Practice in Health and Social Care*. London: Sage.

O'Brien, J (1987) A guide to lifestyle planning. In B Wilcox and T Bellamy (eds) *A Comprehensive Guide
to the Activities Catalogue*. Baltimore, MD: Paul H. Brookes.

O'Brien, J and Lovett, H (1992) *Finding a Way to Everyday Lives: The Contribution of
Person-Centered Planning*. Lithonia, GA: Responsive Systems Associates. Available at
disabilitystudies.syr.edu/resources/reports.aspx.

O'Brien, J and Lyle O'Brien, C (1992) *Remembering the Soul of Our Work: Stories by the Staff of
Options in Community Living*. Madison, WI: Options in Community Living.

O'Brien, J and Lyle O'Brien, C (1998) *A Little Book About Person-Centered Planning: Ways to
Think about Person-Centered Planning, Its Limitations, and the Conditions for Its Success*.
Toronto: Inclusion Press.

O'Brien, J and Lyle O'Brien, C (2002) *Implementing Person-Centered Planning:
Voices of Experience*. Toronto: Inclusion Press.

O'Brien, J, Lyle O'Brien, C and Jacob, G (1998) *Celebrating the Ordinary: The Emergence
of Options in Community Living as a Thoughtful Organization*. Toronto: Inclusion Press.

O'Bryan, A, Simons, K, Beyer, S and Grove, B (2000) *A Framework for Supported Employment*.
York: Joseph Rowntree Foundation.

O'Connor, N and Tizard, J (1956) *The Social Problem of Mental Deficiency*. Oxford: Pergamon Press.

O'Loughlin, M and O'Loughlin, S (2012) *Social Work with Children and Families*, 3rd edition. London: Sage/Learning Matters.

Osgood, T (2005) Managing the tensions between the interests of organisations and service users. In P Cambridge and S Carnaby (eds), *Person-Centred Planning and Care Management with People with Learning Disabilities*. London: Jessica Kingsley.

Oswin, M (1971) *The Empty Hours: A Study of the Weekend Life of Handicapped Children in Institutions*. London: Allen Lane.

Oswin, M (1978) *Children Living in Long-stay Hospitals*. London: Heinemann.

Oswin, M (1984) *They Keep Going Away: A Critical Study of Short-term Residential Care Services for Children with Learning Difficulties*. London: King's Fund Centre.

Oswin, M (1991) *Am I Allowed to Cry? A Study of Bereavement Amongst People Who Have Learning Difficulties*. London: Souvenir Press.

Palley, S (2012) *Promoting Positive Behaviour*. London: Sage/Learning Matters.

Paradigm (2008) *REACH – Standards in Supported Living*. Birkenhead: Paradigm.

Parker, B (2005) *Social work and bereavement support: a perspective from palliative care*. In J Parker (ed.), *Aspects of Social Work and Palliative Care*. London: Quay Books.

Parker, J and Bradley, G (2010) *Social Work Practice: Assessment, Planning, Intervention and Review*. Exeter: Learning Matters.

Partners in Advocacy (2004) *People with Learning Disabilities and Same-sex Relationships*. Edinburgh: Partners in Advocacy. Available at **www.siaa.org.uk/documents/learningdisabilitysame-sexrelationships-accessiblereportssummary.pdf**.

Payne, M (1997) *Modern Social Work Theory*, 2nd edition. Basingstoke: Macmillan.

Pearpoint, J, O'Brien, J and Forest, M (1992) *PATH: Planning Alternative Tomorrows with Hope*. Toronto: Inclusion Press.

Perry, D, Hammond, L, Gaskell, S and Eva, J (2010) *Caring for the Physical and Mental Health of People with Learning Disabilities*. London: Jessica Kingsley.

Perske, R (1972) The dignity of risk. In W Wolfensberger (ed.), *The Principle of Normalisation in Human Services*. Toronto: National Institute on Mental Retardation.

Philip, M, Lambe, L and Hogg, J (2005) *The Well-Being Workshop: Recognising the Emotional and Mental Well-Being of People with Profound and Multiple Learning Disabilities*. London: Mental Health Foundation.

Phillips, C and Thompson, G (2001) What is a QALY? *Bandolier Extra*, 1(6). Available at **www.evidence-based-medicine.co.uk**.

Phillips, F (2001) Poem: 'When You Were Born'. *Down's Syndrome Association Journal*, 95: 18.

Pickford, J and Dugmore, P (2012) *Youth Justice in Social Work*. London: Sage/Learning Matters.

Pitonyak, D (2004) *The Importance of Belonging*. Blacksburg, VA: Imagine. Available at **www.dimagine.com**.

Pitonyak, D (2005) *Loneliness is the Only Real Disability*. Blacksburg, VA: Imagine. Available at **www.dimagine.com**.

Potts, M and Fido, R (1991) *'A Fit Person To Be Removed': Personal Accounts of Life in a Mental Deficiency Institution*. Plymouth: Northcote House.

Priestley, M (2003) *Disability: A Life Course Approach*. Cambridge: Polity Press.

Pring, J (2003) *Silent Victims*. London: Gibson Square Books.

Prison Reform Trust (2012) *Fair Access to Justice? Support for Vulnerable Defendants in the Criminal Courts*. London: PRT.

Race, D (1995) Epidemiology of learning disabilities. In N Malin (ed.), *Services for People with Learning Disabilities*. Abingdon: Routledge.

Race, D (1999) *Social Role Valorization and the English Experience*. London: Whiting & Birch.

Race, D (ed.) (2002) *Learning Disability: A Social Approach*. Abingdon: Routledge.

Race, D (ed.) (2003) *Leadership and Change in Human Services: Selected Readings from Wolf Wolfensberger*. Abingdon: Routledge.

Race, D (2007) *Intellectual Disability: Social Approaches*. Maidenhead: Open University Press.

Race, D, Boxall, K and Carson, I (2005) Towards a dialogue for practice: reconciling Social Role Valorisation and the Social Model of Disability. *Disability & Society*, 20: 507–21.

Ramcharan, P, Roberts, G, Grant, G and Borland, J (eds) (1997) *Empowerment in Everyday Life: Learning Disability*. London: Jessica Kingsley.

Rankin, K (2000) *Growing Up Severely Autistic*. London: Jessica Kingsley.

Rapley, M (2003) *Quality of Life Research: A Critical Introduction*. London: Sage.

Raynes, N, Wright, K, Shiell, A and Pettipher, C.(1994) *The Cost and Quality of Community Residential Care*. London: David Fulton.

Ridley, J and Hunter, S (2005) *'Go For It!': Supporting People with Learning Disabilities and/or Autistic Spectrum Disorder in Employment*. Edinburgh: Scottish Executive. Available at **www.scotland.gov.uk/publications**.

Ridout, P (ed.) (2003) *Care Standards: A Practical Guide*. Bristol: Jordan Publishing.

Rolph, S, Atkinson, D, Nind, M and Welshman, J (eds) (2005) *Witnesses to Change: Families, Learning Difficulties and History*. Kidderminster: BILD Publications.

Roy, M (2000) Sexuality and people with learning disabilities. In M Roy, D Clarke and A Roy (eds), *An Introduction to Learning Disability Psychiatry*. West Midlands Learning Disability Group. Available at **www.users.globalnet.co.uk/~asdame/Book.htm**.

Royal College of Speech and Language Therapists (2003) *Speech and Language Therapy Provision for Adults with Learning Disabilities*. Available at **www.rcslt.org**.

Rumbelow, H (2000) Autistic son's language aid led to abuse charge. *The Times*, 13 July, p.9.

Samuel, M (2012) What the NHS shake-up means for social care. *Community Care* online: **www.communitycare.co.uk/blogs/adult-care-blog/2011/01/what-the-nhs-shake-up-means-for-social-care.html**.

Sanderson, H, Kennedy, J, Ritchie, P and Goodwin, G (1997) *People, Plans and Possibilities: Exploring Person-Centred Planning*. Edinburgh: SHS Trust.

Schalock, R (1996) *Quality of Life, Volume 1: Conceptualization and Measurement*. Washington, DC: American Association on Mental Retardation.

Schalock, R (1997) *Quality of Life, Volume 2: Application to Persons with Disabilities*. Washington, DC: American Association on Mental Retardation.

Schalock, R, Brown, I, Brown, R, Cummins, R, Felce, D, Matikka, L, Keith, K and Parmenter, T (2002) Conceptualization, measurement, and application of quality of life for persons with intellectual disabilities: report of an international panel of experts. *Mental Retardation*, 40: 457–70.

SCOPE (2002) *The Good Practice Guide for Support Workers and Personal Assistants Working with Disabled People with Communication Impairments*. London: SCOPE. Available at **www.scope.org.uk/publications**.

Scottish Executive (2000) *The Same As You? A Review of Services for People with Learning Disabilities*. Available at **www.scotland.gov.uk/ldsr/docs/tsay-00.asp**.

Scottish Executive (2003) *Working for a Change? The Same as You? National Implementation Group: Report of the Short-life Working Group on Employment*. Edinburgh: Scottish Executive.

Seed, P and Lloyd, G (1997) *Quality of Life*. London: Jessica Kingsley.

Shearer, A (1972) *Our Life: Conference Report*. London: Campaign for the Mentally Handicapped.

Shearer, A (1973) *Listen!* London: Campaign for the Mentally Handicapped.

Simpson, D and Miller, L (2004) *Unexpected Gains: Psychotherapy with People with Learning Disabilities*. London: Karnac Books.

Sinason, V (1992) *Mental Handicap and the Human Condition: New Approaches from the Tavistock*. London: Free Association Books.

Smale, G and Tuson, G (1993) *Empowerment, Assessment, Care Management and the Skilled Worker*. London: HMSO.

Smith, K (2011) *The Politics of Down Syndrome*. Alresford: Zero Books.

Smull, M and Sanderson, H (2005) *Essential Lifestyle Planning for Everyone*. Toronto: Inclusion Press.

Social Care Institute of Excellence (2005) *How to Produce Information in an Accessible Way*. Available at **www.scie.org.uk**.

Social Care Institute of Excellence (2011) *Challenging Behaviour: A Guide for Family Carers on Getting the Right Support for Adults*. London: SCIE.

Souza, A (1997) Everything you ever wanted to know about Down's syndrome, but never bothered to ask. In P Ramcharan, G Roberts, G Grant and J Borland (eds) *Empowerment in Everyday Life: Learning Disability*. London: Jessica Kingsley.

Stancliffe, R (1995) *Choice and Decision-Making and Adults with Intellectual Disability*. Sydney: Macquarie University.

Stratford, B (1996) *In the beginning*. In B Stratford and P Gunn (eds) *New Approaches to Down Syndrome*. London: Cassell.

Sutcliffe, J and Simons, K (1993) *Self-Advocacy and Adults with Learning Difficulties*. Leicester: National Institute of Adult Continuing Education.

Swain, J, French, S, Barnes, C and Thomas, C (2007) *Disabling Barriers: Enabling Environments*, 2nd edition. London: Sage.

Talbot, P, Astbury, G and Mason, T (2010) *Key Concepts in Learning Disabilities*. London: Sage.

Taylor, B (2011) *Working with Aggression and Resistance in Social Work*. Exeter: Sage/Learning Matters.

Taylor, T (2003) *Insistent Voices: Stories on Claiming Identity*. Kingston-upon-Thames: Kingston Advocacy Group.

Thomas, D and Woods, H (2003) *Working with People with Learning Disabilities: Theory and Practice.* London: Jessica Kingsley.

Thompson, D (1996) *The Oxford Compact English Dictionary.* Oxford: Oxford University Press.

Thompson, N (ed.) (2002) *Loss and Grief: A Guide for Human Service Practitioners.* Basingstoke: Palgrave.

Tilley, L (2011) *Person-Centred Approaches when Supporting People with a Learning Disability.* Exeter: Sage/Learning Matters and British Institute of Learning Disabilities.

Tilley, R and Bright, A (2003) Votes that could not be ignored: the Elfrida Society's Community Development Project. *Community Living*, 16(3): 13–16.

Titterton, M (2004) *Risk and Risk-Taking in Health and Social Welfare.* London: Jessica Kingsley.

Tizard, J (1964) *Community Services for the Mentally Handicapped.* Oxford: Oxford University Press.

Toft, B and Reynolds, S (1997) *Learning from Disasters: A Management Approach.* Leicester: Perpetuity Press.

Towell, D (ed.) (1988) *An Ordinary Life in Practice: Developing Comprehensive Community-based Services for People with Learning Disabilities.* London: King Edward's Hospital Fund for London.

Treneman, M, Corkery, A, Dowdney, L and Hammond, J (1997) Respite care needs, met and unmet: assessment of needs for children with disability. *Developmental Medicine and Child Neurology*, 39: 548–553.

Tuffrey-Wijne, I (2009) *Living with Learning Disabilities, Dying with Cancer: Thirteen Personal Stories.* London: Jessica Kingsley.

Turk, V and Brown, H (1993) The sexual abuse of adults with learning disabilities: results of a two-year incidence survey. *Mental Handicap Research*, 6: 193–216.

Turnbull, J (ed.) (2004) *Learning Disability Nursing.* Oxford: Blackwell.

United Nations (1971) *Declaration on the Rights of Mentally Retarded Persons.* New York: United Nations.

United Nations (1994) *Human Rights and Social Work.* New York: Centre for Human Rights, United Nations.

Valuing People Support Team (2004) *Workbook on Person-Centred Care Management.* London: Valuing People Support Team, Department of Health.

Valuing People Support Team (2005) *Families, Merseyside Partners.* London: Valuing People Support Team, Department of Health.

Vanier, J (2004) *Letter to the L'Arche Communities.* Available at **www.larchecanada.org/vanbiol.htm**.

Ward, OC (1998) *John Langdon Down: A Caring Pioneer.* London: Royal Society of Medicine Press.

Wassermann, J (1973) *Caspar Hauser: The Enigma of a Century.* New York: Rudolf Steiner Publications.

Weinstein, J (2008) *Working with Loss, Death and Bereavement: A Guide for Social Workers.* London: Sage.

Wertheimer, A (1988) *A Voice of Our Own, Now and in the Future: Report of the People First International Conference, London, September 1988.* London: People First.

Wertheimer, A (1998) *Citizen Advocacy: A Powerful Partnership.* London: Citizen Advocacy Information and Training (now Advocacy Resource Exchange).

White, R, Carr, P and Lowe, N (2008) *The Children Act in Practice*, 4th revised edition. London: Butterworths LexisNexis.

Whittaker, A (1999) *Changing Our Days: Finding Ways to Get What You Want from Life*. London: King's Fund Publications.

Whittaker, A, Gardner, S and Kershaw, J (1991) *Service Evaluation by People with Learning Difficulties*. London: King's Fund Centre.

Whittaker, J and Kenworthy, J (2002) Education services: why segregated special schools must close. In D Race (ed.), *Learning Disability: A Social Approach*. Abingdon: Routledge.

Whittington, C (2007) *Assessment in Social Work: a Guide for Learning and Teaching*. London: Social Care Institute for Excellence.

Williams, C (1995) *Invisible Victims: Crime and Abuse against People with Learning Difficulties*. London: Jessica Kingsley.

Williams, P (1974) *A Workshop on Participation*. London: Campaign for the Mentally Handicapped.

Williams, P (1978) *Our Mutual Handicap*. London: Campaign for the Mentally Handicapped.

Williams, P (1995) Should we prevent Down's syndrome? *British Journal of Learning Disabilities*, 23(2): 46–50.

Williams, P (1998) *Standing By Me: Stories of Citizen Advocacy*. London: Citizen Advocacy Information and Training (now Advocacy Resource Exchange).

Williams, P (2002) Residential and day services. In D Race (ed.), *Learning Disability: A Social Approach*. Abingdon: Routledge.

Williams, P (2004) Incorporating Social Role Valorisation into other contexts of needs assessment, anti-oppressive practice and the application of values. *International Journal of Disability, Community and Rehabilitation*, 3(1): **www.ijdcr.ca/VOL03_01_CAN/articles/williams.shtml**.

Williams, P (2005a) Should the CSCI review its own standards? *Community Living*, 19(1): 18–19.

Williams, P (2005b) The work of Jack Tizard, I: 1950 to 1964. *Learning Disability Review*, 10: 7–11.

Williams, P (2005c) The work of Jack Tizard, II: 1965 to 1979. *Learning Disability Review*, 10: 18–21.

Williams, P (2006) Two inspirational speakers who can strengthen our vision. *Community Living*, 19(3): 18–19.

Williams, P and Shoultz, B (1982) *We Can Speak For Ourselves: Self-Advocacy by Mentally Handicapped People*. London: Souvenir Press.

Wilson, H, Bialk, P, Freeze, T, Freeze, R and Lutfiyya, Z (2012) Heidi's and Philip's stories: transitions to post-secondary education. *British Journal of Learning Disabilities*, 40: 87–93.

Wolfensberger, W (1969) The origin and nature of our institutional models. In R Kugel and W Wolfensberger (eds), *Changing Patterns in Residential Services for the Mentally Retarded*. Washington, DC: President's Committee on Mental Retardation.

Wolfensberger, W (ed.) (1972) *The Principle of Normalization in Human Services*. Toronto: National Institute on Mental Retardation.

Wolfensberger, W (1983) Social Role Valorization: a proposed new term for the principle of normalization. *Mental Retardation*, 21(6): 234–9.

Wolfensberger, W (1992) *The New Genocide of Handicapped and Afflicted People*, 2nd edition. Syracuse, NY: Training Institute, Syracuse University.

Wolfensberger, W (1998) *A Brief Introduction to Social Role Valorization*, 3rd edition. Syracuse, NY: Training Institute, Syracuse University.

Wolfensberger, W (2005) *Guideline on Protecting the Health and Lives of Patients in Hospitals, Especially if the Patient Is a Member of a Societally Devalued Class*, 2nd edition. Syracuse, NY: Training Institute, Syracuse University.

Wolfensberger, W and Glenn, L (1975) *PASS: Program Analysis of Service Systems*. Toronto: National Institute on Mental Retardation.

Wolfensberger, W and Thomas, S (1983) *PASSING: Program Analysis of Service Systems' Implementation of Normalization Goals*. Toronto: National Institute on Mental Retardation.

Wolfensberger, W and Thomas, S (2007) *PASSING: A Tool for Analysing Service Quality According to Social Role Valorization Criteria*, 3rd edition. Syracuse, NY: Syracuse University Training Institute.

Wood, S and Shears, B (1986) *Teaching Children with Severe Learning Difficulties: Radical Reappraisal*. London: Croom Helm.

Wright, D and Digby, A (eds) (1996) *From Idiocy to Mental Deficiency: Historical Perspectives on People with Learning Disabilities*. Abingdon: Routledge.

Young, A (2008) 'The best laid plans': the Mental Capacity Act is having some unforeseen and unwelcome consequences. *Community Living*, 22(1): 22–3.

Zipperlen, H and O'Brien, J (1994) *Cultivating Thinking Hearts: Letters from the Lifesharing Safeguards Project*. Kimberton, PA: Camphill Village, Kimberton Hills.

Index

Added to the page reference 'f' denotes a figure and 't' denotes a table.